James Johonnot, Sarah Evans Johonnot

**Principles and Practices of Teaching**

James Johonnot, Sarah Evans Johonnot

**Principles and Practices of Teaching**

ISBN/EAN: 9783337167868

Printed in Europe, USA, Canada, Australia, Japan

Cover: Foto ©Paul-Georg Meister /pixelio.de

More available books at **www.hansebooks.com**

*INTERNATIONAL EDUCATION SERIES*

# PRINCIPLES AND PRACTICE
# OF TEACHING

BY

JAMES JOHONNOT

REVISED BY

SARAH EVANS JOHONNOT

NEW YORK
D. APPLETON AND COMPANY
1896

# EDITOR'S PREFACE.

This book embodies in a compact form the results of the wide experience and careful reflection of an enthusiastic teacher and school supervisor.

James Johonnot was a power in teachers' institutes to arouse professional aspiration and kindle zeal for improvement. He advocated the new education as based on the methods of Pestalozzi and as finding its material of instruction not merely in the traditional three R's but also in natural science. The chapters in this book on the Objective Course of Instruction, Object-Teaching, Systems of Education Compared, all develop the Pestalozzian method of interesting the pupil in the study of real things. Again, the chapters on the Relative Value of the Different Branches of Instruction, Agassiz, and Science in its Relations to Education, all lay emphasis on the doctrine that natural science should lead in this course of study.

Mr. Johonnot ranked himself on the side of the educational reformers, and this his book belongs under the division which we have described as criticisms of education. The mere routine teacher who follows in a lifeless manner the traditions handed down to him is often goaded into something like vital action by the taunts and scorn of the reformer. It is the only door of hope for him. He must break with tradition, and learn to think and act for himself. Then he can grow.

The first and most needed reform in methods of instruction called for in the educational revival begun by Horace Mann was the substitution of something better for text-book memorizing. Lessons on objects were recommended as the best substitute for lessons on mere words. "Things before words" became the motto. Great improvement in the work of class instruction followed when the teacher began to lay less emphasis on the parrotlike repetition of the words in the book and to insist on the understanding of the meaning, and especially to require illustrations drawn from the pupil's own experience. It became a part of the work of the good teacher to lead his pupils to test and verify by actual experiment the statements of the book, and the method of investigation began to take the place of the method of memorizing the words of the author.

Instruction had sunk to this low level of parroting the words of the book, or, rather, had remained on it as a necessary consequence of the ungraded and unclassified state of the rural schools in sparsely settled districts. A one-room school, with from sixteen to thirty pupils of all ages and of all degrees of advancement under one teacher, might furnish forty different recitations or more in a day, of an average length of five minutes each. The teacher was practically reduced to setting a task for each pupil—a lesson to learn in his book. He was not able to test his pupils' understanding of the lesson in the brief recitation of five minutes. He could only at best try their ability to reproduce from memory the words of the book. It often happened that the exact words of the book were preferred to clear ideas expressed in the pupil's own words.

No complete remedy has ever been discovered for the evils of the ungraded school. It seems, after all, to be necessary in the rural school to set pupils at work on the printed page of the text-book and devise such methods as one can to insure the real understanding of the text; the results will be poor enough at best.

In the village and city schools, on the other hand, there will be increased numbers and the possibility of classification, and as a consequence more time for the recitation. The teacher can probe the pupil's mind and discover his strong and his weak habits of study, where his attention has flagged and where he has lost his way in the preparation of his lesson. By the discussion of the several points of the task, one after another, with the different pupils of the class, all its phases are brought out, and each one acquires alertness and corrects his one-sidedness. He goes to the preparation of his next lesson with a much-increased power to understand it.

Mr. Johonnot as educational reformer helped thousands of struggling teachers who had brought over the rural school methods into village school (or "union school") work. He made life worth living to them. His help, through the pages of this book, will aid other thousands in the same struggle to adopt the better methods that are possible in the graded school.

His early advocacy of natural science in the curriculum of the elementary school contributed to improve the course of study by introducing the elements of natural history and natural philosophy (or physics) into the primary and grammar schools. This branch of study, taught in oral lessons, gives the pupil a glimpse into the great process going on in civilization by which Nature is conquered and rendered of service to man. It makes the instruction in arithmetic and geography far more interesting and profitable than it could be without scientific explanations and applications. Children taught the technique of the natural sciences become able to comprehend the constant allusions to scientific discovery found in the daily newspapers and in the books of the day, and by this they put themselves in the way of acquiring a fund of information regarding Nature and mechanic invention without effort.

The elements of natural science can easily be taught, and, once learned, the child has, so to speak, learned the language of science and can have access at will to the storehouse in which all the discoveries are treasured.

The object-lesson and the study of natural science have been and are the watchwords of reform in methods of instruction—especially of reform in those methods inherited from the rural school. The teacher who aspires to better his instruction will read this book with profit.

W. T. HARRIS.

WASHINGTON, D. C., *August 25, 1896.*

# PREFACE TO REVISED EDITION.

An intimate acquaintance of forty years with the author's thought has enabled me to revise his work without changing its essential principles. In some few instances I have taken the liberty to restate his opinions in more modern phraseology, and to extend somewhat the field of their application.

A brief sketch of the pioneer work in Manual Training has been added to show Mr. Johonnot's influence and close connection with the earliest experiments in this country. The two men, Mr. Love and Mr. Runkle, who were the first to actually introduce it, were life-long friends of Mr. Johonnot, with whom he often held counsel.

In my revision I have also noted and emphasized two points made by Mr. Johonnot, which, though not new, had not before received adequate attention: First, the *interdependence* of the whole body of knowledge is progressively taught in every chapter of his book, and its co-ordination in the Course of Study is continually kept in mind and insisted upon. In view of this unity of knowledge, the shallow complaint so often heard in "high places," that the schools teach too many subjects, is seen to be unworthy of notice.

The second point I have noticed is the peculiar importance accorded by Mr. Johonnot to the word *incidental*. It appears constantly on the scene, now in connection with the training of the intellect, especially when he treats of language in its use, again in the field of taste, and notably in the domain of morals. He evidently distrusts the free use of dogma, and would in a large measure rely for the finer spiritual issues on the culture that "cometh not with observation."

I wish further to state that "markings" and examinations played an insignificant part in his scheme of education. He early realized the many evils incident to stated examinations, and, besides, found them of no educational value. Having the courage of his opinions, as was his habit, he acted on this conviction, and dispensed with them altogether.

In the controversy between Natural Science and Language he could not take part, since he fully appreciated the value of both. Between the two great classes into which the realm of knowledge is divided—Natural Science and The Humanities—he saw no cause for rivalry, and assigned to each a place in the Course of Study, under one form or another, throughout the whole school course. Naturally, he drew special attention to such departments as had suffered most from neglect, viz., Natural Science, Literature, Music, and the Manual Arts, but he expressly and emphatically claimed fully half the time for The Humanities. True, he discarded the old methods, which fed the pupil on the mere dry bones of every subject, and substituted a nurture fruitful of spiritual growth.

I need not call attention to the fact that Mr. Johonnot not only treated at length of the subject-matter of instruction; he consistently advocated the "scientific method" as applicable to all branches of knowledge, to The Humanities as well as to Natural Science. He chose not to belittle a method as old as common sense by dubbing it either Pestalozzian or Baconian.

Finally, I would call attention to the fact that Mr. Johonnot set up no claim to originality; at the same time he was in no sense a "disciple." He did not presume to call the principles he advocated new. Thinkers in ages long past had stated them, but the schools, public and private, and the colleges as well, had not only ignored them: they had nullified them.

SARAH EVANS JOHONNOT.

*September 1, 1896.*

# PREFACE TO FIRST EDITION.

EXPERIENCE is beginning to show that teaching, like every other department of human thought and activity, must change with the changing conditions of society, or it will fall in the rear of civilization and become an obstacle to improvement.

Teachers imbued with modern thought, in comparing the ideals which such thought suggests with the actual results of their efforts in the ordinary routine of instruction, have become dissatisfied; and intelligent outside observers have seen with great concern the continual divergence of education from practical affairs.

Efforts to remove these difficulties have usually been directed toward reforming the methods of presenting the ordinary topics, rather than toward a more radical change; and hence there have grown up a great number of empiric methods, which have found expression in manuals for teachers and in text-books. These have all contributed something to the solution of the problem, and in the aggregate have been of great value to education, especially in the primary grades.

But the remedies have proved inadequate, and the

dissatisfaction remains, taking the form of a widespread feeling that, in some way, the schools are out of joint with the times, and that the instruction which they afford is not the highest and best, either as a disciplinary force, or as a preparation for the duties and occupations of life. This feeling gives rise to a demand that some means shall be devised by which education may profit by the results of modern science and philosophy, and once more take rank as a leading force in civilization.

To meet this demand, the changes required are organic and fundamental, and include the matter which shall be made the basis of instruction and the order of presenting the several subjects, as well as the methods to be pursued.

In this volume, an endeavor has been made to examine education from the standpoint of modern thought, and to contribute something to the solution of the problems that are forcing themselves upon the attention of educators. To these ends, a concise statement of some well-settled principles of psychology has been made, and a connected view of the interdependence of the sciences given, to serve as a guide to methods of instruction, and to determine the subject-matter best adapted to each stage of development.

The systems of several of the great educational reformers have been analyzed, with a view to ascertain precisely what each has contributed to the science of teaching, and how far their ideas conform to psychological laws; and an endeavor has been made to combine the principles derived from both experience and philosophy into one coherent system.

Several of the topics are examined from different points of view, involving a degree of repetition; but in these cases the topics treated either relate to some erroneous notions of education still practised and defended, or the treatment is needed to fully illustrate the general topic under discussion.

Fully aware of the difficulties of the work which he has undertaken, the author presents this volume to the public, in the hope that any shortcomings in the performance may be more than compensated by the thought which may be elicited in a renewed examination and discussion of the subject. Seeking only what is true, he will be first to welcome criticism that shall point out errors of fact or of philosophy.

ITHACA, N. Y., *February* 8, 1878.

# CONTENTS.

### CHAPTER I.

GENERAL OBJECTS OF EDUCATION . . . . . 1

KNOWLEDGE AS RELATED TO SUCCESS: Conditions of Successful Teaching—System, Symmetry, Harmony—Objects of Education—The Means of Education—Divisions of the Subject. PHYSICAL EDUCATION: Physical Development Twofold—Work and Exercise. MENTAL EDUCATION: The Process of Mental Education—Knowledge the Mind's Food—Character and Knowledge—Modes of Exercise—Knowledge of Rights. MORAL EDUCATION: Means of Moral Growth—Means of Moral Strength. GENERAL SUMMARY: Scientific View—Effect of Broader Views.

### CHAPTER II.

THE MENTAL POWERS . . . . . 14

IMPORTANCE OF MENTAL SCIENCE TO TEACHERS: A Common Defect of Teachers—Scope of the Discussion. HOW KNOWLEDGE IS OBTAINED: Ideas of Pressure—Ideas in Regard to the Surface of Objects—Ideas in Regard to Flavor—Ideas in Regard to Odor—Ideas in Regard to Sound—Ideas in Regard to Light and Color—The Senses to be Cultivated—Sensation—Attention—Treatment of Attention—Perception—Nature of Percepts—Treatment of Perception. HOW KNOWLEDGE IS RETAINED: Arbitrary Memory—Suggestive Memory—Associative Memory—Likenesses—Unlikenesses—Dependence—Abuse of Memory—The Right Use of Memory—Perception and Memory—Recollection. HOW KNOWLEDGE IS USED: Imagination—The Depreciation of this Faculty—A Highly Practical Faculty—Dependence of Imagination—Treatment of Imagination—Reason—Judgment. MIXED MENTAL PROCESSES: Comparison—Conception. ORDER IN MENTAL DEVELOPMENT: Principles Confirmed by Observation—Age an Important Consideration. EXPRESSION AS RELATED TO MENTAL DEVELOPMENT: Position Illustrated—The Twofold Office of Language—Importance of Cultivating Language.

### CHAPTER III.

OBJECTIVE COURSE OF INSTRUCTION . . . . . 40

GENERAL VIEW OF PRESENT PRACTICES: Wrong Practices—Examples—Rote-Learning—Nervous Action—Semi-Reflex Action—Studies too Difficult—Faults of Omission. RACE AND INDIVIDUAL GROWTH: Historical Examples. OBJECTIVE OR INDUCTIVE METHOD: Perception—Comparison—Grouping—Objective Classification—Generalization—Law, Principle, Definition—Examples—Benefits of the Objective Method—Spirit of Modern Science.

### CHAPTER IV.

SUBJECTIVE COURSE OF INSTRUCTION . . . . . 55

THE SUBJECTIVE METHOD: Definition—Examples—Divisions of a Subject—Imperfect Divisions—Subjective Classification—Illustrations—Opposing

Theories — Scientific View — Definition of Divisions — Subdivisions. CHARACTERISTICS OF THE SUBJECTIVE COURSE: Relations to Development — Relations to Knowledge — Place in the Educational Course — Misuse of the Subjective Method. THE OBJECTIVE AND SUBJECTIVE COURSES COMBINED: The Two Courses as Related to Discovery and Application — The Two Courses as Related to the Teacher's Work — Errors of Reversing the Two Courses. COROLLARIES: Sources of Primary Ideas — Training the Senses — Securing Attention — Cultivating Perception — Exercises in Memory — Advanced Instruction — Ideas and Words — The Steps of Instruction — Exercise — Completed Processes.

## CHAPTER V.

OBJECT-TEACHING . . . . . . . . 72

GENERAL VIEW OF THE SUBJECT: False Philosophy — Introduction of Object-Lessons — Practical Mistakes — Reaction against Object-Teaching — Real Nature of Object-Lessons. VALUE OF OBJECT-LESSONS: Qualities of Objects — The Physical Sciences — "How not to do it" — Ideal Objects — Order in Thinking — The Ideal and the Real — Interest in Study — Verification of a Law. SUMMARY: Cautions to be Observed — Limits of Object-Teaching — Additional Caution — Conclusion.

## CHAPTER VI.

RELATIVE VALUE OF THE DIFFERENT BRANCHES OF INSTRUCTION . 84

THE END OF EDUCATION: Practical Questions — Responsibility for Change — Conditions of Change. REAL AND APPARENT KNOWLEDGE: Relations of Language — Relations of Mathematics — Direct and Incidental Acquirement — Kinds of Knowledge Required — Branches of Real Knowledge. THE BRANCHES AS RELATED TO DEVELOPMENT: Natural Science as Promoting Development — The Discipline of Memory — The Humanities as Promoting Development — Discipline of the Reflective Faculties — General Effect of Real Knowledge — The Discipline of Conduct. THE BRANCHES AS RELATED TO USES: Uses of Natural Science — Natural Science and Industry — Ubiquity of the Elements of Natural Science — Uses of the Humanities - Conditions of their Successful Use. SPECIAL STUDIES: Importance of History — Chronology — Philology — Archaeology — What is Gained. FOREIGN LANGUAGES: Elementary Study — Foreign Literature — Comparative Philology. THE ANCIENT LANGUAGES: Advantages Claimed — Difficulties Encountered — Mental Discipline — Schiller's Opinion. SUMMARY IN REGARD TO LANGUAGE. GENERAL SUMMARY.

## CHAPTER VII.

PESTALOZZI . . . . . . . . . 105

SCHOOLS OF THE OLDEN TIME: Effect of Printing upon Education — Teachers Employed — Value of Learning to Read — Ideal Schools. PESTALOZZI'S CAREER: Philanthropic Views — The Ideal Reduced to Practice — Experiments at Neuhof — Condition of the Country — School at Stanz — Condition of the School — Things and Representatives — Intellectual Success — Moral Success — School at Burgdorf — School at Yverdon. PESTALOZZI'S PRINCIPLES: Order in Mental Growth — Home Education — The Influence of Mothers — Mistakes in Application — Education of Mothers — Study of Children — Training Imbeciles — Basis of Experience — Object-Teaching — Practical Objections — Conduct and Character — Growth of the System.

## CHAPTER VIII.

FROEBEL AND THE KINDERGARTEN . . . . . 119

FRUIT OF PESTALOZZI'S PRINCIPLES: Education through Work — Agricultural Schools — Limitations of these Schools. THE WORK OF FROEBEL: Philanthropic Motives — Development of the Kindergarten — Obscurity of Expression. KINDERGARTEN PRINCIPLES: Inherited Powers and Tendencies—Education should Commence Early—Education Based on Self-Activity—Spontaneous Activity, or Play—School Exercises should give Pleasure—Physical and Mental Activiy combined—Harmonious Development of the Powers—The Schools demanded by these Principles. PRACTICAL KINDERGARTEN WORK: The Kind of Play—The Method of Play—Original Work—Singing—Playing in the Dirt—The Law of Order—Study of the System. THE KINDERGARTEN AT ST. LOUIS: Necessity of Study and Experiment—Scope of Education—Scope of the Kindergarten—Delicate Adjustments—Philosophy Involved—Questions to be Settled.

## CHAPTER IX.

AGASSIZ; AND SCIENCE IN ITS RELATIONS TO TEACHING . . 135

THE SCOPE AND END OF SCIENCE: Philosophy and Utility—Prof. Tyndall's Opinion—Another View—Prof. Huxley's Opinion—Antagonisms Harmonized—Incentive to Investigation. METHODS OF SCIENCE: Scientific Method in Teaching—Defects in Teaching which Science Remedies—Waking up Mind—Growth of the Scientific Principle. AGASSIZ'S WORK: Early Life—Love of Nature—Vacation Studies—Study of the Glaciers—Spirit of his Work—The Old Methods Distrusted—Reformation Begun—The School at Penikese—A New Era—Unfinished Plans. SUMMARY OF AGASSIZ'S PRINCIPLES: Training the Observing Powers—Importance of Hand-Work—Science the Basis of Education—Knowledge Necessary for Discipline—Authority in Science and Education—Thoroughness in Work and Study Scientific Object-Lessons—Corroborative Views—Uses of Hypotheses—Value of Hypotheses—Hypotheses in Education.

## CHAPTER X.

SYSTEMS OF EDUCATION COMPARED . . . . . 157

INTRODUCTORY. MEMORIZING: Chinese Schools—The Monkish System—English Schools—Grounds of Defense—Securing Attention—Training the Memory—Judgment of Study—Cultivation of Language—Future Use. THE STUDY OF BOOKS: Ideas of what Constitutes an Educated Man—The Worship of Books—Evils resulting from the Abuse of Books—The Place of Text-Books—The Necessity of Text-Books—The Proper Use of Text-Books—Increased Demand for Text-Books. THE STUDY OF THINGS: Cultivation of Perception—Basis of Experience—Materials of Thought. EXPERIMENT AND WORK: Technical Schools—Superiority of Educated Workmen—Work in the Kindergarten—The Next Step Demanded—Manual Training—Hand and Brain Culture. GENERAL SUMMARY.

## CHAPTER XI.

PHYSICAL CULTURE . . . . . . . 178

INTRODUCTORY: Opposing Theories—Factors of Physical Culture—Scope of Instruction—Preparation on the Part of Teachers. FOOD: Kinds of Food—Limitations—Quality of Food—Quantity of Food—Variety of Food—Caution to be Observed—Time for Taking Food—Manner of Taking Food—Miscellaneous Suggestions—Use of Drinks—Pernicious Drinks—Tobacco—Habits of the Teacher. WARMTH: Clothing—Materials for Clothing—Relations of Clothing to Food—Changes of Temperature—Sanitary Suggestions—Houses—Necessary Considerations. LIGHT: Direction of Light—Defective Sight. AIR AND VENTILATION: Sources of Impure Air—Conditions to be Observed—Distribution of Heat—Egress of Air—Ventilating Arrangement—Method of Operation—Practical Suggestions. DIRECT MUSCULAR TRAINING: Calisthenics—Kinds of Exercise—Calisthenic Apparatus—Time given to Exercise—Caution to be Observed. REST: Rest of Change—Rest of Attention—Complete Rest—Daily Rest or Sleep—Amount of Sleep—Rest from Weariness.

## CHAPTER XII.

**ÆSTHETIC CULTURE** . . . . . . . 210

NATURE OF ÆSTHETICS: Standard of Beauty—Ruskin's Views—Experience Theory—Training in Art. FORM: Analysis of Form—Geometric Divisions—Forms Used in Art—Nature the Basis of Art. PROPORTION: Proportion in Architecture—Element of Safety—General Ideas of Proportions—Ideas of Proportion Applied. UNITY: Example in Nature—Unity in Art—Disregard of Unity—Aggregation not Unity. SYMMETRY: Symmetry in Nature—Symmetry in Art. HARMONY: Harmony in Style—Harmony in Nature—Harmony in Art—Want of Harmony. VARIETY: Variety in Nature—Variety in Art—Monotony in Cities—Contrasted Examples. COLOR: Standard of Beauty in Color—Complementary Colors—Variety in Color—Attention to Color. SOUND: Origin of Musical Perception—Æsthetic and Moral Value of Music—Tones in Speech—Unpleasant Tones. GENERAL SUMMARY. ÆSTHETIC TEACHING: The School-room—School Surroundings—Dress—Habits and Manners. DRAWING: Muscular Drill—Cultivating Observation—Perspective and Shading—Use of Color—Industrial Art—Art Proper—National Art.

## CHAPTER XIII.

**MORAL CULTURE** . . . . . . . 245

MORAL AIMS: Neglect of Moral Instruction—Reasons for the Neglect. WHAT IS MORALITY? Basis of Morals. Extent of Needs—Equality of Needs—Basis of Rights—Basis of Duty—Negative and Positive Duties—Standard of Moral Duty—Concrete Examples—Factors of Morality—Individual Morality. MORAL INSTRUCTION IN SCHOOL: Force of Example—Manners—Example of Ill Manners—Limit of Responsibility—Moral Sensibility—Incidental Moral Lessons—Negative Results—Labor and Service—Caution—Recognition of Well-doing. SCHOOL GOVERNMENT: Obstructive Considerations—Changes Desirable—Restraint—Indirect Moral Influences—Dangers of Neglect. DIRECT MORAL TEACHING: Precept and Practice—Use of Common Incidents—Use of Literature—Abuse of Literature—Use of History—Defects in Historic Study—Moral Science. SOCIAL RELATIONS: The Family—General Society—Civil Government—Practical Morality—Applications in Schools—Results of Moral Training.

## CHAPTER XIV.

**GENERAL COURSE OF STUDY** . . . . . . 280

PRELIMINARY: Principles taken as a Basis—The Natural Sciences—Course in Science—Philosophy, or the Humanities—Literature—Geography—History—Mental and Moral Philosophy—Four Subordinate Lines of Instruction—Music—Manual Arts—Language—Mathematics—Course in Music—Course in Language—Course in Manual Arts—Course in Mathematics—Cultivation of Taste.

## CHAPTER XV.

**COUNTRY SCHOOLS AND THEIR ORGANIZATION** . . . 298

COMPARATIVE STANDING: Advantages—Defects—Imperfect Grading—Boards of Control—School-houses—Apparatus and Books—Short Terms—Change of Teachers. QUALIFICATION OF TEACHERS: Scientific Knowledge—General Culture—The Mental Powers—Professional Knowledge—Self-Improvement. DETAILS OF WORK: The Alphabet—Reading—Spelling—Object-Lessons—Rural Affairs.

## APPENDIX.

**THE STORY OF A SCHOOL** . . . . . . 315

# PRINCIPLES AND PRACTICE OF TEACHING.

## CHAPTER I.

*GENERAL OBJECTS OF EDUCATION.*

KNOWLEDGE AS RELATED TO SUCCESS.—"The secret of thrift," says the late Charles Kingsley, "is knowledge. The more you know, the more you can save yourself and that which belongs to you, and can do more work with less effort. A knowledge of the laws of commercial credit, we all know, saves capital, enabling a less capital to do the work of a greater. Knowledge of the electric telegraph saves time; knowledge of writing saves human speech and locomotion; knowledge of domestic economy saves income; knowledge of sanitary laws saves health and life; knowledge of the laws of the intellect saves wear and tear of brain; and knowledge of the laws of the spirit—what does it not save?" The need of special knowledge for all the various trades and professions has long been admitted, but practically the farmer and the teacher have been like the poet—Heaven-taught. We are finally coming to see that the teacher, too, must be specially trained for his profession.

*Conditions of Successful Teaching.*—Before a teacher can set about his professional work intelligently and with assurance of success, he must not only understand its technical details, but he should also have a broad and comprehensive knowledge of the general objects of education, and of the means by which these objects are to be accomplished.

To many, the word *education* has no definite meaning; and to others it only implies an acquaintance with certain stereotyped branches commonly taught in our schools. In our day the science of teaching finds its basis in psychology. The laws of mind have been studied and formulated sufficiently to furnish general guidance to the intelligent teacher. The psychologists, through their minute and careful study of the child-mind, have discovered and applied the laws which should govern the training of children. Every teacher should by some means gain a thorough knowledge of these laws, and should be trained in their application under the guidance of professional instructors.

The mind, in its development, is like a plant which grows from a seed to its full stature. The way in which the growth of a plant results from bringing the germ of the seed into contact with the appropriate substance in which it is planted, is illustrative of the process by which the inherent powers of the mind are brought into contact with material outside of the mind —thus producing growth: but growth, as we shall see, under the laws and limitations of the mental organism itself.

*System, Symmetry, Harmony.*—This illustration may be still further applied. The growth of a plant proceeds systematically, symmetrically, and harmoniously. Stem, bud, leaf, flower, and fruit, come precisely in the succession necessary to accomplish the highest object of the plant. Supplied with appropriate food and culture, the progress of the plant will be distinguished by symmetry and harmony in the development of its different organs. An excessive forcing of stem or leaf will unavoidably result in a limitation of flower and fruit. These organs, therefore, develop in due proportion, and without interference with each other, and, as a natural consequence, avoid loss or waste of force. The harmonious development of the child must follow a similar law or method. The needs of the growing child change as time goes on. These needs must be appropriately supplied in their due order, else instruction retards development.

*Object of Education.*—The object of education, then, is to promote the normal growth of a human being, developing all his powers systematically and symmetrically, so as to give the greatest possible capability in thought and action. These powers must be trained to act harmoniously, so that there need be no waste of effort in any direction.

*The Means of Education* are such agencies as will promote the objects set forth. These means are proper where they contribute to the desired result; they are adequate when they accomplish the result.

All educational means should be measured by this standard of excellence, and they should be adopted or rejected accordingly as they bear this test.

*Division of the Subject.*—Education, in the broad sense, naturally divides itself into physical, intellectual, and moral. The first relates to the development of the body; the second, to the development of the intellectual faculties; and the third, to the development of the emotional nature, moral and æsthetic.

PHYSICAL EDUCATION has for its objects the growth and nurture of the body, and the attainment of bodily strength and skill. Upon the accomplishment of these objects the entire welfare of the human being depends. Without proper bodily growth and nurture, it is impossible to achieve either mental or moral excellence.

*Physical Development Twofold.*—Bodily development is twofold, consisting of physical growth and physical strength. In thought these two can be separated, but in practice they are always associated. While growth and strength go on together, each increment or step of growth must precede an increment or step of strength.

Physical growth depends primarily on a supply of suitable food, and subordinately upon those other material agencies necessary to the preservation of human life. Besides these external conditions, food must be properly digested and assimilated, or converted into bodily tissue. These conditions fulfilled, the body grows, and is nurtured after growth is attained—food being an indispensable agent, and the principal one in promoting the growth.

*Work and Exercise.*—The means used to promote bodily strength—the second object of physical education—are work and exercise. While food in some measure produces strength, its chief object is to promote growth. And while exercise in some degree produces growth, its chief object is to promote strength and skill. Both food and exercise are indispensable to physical development and physical well-being.

Physical well-being, however, is only one of the aims attained through physical training. The psychological value of expression through muscular action is not yet generally comprehended, though Pestalozzi, Von Fellenberg, and Froebel, each in his own way, sought to embody this principle in school methods.

MENTAL EDUCATION.—In intellectual as in physical education, the two objects to be attained are intellectual growth and intellectual strength: the growth of all the faculties of the mind to their full maturity, and the possession of all the strength possible in each individual.

*The Process of Mental Education.*—Though the nature of the mind's action is peculiar, the process of its development is analogous to the process of physical development. Food properly appropriated is the means by which the growth of the body is secured. In like manner the mind grows by what it feeds upon, and the natural aliment that produces mental growth is knowledge.

*Knowledge the Mind's Food.*—The term knowledge is here used in its comprehensive sense, as embracing not only the subjective cognition, or act of knowing, but the things, facts, truths, or material about which this act is employed in bringing the individual into the practical relations of life. As food is indispensable to physical growth, so without knowledge the mind cannot grow. While the mind, from the first, possesses all the germs of mental power, it is the appropriation of knowledge alone that converts its latent and apparently passive capacities into active capabilities.

In accordance with a theory of education fast becoming obsolete, undue value has been ascribed to certain branches of study, notably arithmetic and grammar, as specially valuable for mental discipline. The teacher will observe that this theory and the methods based upon it are wholly discarded in the present work.

*The Character of Knowledge Important.*—The great problem of education has been to adjust the course of study in the manner best adapted to nurture the mind in its various stages of growth, and so to present each subject that the mind can assimilate it with the least waste of effort. Or, to state the problem in another form: "What course of study, and what methods of teaching the same, will best fit the pupil for right living?" Some writers would "darken counsel" by claiming that a course of study dictated by psychology would be quite other than that required to fit the pupil for practical life. Such writers are behind their age, and need not detain our attention.

It will be shown hereafter that the course of study which most effectively moulds the pupil into sympathetic coöperation with his environment is precisely the course prescribed by the laws of mental action, as seen in the growing child.

In his work on moral science, President Hopkins, of Williams, says: "Knowledge is the food of the mind. And as food may overload and enfeeble the body, and is to be received only as there is a capacity of digestion and assimilation, and ultimate reference to action, so knowledge may overload and enfeeble the mind, and should be received only as it can be reflected on and arranged, and so incorporated into our mental being as to give us power for action."

While knowledge in general contributes to mental growth, and while there may be room for choice in regard to the kind of knowledge best adapted to individual development, one specific kind is indispensable, and that is, a knowledge of the conditions of physical well-being. Obedience to physical laws is also a necessity to mental and moral well-being. This knowledge, so momentous to life and everything which makes life worth preserving, includes the careful and systematic observation of all the facts bearing upon the subject; the inferences and laws to be derived from these facts; and the application of laws, through wisely-directed means, to the maintenance of health.

Intellectual strength or power—the second object of intellectual education—is best promoted by exercise. While knowledge in some measure produces strength, its chief object is to promote the growth and nurture of the mind; and while exercise to some extent produces growth, its chief object is to give intellectual strength. The two—knowledge and exercise—are both indispensable to mental development and well-being.

It should not for a moment be supposed that any scheme for the promotion of a true education can be devised that does not involve intellectual work. The improvement of methods of instruction, the perfecting of illustrative apparatus, and all the valuable helps of the best schools, conspire only to avoid misdirection and waste, and to increase intellectual effort, but nothing can supersede the necessity of work as the source of strength.

*The Modes of Exercise*, conducive to strength and best adapted to school-work, are the arrangement of knowledge in logical order, so as to lead to the perception of laws and principles; the expression of knowledge; and the use of knowledge in directly serving the great purposes of life.

These modes of exercise take their practical form in the arrangement of all the facts gained from the study of each branch of instruction in some kind of definite order. The incidents of a journey are arranged in the order of sequence; the events of history in the order of time; and the facts of physical phenomena in the order of causation. The successive topics treated in arithmetic, geography, and the like, are arranged in accordance with relations peculiar to each branch respectively—the arrangement resulting in classification. The knowledge so arranged then finds expression in such language as can be best understood.

The effort of the mind to arrange knowledge, and the subsequent effort to express it clearly, are among the best possible school-exercises for the promotion of intellectual strength. The result of these efforts, when rightly directed, is to put knowledge in the best form for that practical use which still further increases the intellectual life.

*Knowledge and Practice of Rights.*—One other specific kind of knowledge seems to be indispensable to full intellectual development. In consequence of our needs, we have certain rights which are inherent and inalienable. Every human being, before he can arrive at a full mental stature, must not only have a knowledge of these rights, but he must be placed in full possession of them. If his rights are surrendered on the one hand, or infringed on the other, his capabilities are lessened, and he is intellectually both smaller and weaker than he otherwise would have been. This consideration shows the connection between intellectual and moral education.

MORAL EDUCATION considers the relations which exist between the individual and other human beings, and the conduct proper to observe in consequence of those relations. Analogous to the divisions of physical and mental education, moral education consists first of moral growth, and secondly of moral strength. As the moral nature is complex, the agencies that promote moral growth and strength are also complex and require careful analysis.

*Means of Moral Growth.*—These are, *first*, the unconscious affection which reciprocates the love of parents; *secondly*, the sympathy which either springs from personal experience or is awakened by art in some form; *thirdly*, the example of parents and instructors; and, *fourthly*, the investigation of human relations, and the development of the laws which govern such relations.

*The Means of Moral Strength* consist mainly in the application of the moral laws which have been developed, to all cases of conduct. The power of self-control, of subordinating selfish propensities, and of the systematic performance of duty, come from practice alone.; and this power needs to receive distinct encouragement through the whole period of school-life, so that, finally, moral strength may be gained.

The principles of moral development, and the general plan for the introduction of moral exercises into our schools, are given in the chapter on "Moral Education."

GENERAL SUMMARY.—This general survey of the educational field gives us an enlarged view of the nature and scope of education, and it enables us to express these enlarged ideas in the form of a definition. Education has for its objects the development and training of all the powers and faculties of a human being completely and harmoniously; the furnishing of the mind with knowledge of the most worth in the performance of duties; the subjection of all the powers to the control of intelligent and beneficent motive; and the formation of the habit of yielding instant obedience to physical and spiritual laws.

*Scientific View.*—In a paper upon "A Liberal Education," Prof. Huxley summarizes his ideas of the character of an education which is demanded by the science and culture of the times. He says: "The question of compulsory education is settled so far as Nature is concerned. Her bill on that question was framed and passed long ago. But like all compulsory legislation, that of Nature is harsh and wasteful in its operation. Ignorance is visited as sharply as wilful disobedience; incapacity meets the same punishment as crime. Nature's discipline is not even a word and a blow, and the blow first; but the blow without the word. It is left to you to find out why your ears are boxed.

"The object of what we commonly call education —that education in which man intervenes, and which I shall distinguish as artificial education—is to make good these defects in Nature's methods; to prepare the child to receive Nature's education neither incapably, nor ignorantly, nor with wilful disobedience; and to understand the preliminary symptoms of her displeasure without waiting for the box on the ear. In short, all artificial education ought to be an anticipation of natural education. And a liberal education is an artificial education, which has not only prepared a man to escape the great evils of disobedience to natural laws, but has trained him to appreciate and to seize upon the rewards, which Nature scatters with as free a hand as her penalties.

"That man, I think, has had a liberal education who has been so trained in youth that his body is the ready servant of his will, and does with ease and pleasure all the work that, as a mechanism, it is capable of; whose intellect is a clear, cold logic-engine, with all its parts of equal strength, and in smooth working order; ready, like a steam-engine, to be turned to any kind of work, and spin the gossamers as well as forge the anchors of the mind; whose mind is stored with a knowledge of the great and fundamental truths of Nature, and of the laws of her operations; one who, no stunted ascetic, is full of life and fire, but whose passions are trained to come to heel by a vigorous will, the servant of a tender conscience; who has learned to love all beauty, whether of Nature or art, to hate all vileness, and to respect others as himself.

"Such an one and no other, I conceive, has had a liberal education; for he is, as completely as a man can be, in harmony with Nature. He will make the best of her, and she of him. They will get on together rarely, she as his ever-beneficent mother, he as her mouth-piece, her conscious self, her minister and interpreter."

This view of education shows that the instruction prevalent in our schools usually falls far below educational demands. It shows also that teachers frequently take narrow and limited views of their work, and so fail in accomplishing the highest attainable good.

*Effects of Broader Views.*—With these enlarged views in regard to the nature of their work, teachers will pay particular attention to everything that pertains to the physical comfort of their pupils; and they will carefully investigate the laws of physical existence for guidance in the proper care and training of the body. They will make their pupils intelligent in regard to the food they eat, the dress they wear, and every condition which affects their physical welfare.

In mental work they will arrange a course of study in exact accordance with the needs of each stage of mental development; and they will present the knowledge embraced in such a course in the way which science points out. They will not be contented with empiric processes and meagre results. They will be guided by rational and intelligent principles rather than by mere precedent or authority, and in all their work they will conform to the laws of mental development, obtained from a study of mind itself. They will seek to give their pupils greater power to do work in every vocation to which they may afterward be called.

In morals, teachers will aim to have their pupils measure and regulate their own conduct toward others by the standard of human welfare so clearly expressed in the Golden Rule, and to make them intelligent in regard to all human relations. They will so order their work and their own conduct as to stimulate the pupil to devote his life to beneficent use, and to the attainment of that crowning excellence of all education—nobility of character.

The subsequent chapters of this work are devoted to a development of the principles which underlie this broad education, and to a consideration of the means by which it may be attained.

A brief *résumé* of the principles of mental philosophy which underlie this subject will first be given, care being taken to avoid metaphysical discussions on the one hand, and an obscure technical phraseology on the other. These principles furnish a key to all problems in educational work as they arise, whether in regard to subject-matter or methods. Later, the principles thus developed receive additional illustration, and are applied to the details of teaching. The systems of several of the great educational reformers are also carefully examined, and their principles are compared with those derived from the study of mind, as the basis of an intelligent appreciation of their merits and criticisms of their faults.

## CHAPTER II.

*THE MENTAL POWERS.*

IMPORTANCE OF MENTAL SCIENCE TO TEACHING.—All intelligent teaching must be based upon principles derived from a consideration of the powers or faculties of the mind; their modes of action; the order of their development; and the means by which their activity is awakened. Moral, and even physical education, depends largely upon laws which can be known only through an acquaintance with the operations of the mind. Indeed, so completely does this science constitute the ultimate basis upon which all trustworthy investigation where human action is concerned must rest, that it has been called the "Queen of the Sciences."

*A Common Defect of Teachers.*—Notwithstanding the fact that the philosophy of the mind is the basis of all other sciences which involve human action, the common fault of teachers is an almost entire ignorance of the application of mental facts to the work of teaching. In the class-room and in the institute, the constant effort is to ascertain what specific and mechanical methods have proved successful by experiment, rather than to settle by fixed laws what methods must be successful.

The real object of instruction is too often ignored.

The question of primary interest seems to be "How to teach the different branches," instead of "How to develop and train the faculties of the child by the use of these branches." The natural consequence of this superficial view is, that teaching is too often a mere imitative art, of doubtful and varying success. Without a careful and reflective acquaintance with the constitution of the child's mind, the work of the teacher, with his geographies, arithmetics, and grammars, is scarcely less absurd than the performance of a difficult operation in surgery by one who knows all about ligatures, knives, and saws, but understands nothing of human anatomy.

*Scope of the Present Discussion.*—It is not proposed here to give a treatise upon intellectual philosophy, but only such a consideration of mental phenomena as is indispensable to an intelligent understanding of the teacher's work. It has already been shown that knowledge in some form is the aliment upon which the mind feeds, and is necessary in all of the processes of education. We now propose to show the specific relations of knowledge to mind, and the manner in which the different intellectual powers are aroused into activity. In the treatment of this subject the language of appearance or of ordinary life will be employed, instead of the strict phraseology of the sciences.

How Knowledge is Obtained.—The mind in some way becomes possessed of knowledge from the outward world, or from objects. To arrive at the possession of this knowledge, three conditions are necessary: The object respecting which the knowledge is gained; the mind to receive this knowledge; and some organism to serve as a means of communication between the mind and the object. In point of fact, we find that the different ideas derived from objects come through different organs specially adapted to their respective purposes.

*Ideas of Pressure*, and of the weight of objects, are conveyed to the mind by the nerves distributed through the muscles. While nearly all of the muscles of the body are more or less sensitive to pressure, ideas of comparative weight are obtained mainly through the muscles of the arm. The ability of the mind to receive the ideas of pressure and weight is called the *muscular sense;* and the nerves and muscles through which these impressions are made are the organs of the muscular sense.

*Ideas in Regard to the Surface of Objects*, such as rough and smooth, hard and soft, are brought to the mind by the nerves distributed through the skin. These nerves are most sensitive in the ends of the fingers. The same nerves within narrow limits convey ideas of comparative temperature. Excessive heat and excessive cold will destroy the nerves so that the impressions made are nearly identical. With the hand in motion, these nerves give rise to ideas of extension and change of direction, from which are derived ideas of size and form. The capability of the mind to receive these impressions of surface is called *touch*—the fingers being the principal organs of touch.

*Ideas in Regard to the Flavor of Objects*, such as sweet, salt, and bitter, are awakened in the mind by the nerves distributed over the surface of the tongue, and the contiguous parts of the mouth. The surface of bodies only can occasion ideas of flavor, and this surface, at the moment of imparting the impression to the nerves, must be dissolved, or in a liquid state. The capacity of the mind to receive ideas of flavor is called *taste*, and the tongue and palate are the organs of taste.

*Ideas in Regard to the Odor of Objects*, such as musk, rose, or pink, are brought to the mind by the nerves distributed through the cavities of the nose. The impressions which give rise to these ideas of odor are made by an ethereal emanation from an object rather than by the object itself. The capacity of the mind to entertain ideas of odor is called *smell*, the nose being the organ of smell.

*Ideas in Regard to Sound*, such as thunder, musical notes, and speech, are occasioned in the mind by the nerves that ramify through the organism of the internal ear. Sound is neither an object nor an emanation from an object, but is caused by a vibration of the air striking the tympanum of the ear, and this vibration is caused by the motion or vibration of an object. Differences in the rapidity of the vibrations give rise to differences in the pitch of sounds. The power of the mind to receive ideas of sound is called *hearing*. The ear is the organ of hearing.

*Ideas in Regard to Light and Color*, such as red, yellow, and blue, are conveyed to the brain by the mechanism of the eye, and by the nerves passing through the interior of the eye. Light is now generally considered to be the vibrations of an exceedingly attenuated ether which fills the whole interstellar spaces, striking against the structure of the eye.

These vibrations are, in turn, set in motion by the vibrations of a luminous object. The difference in the rapidity of these vibrations gives rise to the ideas of the different colors. By differences in intensity of light; by the distribution of color; by the impressions of extension gained from touch, and by the experience gained from motion, we get corrected ideas of distance, size, and form. The capacity of the mind to receive ideas of light is called *seeing*, or *sight*. The eye is the organ of sight.

*The Senses.*—These six methods by which the mind gets possession of knowledge respecting the outward world are called the *senses*. It will be seen that each sense has its separate function, and that one sense cannot perform the office of another sense.

It has been a question much discussed, whether the organs of one sense can be made to perform the functions of another. For example, can the blind be made to apprehend light and color? and can the deaf ever understand the nature of sound? It is a well-known fact, that the touch of a blind man can be made so sensitive that he can readily distinguish the differences of color in different kinds of cloth. This sensitiveness, however, appears to enable him to distinguish differences in the surface of the fabric which could not be detected by ordinary touch, while it does not convey to him any definite idea of color in the sense in which it is presented to the eye. So of sound. The deaf man may be sensitive to the vibrations of the air, but he can have no adequate idea of the nature of sound as it comes to the ear.

By the loss of one sense the other senses become more acute, but probably the exact functions of one are never performed by another.

*The Senses to be Cultivated.*—As the senses are the only means by which primary knowledge of objects can be obtained, the well-being of every individual demands that the different organs of sense should be so cared for as to be in a healthy and sensitive condition; and the senses themselves should be trained to do their work with precision and skill.

*For example:* the notes in music, the modulations of the human voice in regard to pitch, quantity, and quality, the modifications of tone which constitute speech, and the peculiarities of speech which express the different emotions and passions, must all be addressed to the ear; and that these differences in sound may be fully understood, the ear must receive special training. It is impossible to present these ideas to the mind through the eye, or through any of the other organs of sense.

Ideas in regard to color and form must be addressed to the eye. A verbal description of an object which has not been seen will give a very vague idea of the reality unless the eye has been trained to accurate observation, and has seen something similar to the thing described.

In the study of geography, a large proportion of the descriptive part is worse than useless from the neglect of the early training of the eye. The words of the description, failing to take hold of the experience of the pupil, find no response in the understanding, and the exercise becomes one of words only. To train the eye to an appreciation of natural scenery, architecture, and the like, when accessible real objects are exhausted, recourse may be had to pictures which address themselves to the eye, and by means of which knowledge may be indefinitely extended.

*Mistakes to be Avoided.*—In school, the mistake is often made of endeavoring to convey to the mind ideas belonging to one sense through another. Ideas of form come through the sight and touch alone, and yet many times an effort is made to have pupils comprehend form by mere verbal description addressed to the ear. By an adult, with a well-trained mind, stocked with images derived from experience, such descriptions may be understood, because he is able to translate the language of one sense into that of another; but to a child, who has had little experience, the description becomes a mere verbal formula, conveying no idea except that of sound.

*Sensation.*—The impression which an object makes upon the organ of sense is called *sensation*. In every sensation three things are necessary: an object, an organ of sense, and vitality or life. For example: in seeing, there must be an object to form an image, an eye upon which the image may be formed, and life, so that the image may be transferred to the nervous centres and to the mind.

The eye of an ox may be taken, and the posterior part of the sclerotic coat removed; then, by placing it in an aperture in a darkened room, so that the light from outside will fall upon it as in life, the observer in the room can see upon the retina a picture of all the objects within the visual angle from the aperture where the eye is placed. This image is the mechanical part of sensation, and life only is needed to convert it into sensation proper.

*Attention.*—When a sensation is carried by the

nerve to the brain, the mind may be so engaged in other matters as not to perceive it, and hence the sensation does not become a possession of the mind; or it may be noticed while the mind is in a passive state, or partially engaged in other matters; or it may be received while the mind is in a state of activity, and eagerly seeking it. The attitude of the mind toward sensations in receiving them is called *attention*.

*Nature of Attention.*—Attention is thus seen to be of a twofold character, *active* and *passive*, or, as named by Sir William Hamilton, *primary* and *secondary*. Both of these degrees of attention may be exercised simultaneously. When specially and actively directed to sensations possessing the greatest interest, the attention is primary; while to the subordinate sensations received at the same time, the attention is secondary.

*Examples.*—The mind may be so intent upon the observation of an outward object, upon an occupation in which the hands are engaged, or upon a subject of reflection, that the impressions which are not a part of the subject of contemplation are entirely unnoticed. Household objects, natural scenery, pictures, music, conversation, the roar of the waterfall, and the rush of the locomotive, all make their impression upon the nerves of sense, and these impressions are conveyed to the nervous centres; but upon the absorbed and occupied mind they make no impression, and, as far as mental consciousness is concerned, they are simply non-existent. In this case the principal sensation receives the entire attention, and the subordinate sensations receive none.

Again, the mind may be engaged in examining the

qualities of an object, in the ordinary vocations of the day, or in the examination of a principle in science or philosophy, and at the same time it may be conscious that the wind blows, the rain falls, the fire burns, and of many other things of like character. In this case the principal sensation becomes a possession of the mind through primary attention, and the subordinate sensations through secondary attention.

The attitude of the mind in listening to conversation, to a speech, lecture, or sermon, affords another illustration in point. The mind of the listener is intent upon the subject discussed; but it often happens that, besides the thought, he is conscious of peculiarities of tone, defects in articulation, and inaccuracies in construction, on the part of the speaker, and of conversation carried on by members of the audience. Here the primary and secondary attention are both busy in receiving and recording impressions.

In this matter a caution is to be observed on the part of both the speaker and the listener. Where the peculiarities and inaccuracies of the speaker are of so pronounced a character as to compel the attention of the listener to them instead of to the thought, the effect of the speech is lost, and the time spent in its delivery is wasted. Hence the form and manner of the speech should receive equal care with that bestowed upon the thought.

On the other hand, where the power of verbal criticism is developed in advance of the ability to receive and assimilate thought, the listener will occupy himself in the form and words of the address, while the thought passes unnoticed. The primary attention is fixed on language; and this habit once formed, the mind busies itself upon petty subjects and details, and becomes incapable of receiving the thought which the language is designed to convey.

*Attention to be Trained.*—As no sensation can be received by the mind without attention, it will be seen that habits of systematic attention are among the most fundamental needs of education. Not only should these habits of attention be cultivated, but the mind should be trained to change passive into active attention at will.

*Treatment of Attention.*—In class-recitation, the attention of the pupils must be secured, or the lesson is a failure. The first requisite in securing attention is to have every pupil assume a proper attitude: erect, easy, and with eyes fixed on the teacher. Everything that is within reach of the hand, and that is calculated to divert attention, should be put aside. Lounging, and a listless attitude and manner, should not be permitted.

Should the members of the class generally be interested in something foreign to the lesson, like a game in which they have been engaged, a story that has just been told, or an interesting piece of news, the teacher should seek to turn their thoughts in a new channel by some anecdote or pleasantry, which will gradually lead to the work on hand.

*To Keep the Attention,* when once secured, the teacher must thoroughly understand the subject; must know how to adapt his instruction to the condition of the pupil; and he must be able to present the subject in such an interesting manner, that the mind will be constantly stimulated to reach out for new ideas. The new ideas presented must be related to those which the pupil already possesses, and not so far in advance but that these relations may be readily discovered.

*Perception.*—The act of the mind in becoming fully conscious of a sensation after attention is secured is called *perception*, and the sensation itself is called a *percept*.

*Nature of Percepts.*—The percept may be single and unrelated, arousing no action in the mind beyond the mere sensation received, and, when used by the mind, reflected back as received; or it may be complex and related, leading to comparisons and inferences, and becoming an element of intelligence.

*Examples.*—One class of nursery rhymes consists merely of jingle without sense. When heard, they are received as unrelated percepts, and are given back in the same manner as received. "Intra mintra cutra corn" conveys no idea to the mind save that of sound. All formulas of words, the meaning of which is not understood, are of the same kind, and are received by the mind and reflected back, without arousing further mental action, or becoming elements of real intelligence.

Observations of objects and of phenomena, and language that contains thought which is understood, are complex percepts, stimulating mental activity, and entering into mental processes.

*Reception of Knowledge.*—The act of perception completes the process of obtaining ideas from the outward world, and transforms the qualities and relations of objects impressed upon the senses into intelligence, which contributes directly to mental growth.

The group of activities necessary to the various

stages of obtaining knowledge from objects, including sensation, attention, and perception, are called the *perceptive or receptive power of the mind.*

*Treatment of Perception.*—As through perception alone does the mind receive impressions of the world outside of itself, and as the facts derived from perception are the materials upon which the mind feeds, and by which the higher powers are brought into activity, the importance of perceptive training of the most thorough kind is at once manifest. The habitual neglect of this training in schools is one of the principal sources of their weakness, and is one point to which efforts at reform, at this time, should be principally directed. The details of perceptive processes, and the agencies to be used, are treated more fully in the chapter upon "Object-Teaching."

How Knowledge is Retained.—The mind has the power not only of obtaining knowledge, but of storing it for use by a process which is known by the general name of *memory.* That memory may perform its functions without failure, it is necessary that an idea should be forcibly impressed upon the mind at once, or that it should be repeated a sufficient number of times to make a deep impression.

*Arbitrary Memory.*—A single unrelated perception of ordinary force makes but a faint impression upon the mind, and one that is easily obliterated. Each of a series of unrelated perceptions makes its own impression without deepening that of another. The effort to retain such perceptions must be complete in each instance, success in one case affording no aid in another. The power of retaining single or unrelated perception is known as *arbitrary memory*.

*Suggestive Memory.*—Two or more dissimilar perceptions may be made upon the mind, nearly or quite simultaneously, connected by time, place, circumstance, or sequence. These connected perceptions make a stronger impression than either would separately, and they are laid away together. The effort to retain the series is no greater than to retain a single one, and the connection is such that the one always suggests the other. This form or degree of retaining bears the name of *suggestive memory* or *suggestion*.

*Associative Memory.*—The impression made by a single perception is deepened by another following in the same channel; and when many perceptions are made to follow each other, the impression is deep and lasting. The relations which bind perceptions closely together are likenesses, unlikenesses, and dependence.

*Likenesses.*—Perceptions of the same kind appear to pass through the mind in the same channels, arousing the same kind of mental activity. In this manner objects having the same qualities are connected in the mind. Honey and sugar are connected by the common quality of sweetness; bleached cloth and snow by whiteness; the roar of the cataract and thunder by loudness; and anger and tempest by fierce commotion. When the likeness of a new perception to an old one is clearly seen, the two are at once associated and are stored together. The effort necessary to retain the new is diminished as the likeness to the old is comprehended, and the two are made to pass through the same channel.

*Unlikenesses.*—Perceptions of one kind arouse in the

mind ideas of an opposite character, and contrasted ideas become associated, deepening the impression of each. Ideas of sweet suggest ideas of sour; black, of white; large, of small; rough, of smooth; high, of low; rapid, of slow. These ideas of opposites are stored together, and the one suggests the other. When the one is retained, the effort to retain the other is inconsiderable, and contrast or unlikeness becomes an important element in developing the retaining power.

*Dependence.*—One idea is seen to depend upon another; and by a recognition of this dependence, the ideas pass through the same channel, each deepening the impression of the other. Fire is seen to depend upon fuel; the light of the day upon the sun; breathing upon air; the warmth of the body upon clothing; harvest upon seed-time. Ideas linked by dependence are stored together in the mind, the one suggesting the other. When the relation of dependence is once seen, the effort necessary to retain is greatly diminished.

This mode of retaining by relations, or this degree of the retaining power of the mind, is called *associative memory* or *association*.

As the amount of knowledge retained by association increases, the effort necessary to retain new ideas of the same character decreases, and the mind is relieved of the special effort necessary to every act of arbitrary memory.

*Abuse of Memory.*—It is claimed, for many studies that are shown to be intrinsically worthless, that they are excellent for developing and strengthening memory. From the above considerations it may be inferred that those studies which are the best for supplying the mind with knowledge are the best for strengthening the memory. In many school-exercises there is an effort made to have the pupil retain knowledge by the use of arbitrary memory alone. This is exemplified in the ordinary method of teaching the alphabet. In this exercise the attention is directed to arbitrary characters which have no possible relation to anything ever before seen.

The facts of geography and history are sometimes taught in the same manner, by an appeal to arbitrary memory alone. The result is that the facts, isolated in thought, make very little impression upon the mind, and are quickly forgotten. A lesson learned in this manner may be retained a sufficient time for recitation; but as it consists of disconnected facts, it exhausts the mind in its effort to retain, and leaves no substance of mental growth.

Memorizing the words of a text-book affords another illustration of waste of power in this direction. The attention is fixed primarily upon the words, and the idea may or may not be understood. With no thread of thought connecting them with any other knowledge, the ideas must be retained, if retained at all, by arbitrary memory, resulting in mental exhaustion, and little or no permanent good.

*The Right Use of Memory.*—In all school-exercises in which the lesson of to-day has some relation to the one of yesterday, and these relations are pointed out and understood, they become sources of association, relieving the mind from the strain which each effort of arbitrary memory imposes. The idea is first understood, and then it is associated with the word that expresses it. The two are then linked to other expressed ideas of a similar character in a chain, so that they are not only remembered, but they are always in the proper order for use.

Macaulay, in his review of the life of Bacon, says: " He acknowledged that the memory may be disciplined to such a point as to be able to perform very extraordinary feats. But on such feats he sets little value. The habits of his mind, he tells us, are such that he is not disposed to rate highly an accomplishment, however rare, that is of no particular use to mankind. As to these prodigious achievements of the memory, he ranks them with the exhibitions of rope-dancers and tumblers. 'The two performances,' he says, 'are much of the same sort: the one is an abuse of the powers of the body, the other is an abuse of the powers of the mind. Both may, perhaps, excite our wonder, but neither is entitled to our respect.'"

*Perception and Memory.*—From the foregoing discussion it will be seen that distinct perceptions depend upon the acuteness of the senses, the distinctness of impressions made upon them, and upon the degree of attention which the mind gives to the sensations made. Memory demands all these conditions with the additional one of connected perceptions; and it is thus seen that the course of training best calculated to develop the perceptive powers is the best for the training of the memory. Exercises for the express purpose of strengthening the memory are not only unnecessary, but obstructive in the processes of education.

*Recollection.*—The mind has power to recall past perceptions that have been preserved by memory, and to bring them up for review or other use. This power of the mind is called *recollection*. The various degrees of memory and recollections are known by the general name of the *retentive power of the mind.*

How Knowledge is Used.—The knowledge received from the outward world through the perceptive powers, and stored by the retentive powers, becomes the basis for the action of the mind independently of the objects from which the knowledge was derived.

*Imagination.*—The perceptions derived from objects come to the mind in a certain order and in a certain combination, and are therefore associated in this order and combination. The mind has the power to sever the links by which these ideas are connected in their first presentation, and to rearrange them and link them into new combinations. The elements used in this process are all derived from perception, but the combination may be something entirely unlike anything ever perceived, and essentially a new creation. This rearranging or creative power of the mind is called *imagination.*

*The Depreciation of this Faculty.*—Many teachers in their practice seem to regard imagination as an entirely unnecessary appendage. They look upon it as a mere fancy, adapted to ornamental rather than useful purposes. As a general fact in schools, the culture of the imagination is systematically neglected, and in consequence one great human power remains uncultivated and unused.

The sentiment has also gained wide popularity that, while a cultivated imagination may be of use to the painter and poet, it would be a positive hinderance in the performance of the sterner duties of life. No mistake could be more fatal to a true education than to carry this sentiment into common practice.

*A Highly Practical Faculty.*—Imagination is the faculty of the mind which more than any other enables man to master the forces of Nature, and raise himself above the domain of sense. By its operation and that of reason combined, the investigator is enabled to achieve the highest results in science and philosophy. By means of it the poet builds the verse which becomes a monument of immortal beauty, and the inventor creates a machine which ameliorates the condition of the whole human family. It is the moving force in every step of human progress, by constructing ideals which are higher and better than any that have yet been realized. It is equally the moving force by which each individual is able to reach upward to a higher state of truth, goodness, or beauty. It is a faculty that needs the most thorough cultivation in every human being, without regard to his condition or vocation in life.

*Dependence of Imagination.*—As the imagination must make use of materials furnished by perception, it is readily seen that perception comes first in order, and that the value of imaginative results must largely depend upon the breadth of perception. Without the training of the perceptive powers, and the storing of the mind with perceptive ideas, there is danger that the imagination will exceed its ordinary functions, and create facts, as well as combine real facts into new images.

President Porter says: "The imagination is capable of steady growth, and requires constant cultivation. The creative imagination, when most gifted, can at first only rise to a certain height above the materials which experience gives. Its succeeding essays are founded upon those which have been made before; and it proceeds by successive steps, more or less long and high, till it attains the most consummate achievements that are ever reached by man."

*Treatment of Imagination.*—In the culture of the imagination two points are to be considered: first, that the power be aroused to action; and second, that its action be placed in proper check and control. The first object is gained when the teacher understands the nature of imagination, and is able to provide exercises that will oblige the pupils to make new combinations. The second object can be gained only by a course of instruction that will provide objective study in sufficient variety and extent to fully employ the inquiring activity of the mind, and leave no deficiency in perception to be made up by imagination; and that will so train the higher powers of the mind, that imagination will always be directed to productive results. The processes of culture for the imagination are more fully described in succeeding chapters.

*Reason.*—The mind has power to perceive relations which exist between different objects and processes of thought. It sees the truth common in a complex series of terms, and perceives the sequences of events and of natural occurrences. It traces effect to cause and cause to effect. From relations found in a few instances, it infers general laws, and it subjects its inferences to tests which verify the law. It applies laws in new instances, and brings all the laws of mind and matter into one coherent system. It directs imagination in its rearrangements so as to accomplish definite results. The power of the mind to enter upon these processes, and to accomplish these results, is called *reason*.

Definite instruction in regard to reasoning processes will be found in the chapters upon "Objective and Subjective Teaching."

*Judgment.* — In addition to the faculties already enumerated, the mind has power to decide in regard to any matter brought before it. This decision may have reference to mere perception, or it may involve the most complex processes of imagination and reasoning. In the former case the process is simple, but in the latter it becomes the highest function of which the mind is capable. This power of the mind, when applied to the various uses which reason has devised, points out the best, and also the best which is available, under all the circumstances of the case. It finally disposes of all matters brought before the mind, and from its decisions there is no appeal. This power of the mind is called *judgment*.

*Other Use of the Term.* — Some authors prefer to consider the power of deciding, or of judgment, a part of each of the faculties with which it is associated, rather than a distinct faculty of the mind. For example, the judgment in regard to two perceptions is simply a necessary part of the completed perceptions; and the judgment in regard to two processes of thought is a necessary part of the completed reasoning. So far as the practical application to the science of teaching is concerned, it is entirely unimportant which of these views is taken. The only relevant questions are: Has the mind the power of deciding? and, When is the power exercised?

*Comprehensive Term.* — The several activities by which the mind uses knowledge, apart from the objects in regard to which such knowledge is gained, including imagination, reason, and judgment, are known as the *reflective powers of the mind.*

MIXED MENTAL PROCESSES. — Besides the mental powers for gaining, retaining, and using knowledge, which have just been considered, there are various mental processes, involving two or more of these powers, to which special attention should be given. In some instances these processes are so important and elementary that they are frequently denominated faculties of the mind, and are so classified in mental analysis. In nature and function, however, they are generally considered as mixed or complex mental processes.

*Comparison.*—The power of the mind to distinguish likenesses and unlikenesses, either in objects or in processes of thought, is called *comparison.* When two objects are compared, both of which can be observed at once, the process seems to involve perception directed to two things instead of one, and a judgment in regard to the qualities observed. When one or both of the objects cannot be observed at the time, memory is brought into activity as an auxiliary. When comparison is directed to processes of thought, all the powers of the mind, including perception, memory, imagination, reason, and judgment, may be required.

*Conception.*—The power of the mind to form a picture of past perceptions or ideal combinations is called *conception,* and the picture is called a *concept.* A conception of past ideas is merely a vivid recollection. A conception of ideal scenes, or combinations of ideas, demands the exercise of memory to recall the elements out of which the combination is formed, and an effort of imagination to arrange these elements so as to produce the picture. A conception of objects described, but which have never been perceived, involves perception of familiar objects, memory of the ideas perceived, imagination to rearrange the familiar ideas, and reason to make the new combination conform to the description given.

ORDER OF MENTAL DEVELOPMENT.— The order of the development of the mind may be determined by considering the relations of knowledge to the mind, and by the study of the phenomena of mind in its gradual change from infancy to maturity.

In regard to the relations of knowledge to mind, it will be seen, from the foregoing presentations, that knowledge must be obtained before it can be retained, and that it must be both obtained and retained before it can be used.

In obtaining knowledge of objects, sensations must be experienced before attention can be given, and both sensation and attention must precede perception.

In retaining knowledge, the successive steps must follow the corresponding steps of perception. First a single sensation is impressed upon the memory, then groups of sensations, and at a later period the principle of association obtains.

The higher forms of association become possible only when the mind is comparatively well furnished with facts.

Arranged according to the character of the knowledge upon which they are exercised, the respective functions of the imagination, reason, and judgment seem to follow each other in the order in which they have been presented.

*These Principles Confirmed by Observation.*—By a careful study of the gradual growth of mind from infancy to maturity, it is found that the mental activities at each stage of growth exactly correspond to the principles of development evolved from a study of the relations of knowledge to mind.

In childhood the senses and the observing powers are keen and active, and the mind eagerly takes in and retains impressions from the outward world. During this period, mental activity is chiefly directed to the perception of the qualities of objects and their simple relations.

As the mind grows, the interest gradually changes from these qualities and simple relations to the more obscure and complex relations of objects. Finally it rises to the relations of thought, until at maturity the reflective powers are not only most active, but they guide and control the entire action of the mind.

*Age an Important Consideration.*—In furnishing the mind with its appropriate knowledge, the particular period of life through which the individual is passing is to be considered as no less important than the stage of mental development at which he has arrived. Perceptive studies, or those that appeal directly to the senses, are best adapted to childhood, because they alone satisfy the mental power most active at the time, and furnish the materials upon which the higher mental powers exercise themselves at a later period: studies, on the contrary, that appeal chiefly to the reasoning faculties, have no place in the primary school, but belong to the advanced course of study. At a period near maturity, or at middle age, the mind is usually more interested in reflective than in perceptive processes; and if the perceptive period has passed without its legitimate work, the mind is poorly supplied with the materials of thought, and the reflective powers, operating upon narrow and insufficient grounds, reach no just or valuable conclusions.

EXPRESSION AS RELATED TO MENTAL DEVELOPMENT. —The activities of the mind are so intimately associated with language that it is scarcely possible to consider the two as separate. All ideas and thoughts have their representatives in words and sentences, and some philosophers have contended that it is impossible to think without thinking in language.

Without adopting this extreme view, however, we see that in all mental operations language acts an important part. No sooner does a new idea present itself, than the mind at once seeks for a word to express it. Should no suitable word be found, the idea is expressed by a combination of words, or by a word coined for the occasion. The mental act of receiving ideas and preparing them for use is not complete until they are not only fully possessed by the mind but fitly expressed in words.

*This Position Illustrated.*—In his work on Logic, Sir William Hamilton says: " A country may be overrun by an armed host, but it is only conquered by the establishment of fortresses. Words are the fortresses of thought. They enable us to realize our dominion over what we have already overrun in thought; to make every intellectual conquest the basis of operations for others still beyond. Or another illustration: You have all heard of the process of tunneling through a sand-bank. In this operation it is impossible to succeed unless every foot—nay, almost every inch—in our progress be secured by an arch of masonry, before we attempt the excavation of another. Now language is to the mind precisely what the arch is to the tunnel. The power of thinking and the power of excavation are not dependent on the word in the one case or the mason-work in the other; but without these subsidiaries, neither process could be carried on beyond its rudimentary commencement. Though, therefore, we allow that every movement forward in language must be determined by an antecedent movement forward in thought; still, unless thought be accompanied, at each point of its evolution, by a corresponding evolution of language, its further development is arrested."

*The Twofold Office of Language.*—The advance of ideas and of language, then, must go on together. Language is used for the double purpose of expressing and of preserving knowledge. Should ideas fail of finding expression, they are imperfectly preserved or entirely lost. Should expression be sought in advance of ideas, the words uttered would be senseless as the chatterings of a parrot. In each step of progress the idea precedes the expression, but should be immediately followed by the word. The two henceforth become so blended that they cannot be separated in practice, and scarcely so in thought.

The importance of cultivating language along with thought, in teaching, even to the extent of carrying this twofold training into every branch of instruction, cannot be too strongly urged. At least half of the time of recitation should be given to expression, so that the pupil may have the advantage of language in both mastering and remembering the thought. When this method is habitually practised, language is usually acquired by secondary attention, while primary attention is fixed on the thought. Perspicuity of expression follows clearness of thinking, and mistakes in expression usually result from want of clearness in the thought. The most effectual method of correcting such mistakes is by discussing the thought until it is clearly understood, and then requiring it to be expressed again. By following this plan of criticism, in practical instruction, much onerous labor is saved the teacher, and many of the distinctive exercises in language of maturer years are rendered unnecessary.

It must also be borne in mind that words are not the only means of expression. Mathematical symbols are used as language to express certain forms of thought. Drawing and painting are both but a means of expression. Laboratory work and manual work of various kinds must be employed both in acquiring knowledge and in putting it to use. In all school-work the teacher must make sure that the "mental circuit" is complete. The pupil must be held to the subject in hand till he can give it adequate expression in some form.

# CHAPTER III.

### *OBJECTIVE COURSE OF INSTRUCTION.*

GENERAL VIEW OF PRESENT PRACTICES.—Until within a comparatively recent period, little attention has been given to the principles which must govern every intelligent effort to impart instruction. Teachers have been content to follow the methods in which they themselves were taught, until the process of teaching has become a merely mechanical routine.

Preliminary to the examination of philosophical methods of teaching, we shall notice some of the practices—they can scarcely be called methods—which are always to be avoided.

*Wrong Practices.*—The great, conspicuous, evil practice in our schools, once almost universal, and still widely prevalent, is that of obliging pupils to commit to memory the words of the text-book. This practice seems to have its origin either in the ignorance or the indolence of the teacher, and is one calculated directly to stultify, rather than expand, the mind. It fixes the primary attention on words rather than on thoughts, which words are arranged to express. The words memorized to-day are forgotten to-morrow, and often the thought is never obtained. This process, by substituting apparent for real knowledge, so far consumes the time of the pupil that the attainment of real knowledge is rendered nearly or quite impossible during the school period.

*Examples of this Practice.*—Pupils are frequently obliged to recite, *verbatim*, the outlines of history, and teachers often defend the practice of rote-teaching in this study after they have given it up in the other branches of instruction. Upon examining a class instructed in this manner, in one of the most noted schools in the country, a few years since, it was found that the pupils could glibly repeat the lesson of to-day; that they could recite about half of that of yesterday; but that they could not remember one word of the lesson of a week ago. While this was the fact in regard to the words of the lesson, it was found that the thoughts which the words were supposed to represent had been entirely neglected—no one in the class having any knowledge of the sequence or relations of events.

A little girl of eleven years came home late one day, and, on inquiry, said she was detained because she could not recite her lesson in geography. As she had forgotten but one word, however, she soon learned it, completed the lesson, and was dismissed. When asked what the word was, she could not tell, although she came fresh from her recitation only across the street. Upon examination, the following was found to be the sentence which made the difficulty, and which she and the other members of the class were obliged to repeat: "The Danubian provinces of Servia, Moldavia, and Wallachia are nominally independent of the Sublime Porte."

Further investigation proved that the teacher had made no effort to explain the meaning of any one of the terms used, that no maps were employed in the recitation, and that the members of the class were as profoundly ignorant of the subject they were supposed to be learning as though it had been written in Choctaw.

*Rote-Learning.*—The memorizing of definitions, principles, and rules in science, before the facts upon which they are based are known, is equally repugnant to the well-settled principles of mental development.

Herbert Spencer says: "The once universal practice of learning by rote is daily falling more into discredit. All modern authorities condemn the old mechanical way of teaching the alphabet. The rote-system, like other systems of its age, made more of the forms and symbols than of the things symbolized. To repeat the words correctly was everything, to understand the meaning nothing; and thus the spirit was sacrificed to the letter. It is at length perceived that, in this case as in others, such a result is not accidental but necessary; that in proportion as there is attention to the signs, there must be inattention to the things signified."

*Nervous Action.*—Dr. Carpenter, in his "Mental Physiology," clearly shows the manner in which impressions upon the nerves are received and treated. The nervous centres consist of the cerebrum or anterior brain, the principal nervous mass, and of the subordinate centres, the sensorium or base of the brain, the spinal cord, and the ganglions. Impressions made upon the nerves, and carried to the cerebrum, become a possession of the mind and are transmuted into intelligence; those carried to the spinal cord or ganglions produce reflex or automatic actions which do not involve intelligence; and those carried to the sensorium and no farther, produce a semi-reflex action in which there are only faint traces of intelligence. Impressions made upon the sensorium are reflected back in the same manner as received, as when words or formulas are repeated when not understood.

*Semi-Reflex Action.*—The following quotation from a late article in the London *Times* reviewing the work of Dr. Carpenter further illustrates this principle, and shows its application directly to the work of teaching.

" There are probably few teachers who have not heard something about the possibility of 'learning by rote,' which is one form of mere sensorial activity in which certain sounds have become associated with the sight of certain written or printed symbols, and are uttered when these symbols are seen and remembered; but there probably is not one in a thousand who understands what 'learning by rote' is; how it is accomplished by the nervous centres; how it differs from learning with the intelligence; and how it may be detected and exposed under whatever guise it may be concealed.

" The great majority of teachers think that they have banished learning by rote when their pupils are able to explain their first answer to a question by a second one; the second, in most cases, being as purely sensorial a symbol as the first, and the original sight symbol, with its two vocal equivalents, being really, as far as ideation is concerned, an unknown quantity, for which either of the two other unknown quantities may be substituted.

" One of the most familiar illustrations of sensorial

action is that which was recorded by the late Mr. Brookfield, in which two children, aged about eleven years, who did their arithmetic and reading tolerably well, who wrote something pretty legible, intelligible, and sensible about an omnibus, and about a steamboat, were called upon to write the answers of the Church Catechism to two questions. The children had been accustomed to repeat the Catechism during half an hour each day in day-school and Sunday-school, for four or five years, and this is what they wrote:

"'My duty toads God is to bleed in him to fearin and to loaf withold your arts withold my mine withold my sold and with my sernth to whirchp and to give thanks to put my old trast in him to call upon him to onner his old name and his world and to save him truly all the days of my life's end.'

"'My dooty tords my nabers to love him as thyself to do to all men as I wed thou shall do and to me to love onner and suke my farther and mother to onner and to bay the queen and all that one pet in a forty under her to smit myself to all my goones teaches spiritial pastures and marsters to oughten mysilf lordly and every to all my betters to hut no body by would nor deed tò be treu in jest in all my deelins to beer no malis nor ated in your arts to kep my ands from peckin and steel my turn from evil speak and lawing and slanders not to civet or desar othermans good but to learn labour trewly to get my own leaving and to do my doody in that state if life and to each it his please God to call men.'

"It will be observed that these written answers, if recited with sufficient rapidity, in the customary schoolroom patter, really bear a horrible likeness to the sounds of the genuine one; and there can be but little doubt that the writers and their classmates had so recited them for years, to the entire satisfaction of all who were 'pet in a forty' over them.

"Even in Mr. Brookfield's report, from which the examples are taken, there is no evidence of any perception that they represent a nervous action which, as a result of teaching, is wholly wrong in kind, and not only in degree, and which, so far as it is permitted to continue, is not merely an expression of waste of time, but of the growth of habits, directly antagonistic to, and incompatible with, those which it should be the chief object of instruction to encourage.

"Until this is recognized and acted upon, and until teachers have some knowledge of the profound difference between the two kinds of action as modes of mental operation, it is hopeless to expect from schools an amount of cultivation of the intelligence at all commensurate with the magnitude and costliness of the machinery which is employed."

*Studies too Difficult.*—Another habit, which is very prevalent and which is almost as pernicious, is that of assigning to pupils studies too difficult for their comprehension. Without really understanding a single principle of the subject taught, they career along, occasionally catching a gleam of knowledge, but falling far short of what might be accomplished in the same length of time by rightly-directed efforts.

*Examples.*—The prevalent method of teaching mental arithmetic to small children is a case in point. Because mental arithmetic has been proved to be a most excellent discipline for the mind at the proper time, it therefore seems to be assumed that it will be of great value at all times. Hence it has been extensively introduced into primary schools. By the study of it young pupils have been obliged to go through reasoning processes which would severely tax the mental powers of adults, and this, too, before their reasoning faculties were developed sufficiently to readily understand the subject. The result has been that frequently pupils have learned the formulas by which the examples are analyzed, just as they would learn any other form of words, while the real reasoning contained in the process was never understood.

In grammar the same mistake is often made. Through the erroneous notion that a knowledge of English grammar ensures correct speaking and writing, text-books in grammar are put into the hands of young children, and their minds are crammed with definitions and rules concerning the philosophic structure of language, and this before their mental powers are so far developed as to comprehend the principles which are sought to be given. The matter memorized, having failed to reach the understanding, becomes a hinderance rather than a help to education.

In reading-classes the same fault obtains. Pupils are permitted, through the ambition or weakness of their teacher, to read in books entirely above their comprehension; and the result is, that they fail to obtain any knowledge from their reading, while the delivery, as a necessary consequence, becomes expressionless and monotonous.

*Faults of Omission.*—The next great fault is a defect or omission rather than a positive evil. The primary exercises for training the observing powers are neglected to such an extent that, as far as the schools are concerned, pupils might almost as well be born deaf and blind. The objects with which they come daily in contact, the phenomena which constantly appear before their eyes, the facts of Nature and of consciousness upon which all science and philosophy are based, are nearly, if not entirely, neglected. At the same time the studies pursued have little connection with matters of common interest, and, as a consequence, fail of bestowing that practical knowledge and breadth of culture necessary to the highest success.

*Examples.*—Generally, in schools, very little if any attention is given to the open book of Nature, which contains lessons of such transcendent importance and interest. One series of the lessons thus neglected is the peculiar stratification, marking, and fossils of the rocks, each of which is a key to a history more profound than that recorded in any human chronology. Another similarly neglected series is found in the wonderful variety of plants, each one an object of beauty, and all together, in their manner of growth, in their distribution, and in their peculiar habits, furnishing lessons which cannot fail to leave their impress of mental growth, and to become sources of never-ending delight while life and sense last. The curious and strange forms of animal life, the metamorphoses of insects from creeping worms to gorgeous butterflies, the peculiar habits of beasts and birds, and the instincts which so nearly approach reasoning, are all replete with these interesting lessons, and they are usually so neglected that the mind fails of comprehending the evidences of intelligence found in the infinite variety and profound laws of the universe.

Carlyle says: "For many years it has been one of my most constant regrets that no schoolmaster of mine had a knowledge of natural history, so far, at least, as to have taught me the grasses that grow by the wayside, and the little winged and wingless neighbors that are continually meeting me with a salutation which I cannot answer, as things are. Why did not somebody teach me the constellations, too, and make me at home in the starry heavens which are always overhead, and which I don't half know to this day? I love to prophesy that the time will come when the schoolmaster will be strictly required to possess these two capabilities, and that no ingenious little denizen of this universe be thenceforward debarred from his right of liberty in these two departments, and doomed to look on them, as if across grated fences, all his life."

RACE AND INDIVIDUAL GROWTH.—The study of history shows that the progress of the race, when the whole human family is taken into consideration, has been a continuous growth or change in a definite direction, and according to certain established principles in the evolution of mind. Commencing at a period when physical Nature tyrannized over man, the change has been continuously in the direction, first, of subduing Nature, then of quickening and refining the senses; after this, of exalting the reason above the senses, and of converting meagre notions into definite, connected, and well-defined thought.

By a careful study of mental development, we find

that the individual passes through changes analogous to the changes that affect the race. In infancy there is the same helplessness in regard to Nature, the same bluntness of the perception, the same subordination of the reason to the senses, and the same vagueness of ideas and thought. From infancy to maturity, the progress is continuous toward making Nature a servant rather than a master, of making thought systematic and definite, and of rendering each step in intelligence a help toward the attainment of higher intelligence.

*Historical Examples.*—In the history of the Israelites, as given in the Old Testament Scriptures, we may see the development of a people from a very low condition of slavery and ignorance to a point of intellectual strength and refinement made remarkable by their distinguished prophets, poets, and teachers. When we compare the character of the people just liberated from Egyptian bondage with their mental and moral condition at the time of the birth of Jesus, the contrast is very striking. The educational means used in the work of this development (we have here nothing to do with the spiritual cultus of the Jews) is equally worthy of note. At first, the stupid and sensuous mind could be aroused and instructed only by addressing the senses. Gradually the tyranny of sense yields to the higher power of an unfolding imagination, and finally the old system of symbol and song passes away, and the reason of this people is addressed by the statement of principles and the analysis of mental facts. Yet, even in this new system of education, the Great Teacher is careful not to violate the laws of mental growth. To the untutored pupils whom He gathered about Him, He said : " I have many things to say unto you, but ye cannot bear them now."

An equally remarkable development is illustrated in the history of the English nation, which, with its settled principles of government, its reflective literature, its art, and philosophy, springs from an uncouth Anglo-Saxon origin. The advancement of a nation may be judged from the progress of its literature; for the literature of a people indicates, at each period, the steps of its psychical development. The beginnings of a nation's literature may be traced to an attempt to record the simplest facts of observation and sense, or the combination of these facts into rude imaginative creations. Hence legend, story, poetry, and the drama, always precede systematic history, dialectics, or philosophy. In the history of every enlightened nation, the presentation of fact and the representation of picture in answer to the question " What ?" have always taken precedence of the explanation of facts or the analysis of principles in answer to the question " Why ?" The age of Homer comes before the ages of Thales, Pythagoras, and Aristotle. The primitive literature of Rome appears in the form of minstrelsy. The literature of England passes through the simple poems and tales of Piers Ploughman, Mandeville, and Chaucer, before it reaches the stern philosophy of Bacon, or the ripe fruit of the literature of the Elizabethan age.

So also in regard to the development of government. The blind struggle of centuries brought at last the Great Charter; but defined principles of government were of much later date. Upon this point Macaulay says: " It is only in a refined and speculative age that a polity is constructed on system. In rude societies the progress of government resembles the progress of language and of versification. Rude societies have language, and often copious and energetic language; but they have no scientific grammar, no definitions of nouns and verbs, no names for declensions, moods, tenses, voices. Rude societies have versification, and often versification of great power and sweetness; but they have no metrical canons; and the minstrel, whose numbers, regulated solely by his ear, are the delight of his audience, would himself be unable to say of how many dactyls and trochees each of his lines consists. As eloquence exists before syntax and song before prosody, so government may exist in a high degree of excellence before the limits of legislative, executive, and judicial power have been traced with precision."

From the study of the development of the race we obtain a knowledge of those general principles which control the development of the individual; and conversely, the careful examination of individual growth will serve to throw light on obscure points in the historical development of the race. The knowledge gained from this twofold examination of individual and race development has scarcely yet been organized into a science; but enough is now understood to be of the greatest service to the teacher in preparing his course of study and in determining the methods to be pursued.

OBJECTIVE OR INDUCTIVE METHOD.—The first step in mental growth and consequently in education is to obtain knowledge. This knowledge comes in the form of perceptions of the qualities of objects, or facts in regard to the relations of objects. The primary perceptions or facts come through the senses. This primary knowledge becomes the basis for all subsequent operations of the mind.

The second step is a comparison of two or more perceptions and the recognition of their likenesses and unlikenesses. This comparison begins with objects the qualities of which, such as form, size, and color, are like or unlike. The facts concerning objects and their relations are also compared in the same manner.

*Grouping.*—When objects are alike, they are associated in thought, and form a *group*. Qualities of objects may be considered apart from the objects themselves, and associated by their likeness, forming a *group of qualities*—as square, large, and red. Facts concerning objects may in like manner be compared, and formed into a single group by their likenesses.

When objects are unlike, they are separated in thought and are placed apart, forming the basis of *different groups*. Qualities of objects, and facts concerning objects, are in the same way separated by their unlikenesses and formed into different groups. Unlikenesses as well as likenesses form the basis of association for the assistance of memory.

*Objective Classification.*—In comparing a large number of objects, several being found alike may constitute a group; several others unlike the first may also be alike and form another group, and this process may continue until a number of distinct groups are formed. The basis of each group is likeness, and the basis of the several groups is unlikeness. When these several groups, unlike in particular qualities, are alike in some general characteristics, the different groups are called *classes*, and the process of forming them is termed *Objective Classification.*

*Generalization, Law, Principle, Definition.*—The characteristic in which the different classes are alike is a *general truth*, and the process or power of obtaining a general truth is called *generalization.* When the general truth expresses invariable relations, it is called a *law.* Assumed as the basis of further mental operations, a law is called a *principle.* When the general truth expresses a description, or fixes the limits of a subject, it is called a *definition.*

*Examples.*—A number of objects may be compared. From their likenesses we call one group *hats*, another group *boots*, and still another *coats.* The articles in each group are alike in regard to the particular use for which they are made; and the groups are unlike because the uses of the articles in the different groups are not identical. By a further investigation, however, we find that hats, boots, and coats are all clothing for the protection and comfort of the body—the general truth arrived at being the idea expressed by the word clothing. A description of this idea is a definition.

A phenomenon is observed, like the falling of an apple. This fact is compared with the falling of other substances, and a number of facts are grouped together by their likenesses. We observe, also, that bodies, like the articles on a table, do not fall to the ground. We have now two groups, and the difference we observe between them relates to their support. By a further investigation we find that all bodies not supported fall to the ground, and this conclusion is a law. By a wider investigation, involving a greater number of facts and relations, we infer that all bodies have a tendency to approach each other, and this inference is also a law—but a law of wider application than the preceding one.

This process of beginning with simple perceptions, and ending in the discovery of a law or in the expression of a definition, is *primary*, because it embraces the first steps which the mind must take in the acquisition of knowledge; it is *objective*, because it begins with an object; it is *synthetic*, because it aggregates or puts together; and it is *inductive*, because it leads into a law or principle.

*Benefits of the Objective Method.*—In regard to mental development, the objective course contributes mainly to mental growth, and without a wide accumulation of knowledge systematically arranged by the inductive method, the mind can not attain its full stature. By this method the faculties are exercised in the exact order in which they are successively brought into activity by a natural and normal development. The method itself has a tendency to arouse this activity in its natural order.

In regard to knowledge, the objective method is the very way in which all definite ideas of the outward world are obtained. It is also the course of discovery. By means of it each individual learns the facts of the universe, and becomes acquainted with the laws which control all phenomena. Through it the human race gained its first knowledge of Nature, and took its first steps in civilization.

*Spirit of Modern Science.*—The great revolution effected by Bacon is largely attributable to the ends which he proposed as the proper ones for all scientific and philosophic investigation. These ends consisted *first*, in multiplying human enjoyments and in mitigating human suffering. The ancient philosophy which ruled over the thoughts of men, up to the time of the great inductive philosopher, "disdained to be useful, and was content to be stationary." Bacon valued knowledge in the direct proportion as it promoted utility and human progress.

The change in the ends proposed necessitated a change in methods. When the end of philosophy was an ideal and unattainable exaltation of spirit above material needs and desires, the methods pursued were purely speculative, and independent of the facts of Nature or consciousness. When the end was the promotion of human welfare, then these facts were of the most profound significance, and nothing could be considered "too insignificant for the attention of the wisest which is not too insignificant to give pain or pleasure to the meanest."

From this change in the ends and methods of thought and investigation, modern science had its birth, and since that time has performed its wondrous mission of beneficence to humanity. Its progress, however, has been marked by a continuous battle with the inertia and with the reactionary forces of society—a conflict still far from being ended.

The introduction of the objective course into schools is but the recognition in education of the ends and methods which have proved of such eminent advantage in science. And when both are thoroughly understood and appreciated by our teachers, we may expect a result as beneficent as that already effected in science, and one much more universal in its application.

# CHAPTER IV.

### *SUBJECTIVE COURSE OF INSTRUCTION.*

THE SUBJECTIVE METHOD.—When all the available facts bearing upon a subject have been acquired, compared, and classified, according to the objective method; and when generalizations have been made resulting in laws or definitions, then the subject has become a possession of the mind, and needs to be arranged in such order as to be most easily and effectively used. At this point the knowledge under consideration becomes the basis for the subjective course.

This knowledge is expressed either in the form of a law, or a definition. When expressed as a law, the subjective course consists of successive applications of the law to new departments of thought and research. The results of these applications of law are at once a verification of the law and the placing of phenomena in the order of dependence. The application of laws in the investigation of science and philosophy is governed by the rules of deductive logic.

*Definition.*—When subjective knowledge starts from a definition, the first thing to consider is the definition itself. The essential elements of a true definition are *simplicity* and *truth*. The definition must be expressed in language more perspicuous and simple than the word or thing to be defined; and it must embrace and express the truth, the whole truth, and nothing but the truth.

*Examples of Definition.—Addition is Addition.* This is not a real definition, because the word to be defined is used in the definition—thus producing mere tautology.

*Addition is the Process of Adding two or more Quantities.* In this case the word defined is repeated in one of its forms, and nothing simpler or more easily understood is given. This is called "defining in a circle."

*Addition is the Aggregation of the Individualities that Compose an Entity.* Here the words employed are more difficult of comprehension and less simple and perspicuous than the word to be defined.

*Geography is a Description of the Moon.* This definition is at fault because it is not true.

*Geography is a Description of Europe.* This definition does not express the whole truth.

*Geography is a Description of the Earth.* This definition expresses more than the truth.

In all subjective work the importance of definition can scarcely be over-estimated. Every definition, before it is finally accepted, should be tested by the principles already illustrated.

*Division of a Subject.*—The second step in the subjective course is the division of a subject into distinct parts. This division must be made on a single basis, and the several parts must represent *real differences*.

These divisions may be natural, as the division of

stars into fixed stars and planets; or they may be artificial and conventional, as the divisions in the census-tables—separating persons by their ages into classes embracing those under ten years and those over ten years of age.

*Imperfect Division.*—Whenever it is found, on a thorough examination of each of the parts, that they fail to exhaust the subject, the division is faulty, because the parts are insufficient in number. And when the parts are found to overlap each other, and partially to treat of the same department of the subject, the division is imperfect, either from having too great a number of parts, or from a failure to observe the relations which subsist between the basis and the parts.

*Subjective Classification.*—The several parts into which the subject is divided are next arranged for examination in the order of their dependence—the part which is independent receiving the first attention, the one depending on the first coming next in order, and so on. This division of a subject into its constituent parts upon a single basis, and the arrangement of the parts according to the laws of dependence, is known as *subjective classification.*

*Illustration.*—Take, for example, grammar. The subjective treatment would call first for a definition which would exactly limit the subject. Upon the basis of the words that compose the language, grammar is divided into Orthography, which treats of the formation of words; Etymology, which treats of the classification of words; Syntax, which treats of the formation of sentences out of words; and Prosody, which treats of the classification of sentences. In the order of the examination of these parts, it will be seen that words must be formed before they can be classified; that they must be formed and classified before they can be made into sentences; and sentences must be formed before they can be classified. Hence, Orthography is the independent term, Etymology is the term depending upon Orthography alone, Syntax the term depending upon Orthography and Etymology, and Prosody the term depending upon all of the preceding.

*Opposing Theories.* — A controversy has arisen among scientific men in regard to the classification of natural history: one party insisting that the divisions shall be grouped around types, while the opposite party is equally strenuous that all divisions shall be founded upon *definition*. From the analysis here made, it will be seen that the classification resulting from the process of discovery is objective, and of necessity is based on types; while the classification which comes from a more extended knowledge, viewed as a whole, is subjective, and is based upon definitions.

*Scientific View.*—Huxley says: " So long as our information concerning them is imperfect, we class objects together according to resemblances which we feel but cannot define; we group them around types, in short. Thus, if you ask an ordinary person what kinds of animals there are, he will probably say: Beasts, birds, reptiles, fishes, and insects. Ask him to define a beast from a reptile, and he cannot do it; but he says: 'Things like a cow or a horse are beasts, and things like a frog or lizard are reptiles.' You see, he does class by type, and not by definition. But how does this classification differ from that of the scientific zoölogist? How does the meaning of the scientific class-name of 'mammalia' differ from the unscientific name of *beasts?* Why, exactly because the former depends on a definition, and the latter on a type. The class mammalia is scientifically defined as 'all vertebrated animals that suckle their young.' Here is no reference to type, but a definition rigorous enough for a geometrician; and such is the character which every scientific naturalist recognizes as that to which his classes must aspire—knowing, as he does, that classification by type is simply an acknowledgment of ignorance and a temporary device."

*Definition of Divisions.*—The third step in the subjective course is the treatment of the several parts as though each were a new subject. These parts are to be taken in the order of their arrangement, and each one defined—the definition to conform to the standard already described. The name given to each part, as far as possible, should indicate the basis upon which the division is made.

*Sub-divisions.*—The fourth step is the separation of the divisions or sub-divisions, following the same law and the same order as the first general divisions of the subject. These steps of successive definition and division follow each other alternately until the ultimate facts, which lie at the foundation of the whole subject, are reached.

CHARACTERISTICS OF THE SUBJECTIVE COURSE.—This process of beginning with the knowledge of a subject, expressed as a definition, and ending in ultimate facts, is *secondary*, because it comes after the primary course;

it is *subjective*, because it begins with the subject already in the mind; it is *analytic*, because it takes apart; and it is *deductive*, because it leads from a law or definition.

*Relations to Development.*—In regard to mental development, the subjective course contributes mainly to mental strength, and without it the individual, though of mature years, is still a child in thought. The effect of the subjective treatment upon the mind is analogous to the effect of muscular exercise upon the body. While to some extent this process may contribute to growth, its principal effect lies in the increase of power.

*Relations to Knowledge.*—In regard to knowledge, the subjective course points out the way in which knowledge may be used. It is the course of application. By means of it each individual learns to bring phenomena under the domain of law, and to see in all phenomena the evidence of law. Through it the race turns knowledge to profitable account, and makes it contribute to the promotion of human welfare.

*Place in an Educational Course.*—The subjective course rounds out and completes education. It points out the way in which objective knowledge can be rendered practically useful. With a broad foundation of facts observed and laws discovered, this course coördinates them all, opens the way for new investigation in higher fields of thought, and becomes emphatically the course of wisdom. Keeping in view that the end to be attained is human welfare, it converts all knowledge into philosophical agencies, and regards knowledge as valuable in proportion as it can be made to conduce to this end.

*Misuse of the Subjective Method.*—By attempting to use subjective methods without a sufficient objective foundation, human thought has been led into unreal and fanciful speculations, which have often been dignified by the name of philosophy. Mental processes sustained by a narrow basis of fact require the same expenditure of vital force as those built upon broader foundations, but they lack *fruit*. To use the expressive language of Macaulay: "A pedestrian may show as much vigor on a tread-mill as on a highway; but, on the road the vigor will assuredly carry him forward, and on the tread-mill he will not advance an inch. Many of the old philosophies were tread-mills, not paths. They were made up of controversies which were always beginning again. They were contrivances for having much exertion and no progress. During the time of their continuance the human race accordingly, instead of marching, merely marked time. Words, and mere words, and nothing but words, had been the fruit of all the toil of all the most renowned sages of sixty generations."

By enlarging the basis of thought, the same vigor in thinking has created all the many improvements which have contributed so much to the welfare of the race. This changed method is seen in the mental and moral spheres, as well as in the sphere of physical action; and now the question which is most frequently asked by philosophers is: "How will this thought affect the condition of men?" The old fruitless philosophies, with their narrow formalisms and unattainable ends, became firmly intrenched in the schools, where they have had supreme control until within a comparatively recent period. Missing the great ends of education, these schools have often borne fruit of words only. The faults of the systems were precisely the faults of the philosophies upon which they were founded, and the remedy for these faults is to be found in a generous objective course to precede all efforts at subjective reasoning.

THE OBJECTIVE AND SUBJECTIVE COURSES COMBINED.—From the foregoing discussion it will be seen that to a complete education, both the objective and subjective courses are indispensable, and therefore neither can be considered of more importance than the other. It will also be seen that in regard to time the relative place of each has been determined by the laws of mental action.

It should be borne in mind that in any given subject it is not necessary that the whole of the objective course be completed before the subjective is begun. Every part of the objective work may be separately put into subjective forms.

*Example.*—In the study of arithmetic, the pupil may be taught how to put numbers together so that the result shall be the same in value as the numbers first taken. He may derive his first knowledge of this process from objects; then, he may use concrete numbers when the objects are not present; and finally, he may be led to use abstract numbers. When the mental process has been mastered, he may be taught the value of figures; the method of expressing numbers by figures; the manner of arranging figures for addition; the convenient method of adding the numbers represented by the individual figures so as to produce the correct result; the means of expressing this result, and the manner of verifying it. He may then be led to describe the process he has gone through, and this description becomes the rule for future use. Then he learns that the whole work which he has done is *addition*. A brief synopsis of this work, which he thoroughly understands, is a definition. This work is objective. It begins with the facts, and proceeds through a series of comparisons and generalizations until the definition is at last reached.

The subjective course can now be brought into operation. The definition is formally and accurately stated, and the subject is divided into its several departments of *methods of writing the numbers, operations, rule, proof.* Each of these is, in turn, divided until the facts of addition are reached. What is true of addition is true of each one of the divisions of arithmetic; after the objective development, each may be stated in subjective forms. When arithmetic in all its forms has been examined in this manner, it may be treated subjectively as a whole, and the relations of the various parts to each other and to the whole may be ascertained.

*The Two Courses as Related to Discovery and Application.*—The objective course dealing with objects and minutiæ reaches laws and principles, by occupying a comparatively narrow field of investigation. The subjective course, by applying the principles discovered to every possible case, widens this field, and in this way enlarges the conceptions which follow investigation.

The objective course furnishes the materials indispensable to sound thinking and correct conclusions. The subjective appropriates these materials and conclusions, and applies them to specific ends.

The objective course busies itself with finding out what are the facts in the case, and what these facts signify. The subjective employs itself in arranging the facts in order, and in devoting them to such uses as will most effectually serve humanity.

*The Two Courses as Related to the Teacher's Work.*—In this work the objective course is necessary in developing the perceptive powers; in cultivating habits of close attention on the part of pupils; in showing the way by which laws are discovered, and in pointing out the method in which the mind must act to reach just conclusions in any field of research or investigation.

The subjective course is indispensable to the teacher for arranging knowledge and placing it in its order of dependence. This arrangement enables him to determine the successive steps necessary in both the objective and subjective methods of presentation; and further enables him to make the most effective application of knowledge to human affairs.

By the application of subjective principles, both teacher and pupils are enabled to become intelligent in regard to the results of investigations which they have not made objectively. To make this latter result possible, however, two things are necessary: *First*, that the principle itself shall be obtained by a strictly objective process; and *secondly*, that the new investigation shall be similar to the one already accomplished, and one to which the principle fully applies.

*Example.*—In the study of physics, by observation and experiment, we may find that water presses equally in all directions, and that the pressure is in direct ratio to its depth. We may now infer that other fluids like water will be subject to the same laws, and we do not need to make experiments with each one. When we find it stated that gaseous fluids are subject to similar laws, we accept the statement, although we have made no experiments upon these fluids. By the study of the facts in the first instance we derived the law; and henceforth, whenever we find an application of this law in a new direction, we fully understand the matter, and do not require that the demonstration shall be made in each specific instance.

*Errors of Reversing the Two Courses.*—A law assumed or taken on trust, without any knowledge of the process by which it was obtained, is of comparatively little worth in mental development. The enunciation of the law is often a mere formula of words which conveys no information to the mind. For example, many pupils have learned that the attraction of bodies is directly as the matter they contained, and inversely as the square of the distance, without in the least comprehending the nature or the magnitude of the law contained in the formula which they have memorized.

By a series of mathematical steps, it is easy to demonstrate to a pupil that "in similar figures the homologous sides are proportional;" but to have this proposition simply learned would not be of the slightest value to the student in geometry. So in astronomy: by careful study of the facts concerning the solar system, we can understand "that the planets in their motions around the sun pass over equal spaces in equal times;" but this formula, which is the expression of an important law when understood, is simply verbal lumber when not understood.

COROLLARIES.—From the laws unfolded in the two preceding chapters, several corollaries can be drawn, which may be taken as principles both in arranging courses of study and in devising methods of instruction.

*Sources of Primary Ideas.*—The first of the corollaries is, that *all primary ideas of the outward world must come through the senses.* This principle will lead to the careful and thorough training of each of the senses, and to the cultivation of observation and perception. It will base all knowledge on personal experience, and avoid the absurd practice of endeavoring to make one sense do the work of another, and of presenting ideas beyond the comprehension of the child.

*Training the Senses.*—The second corollary is: *The senses should be trained and made acute by systematic object-teaching.*

This principle is derived from the general discussion of the subject, and may be inferred directly from the last corollary. As our knowledge must needs come through the avenues of sense, then it follows that one of the most important factors of intelligence is acuteness of sense. The senses that most enter into intellectual processes are sight, hearing, and touch, and in no way can they be trained to great sensibility, except by means of sights, sounds, and manipulations which appeal directly to them. Only to a very limited extent do our present school-exercises contribute to this accurate training of the senses.

*Securing Attention.*—Third corollary. *Attention is best secured by proper and related object-lessons.*

A child is always more interested in something that appeals to his senses than in abstract matters. By adapting the lessons to the capacity and immediate interests of the child and by appealing to his curiosity, the teacher can always succeed in getting attention. In the process of growth the mind becomes interested in more abstract matters, and the object-lessons may be gradually omitted.

*Cultivating Perceptions.*—Fourth corollary. *Perceptive knowledge should be made the basis of primary instruction.*

This follows from the fact that the perceptive powers are relatively most active in childhood, and hence the school course should provide the material best suited to awaken these powers to activity. It equally follows from the fact that such knowledge is needed for the next step in mental growth, and that a failure to improve the season and opportunity is fatal to the highest improvement.

*Exercises in Memory.*—Fifth corollary. *Memory is best cultivated by forcible, repeated, and related perceptions and ideas.*

This follows from the general fact that the deepest impression is retained the longest, and it shows that the faculties are so related that, in the primary stages, that course of training which is best for one is best for all. It also effectually disposes of the nonsense that rote-teaching should be practised because it "strengthens the memory."

*Advanced Instruction.*—Sixth corollary. *Subjects appealing mainly to the reason and judgment belong to the advanced course of instruction.*

This principle is so obvious, that there would be no necessity of stating it were it not for the fact that it is so often violated in practice. Many studies are admitted in the primary-school course which have no place there, and little children are given tasks which would tax the ability of mature minds. The result is, that teaching must of necessity become mechanical, because the logical formulas are simply understood as sounds, and not as ideas.

*Ideas and Words.*—Seventh corollary. *Ideas should precede words.*

This principle follows from the nature of language, and the relations of language to thought. While the statement is all that is needed to establish its truth, a more detailed explanation is necessary to show its application in certain cases. The principle includes the following minor statements: *Objects should precede names; thoughts should precede sentences; knowledge should precede definitions.*

This last proposition, besides being included in the general principle, may be directly inferred from the laws of mental development, and from the nature of the objective course.

By reversing this process, and giving definitions or attempting to give them before the thing defined is well understood, several of the fundamental principles of teaching are violated, time and effort are wasted, and the powers of the mind are permanently injured by a most unnatural process.

*The Steps of Instruction.*—Eighth corollary. *Instruction should proceed from the known to the unknown.* This truth also shows that the attainment of all knowledge should have a basis in personal experience. By directing the observing powers to the objects and phenomena nearest at hand, the mind becomes possessed of real knowledge; and from this sure basis of home knowledge it gradually extends outward toward the unknown. Each item of the unknown in converted into the known, and each step taken is a firm step in advance.

This principle includes the following elements: *Instruction should proceed from the concrete to the abstract; from the simple to the complex; and from facts to principles.* In examining a single object, instruction may go from the general to the particular, but with a number of objects it passes from the particular to the general.

*Exercise.*—The ninth corollary is: *Exercise should be left to the pupil.* The race, in its education, was obliged to gain knowledge by experiences which nearly as often retarded as promoted direct development. The teacher's work should remove these obstacles, and should so direct the pupil in the use of his own powers that the greatest progress may be made with the least waste. In the exercise of this directive power the teacher must avoid the very prevalent fault of telling too much, and by so doing of depriving the pupil of an opportunity for that mental exercise which is indispensable to his highest good.

To the end that the pupil shall receive the utmost benefit, the teacher must always carefully select the materials to be used, and so arrange the conditions that with ordinary observation the pupil will discover the desired truth. This end can be defeated either by rendering the process too obscure for the mental vision of the pupil, or by injudicious haste in verbal explanation. When the teacher has so excited the curiosity of the pupil that he is led to inquire, the desired end is more than half attained.

*Completed Processes.*—Tenth corollary. *Each process of instruction should include full perception, distinct understanding, clear expression, and, where possible, the passing of thought into act.*

In much of school-work the processes stop at one or the other of these steps, few being carried to the final consummation. Some—as rote-lessons—never reach perceptions, but are reflected back from the sensorium as automatic action; some—as most of the lessons in primary grammar—fail to reach the understanding, but remain as vague perceptions. In very few schools is the practice of clear expression enforced at all times; and yet, from the necessity of forcible impressions, and from the relations of thought to the language, expression is seen to be an essential factor in both the reception and the retention of knowledge, and to a clear understanding.

The last step, the passing of thought into act, is as yet seldom found in any schools except in the kindergartens and the schools of technology; still, it will be seen that the step is *necessary* to the full perception and distinct understanding of many subjects; to the physical training that coördinates study and work; and to the application of ideas and thought to common affairs and duties.

# CHAPTER V.

## *OBJECT-TEACHING.*

GENERAL VIEW OF THE SUBJECT.—Primary teaching, until within a comparatively recent period, has consisted chiefly of mere routine work. The previous experience of the pupil was ignored, instead of being made the foundation of his school-work. From the observation of things with which he was partially familiar, and in which he took an interest, his attention was forcibly turned to the consideration of the arbitrary characters which make up the alphabet. School-work was considered as not only having no particular relation to previous experience, but as something directly opposed to it.

*False Philosophy.*—The philosophy somehow obtained that, the more difficult an exercise was made, and the more it differed from ordinary occupations and thoughts, the greater was its value as a mental exercise. In consequence, the school-lessons were little more than memorizing exercises, and the schoolroom had few attractions for the majority of children.

*Introduction of Object-Lessons.*—While these mechanical and unnatural methods were in practice, object-lessons were introduced. The decided superiority of the new method over the old, in arousing attention and in exciting interest, was soon manifest. The new instruction appealed to experience, and excited the observing powers to intense activity. It fed the mind upon real knowledge, and raised it out of the slough of inattention and listless inactivity produced by the old process of mere routine.

*Abuse of Object-Lessons.*—These substantial results gained for the new system extensive notoriety, and led to an excessive estimation of its value. Object-lessons were found excellent in certain grades and under certain circumstances, and it was therefore assumed that they would prove as good for all grades and under all circumstances. Experiments on a large scale were at once entered upon, in which object-lessons were made to take the place of nearly every other kind of study. Since it was found that the primary knowledge of the outward world could be best obtained through lessons in which the object was present, it was concluded that advanced knowledge could best be obtained in the same manner. Hence there grew up an undue estimation of personal experience, and an unwarranted depreciation of the experience of others as found recorded in books. The protest against the study of books was carried to an extreme, and the new method became nearly as one-sided as the old.

*Practical Mistakes.*—Mistakes were also frequently made in the methods of applying object-teaching. Pupils were often required to obtain from objects ideas with which they were already familiar—making their tasks of no more interest than the old routine of the books. Facts were communicated by the teacher which the pupils could readily discover for themselves. The lessons assigned, instead of being in a connected series, were often so isolated and fragmentary that no relations could be discovered between them, and much of their real value, therefore, was lost.

*Reaction against Object-Teaching.*—These faults of over-valuation, and of methods of application, caused many teachers to look with distrust upon the whole system of object-teaching. The real results in many cases falling so far short of what was generally expected, led to a reaction, in which the whole system of object-lessons was declared a failure. As usual in such cases, the truth seems to lie between these extremes.

*Real Nature of Object-Lessons.*—In a preceding chapter, it has been shown that the first ideas of the outward world must come from objects and through the senses. This necessary and indeed indispensable process, which occupies the attention during a large share of the earlier years of life, is object-teaching. When a similar process is introduced into school, and the qualities of objects become known from the examination of the objects themselves, the performance is an object-lesson.

VALUE OF OBJECT-LESSONS.—By systematizing object-lessons, the observing powers are cultivated and trained, qualities of objects become known that were unnoticed before, the mind is filled with that knowledge which is essential to advanced thought, and a much wider basis is given to culture than is usual in school-work.

*Qualities of Objects.*—The forms of objects, and

ideas in regard to differences of form, are readily obtained through the examination of objects. For the purpose of impressing these ideas of form, every school should be supplied with a variety of the regular plane and solid figures, so that children may become familiar with them at a very early period. The different colors, with their varieties of hues, tints, and shades, can be best known by examining objects which represent these colors; and the only way to train the senses to a nice appreciation of color is through this examination, which is an object-lesson. The mind is best trained to understand ideas of position, size, and number in a similar manner.

*The Physical Sciences.*—The first steps in every science are those which make us acquainted with the facts upon which it is based. In all the physical sciences, the primary facts are obtained from the observation of objects. This is object-teaching. Without this observation, and the facts which result from it, correct inference is impossible, and science can never advance beyond its rudimentary state.

*Illustrative Examples.*—In mineralogy and geology, which treat of the inorganic world, the first step is to carefully examine specimens of the principal rocks which compose the crust of the earth. By this examination, we become acquainted with the structure and qualities of each specimen, and the differences between them. This knowledge is at once fundamental and necessary, and each exercise in school designed to give a pupil this knowledge constitutes an object-lesson.

In botany and zoölogy, the same principle holds true. In these cases, plants and animals respectively must be subjected to careful examination, and their peculiarities of structure and parts noted. This investigation is preliminary to any clearly-defined knowledge of them. No speculations, however profound, can be substituted for these elementary facts, which can only be obtained through the process of object-teaching. Physics, chemistry, and indeed the whole circle of the sciences, will afford additional illustrations of this truth.

"*How not to do it.*"—In endeavoring to teach science, a method has extensively prevailed which admirably illustrates the process of how not to do it. The student is referred to a book, instead of to natural objects, to procure his preliminary ideas in regard to the subject. He is required to accept authority, in the place of making personal investigation. He learns a formula of words, which is said to be a law, or rule, or definition, when he is utterly ignorant of the facts upon which the law, or rule, is based, and of the knowledge embodied in the definition. The whole performance is a substitution of apparent for real knowledge, and, whether resulting from ignorance or design, is a practical fraud, by which not only are time and labor lost, but the mind becomes so deteriorated as to be unable to distinguish between the spurious and the real, the false and the true.

*Ideal Objects.*—In its enlarged sense, the term *object* means anything to which thought is or may be directed. It is not necessarily confined to things which manifest themselves through the senses. The mind may consider a physical object, like an apple, a physical quality, like color, a mental process, like perception, or a moral power, like conscience; and in each instance, that upon which the mind is employed is an object. Whether the object is real, like an apple, or ideal, as a mental power or fact, the mind must become acquainted with all its qualities, characteristics, and relations; and the process of obtaining this knowledge is both objective and inductive. When this process is carried still further in the investigations of science it culminates in laboratory experiments, both physical and psychological. In this sense, objective work is the necessary foundation of every department of thought.

*Order in Thinking.*—To ascertain laws, to discover truth, and to promote human welfare, mental operations must proceed in a strictly definite order. As the materials of thought are primarily derived from the observation of external objects, so the order of thought springs from the observation of the sequence, causation, and dependence of objects and phenomena in the outward world. These ideas, essential to logic and all connected thought, are most forcibly presented, and make the deepest impression on the mind, by systematic object-lessons, in which relations, as well as qualities, are presented.

*The Ideal and the Real.*—Descartes, in his philosophy, maintains that the only reality of which we are absolutely certain is that *we think*. Through our senses we observe objects, and we ascribe to these objects real existence; but of this reality we cannot be perfectly sure, for our senses may deceive us, and that which we think exists may be only an appearance. In the shimmer of the light over the parched sands of the desert, the thirsty traveller sees water, to all appearance as real as the little lakes that lie among the hills of more favored regions. It is an appearance, however, that mocks the sight; and the only real thing to the traveller is that *he thinks* he sees the water.

The next position taken by the philosopher is that the materials and order of thought are furnished by the outward world. In our daily experience we observe the sequences of Nature. Night follows day; the sun unfailingly appears to pursue his course through the heavens; vernal flowers succeed winter snows; all vegetable life has an orderly course from germ to maturity, and from maturity to decay; animals have their birth, their growth, and their decrepitude, and everywhere is orderly sequence. This observation leads the mind to ascribe order to every kind of phenomena, and develops in it the logical faculty.

These positions show the ground for the reconciliation of the apparently antagonistic ideal and real schools of philosophy, and at the same time serve as a guide to educational processes. The materials of thought must come from the outward world. The more we study natural phenomena, and rise to a comprehension of the laws that control them, the more thoroughly is our logical faculty developed, and the better are we prepared to perform the duties of life.

*Interest in Study* is greatly increased by well-arranged object-lessons. The impression upon the mind, made directly through the senses, is much more vivid and lasting than when made indirectly through words. When the object is present, an appeal is made to several of the senses, and thus deepens the impression desired and makes it easier of retention. By this means, also, vague and crude impressions are changed into clear and definite conceptions, and the field of experience is extended on every side.

*Verification of a Law.*—A law which has been discovered inductively may need verification, or, as in the subjective course, it may become necessary to apply it to a great variety of new circumstances. In either case there must result an examination which will reach down to the ultimate facts, and this will involve object-lessons.

*Examples.*—In observing a common balance, we find that the arms are of equal length, and that equal weights balance each other. By experiment we find that, if one arm is decreased, the weight must be increased to balance the weight upon the other side. From these observations we may infer that, to produce an equilibrium, the product of the weight, multiplied by the length of the arm, must be equal. This generalization from the observed facts needs additional verification before it can be accepted as a law. Will it be true of all lengths of the arms ? Is it true of bent as well as straight arms ? Is it true of compound as of simple arms ? To answer these questions and others of the same sort, and before it is safe to assume that the inference made is a general law, experiments must be made with objects to verify the generalization in every case; and when the verification has covered the ground of all supposable conditions, it is accepted as a law.

Leverrier, noticing the perturbations of Uranus, from the established laws of gravitation inferred that its motions were affected by a hitherto undiscovered planet; and carrying out his inferences more in detail by the aid of mathematics, he inferred the place of the new planet at a given time. The astronomical observer turned his telescope in the direction indicated, and discovered Neptune, thus verifying the inferences of the astronomer.

SUMMARY.—From the foregoing discussion it will be seen that object-lessons are of use in the following particulars:

*First*, they furnish the best means known for the exercise of observation and the training of the perceptive powers.

*Secondly*, they constitute the first steps in the unfolding of every science; and especially are they indispensable in the study of natural history and the physical sciences generally.

*Thirdly*, they give to the mind the first ideas of orderly and methodical thinking.

*Fourthly*, they are potent in exciting the mind to activity, and in arousing that curiosity and zeal which lead to new discovery.

*Fifthly*, they furnish the means by which laws may be verified and principles may be applied.

In consequence of these advantages, the time formerly spent in mastering the branches taught in the primary schools may be greatly abridged; and pleasant, healthful occupations may be substituted for burdensome and barren tasks.

*Cautions to be Observed.*—In consequence of errors committed in the methods of conducting object-lessons, the good which would have resulted from their proper use has not been realized, and discredit has been thrown upon the whole system. These errors have arisen from a violation of one or more of the following simple rules in regard to their proper use, which rules may be directly inferred from the nature of the system itself.

*First:* No object-lesson should be given from a book. The very name of the exercise would seem to be sufficient to render this rule unnecessary; but there have been teachers so profoundly stupid as to oblige pupils to commit to memory the model lessons given in manuals of teaching.

*Secondly:* In giving an object-lesson, the teacher should have a distinct end in view, and the lesson should be considered a failure unless this end is attained. Objectless object-lessons are always to be avoided.

*Thirdly:* Object-lessons should be given in a systematic course, each one conveying its own teaching, and bearing some palpable relation to the one that has preceded and the one that follows, thus leading the pupil to the discovery of the relations, and enabling him to associate them in memory. Desultory object-lessons are of little worth.

*Fourthly:* Object-lessons giving pupils ideas and thoughts with which they are already familiar are to be avoided. The interest of a lesson depends very much upon its novelty; and if this element is wanting, there is very little left to create a permanent impression.

*Fifthly:* In giving an object-lesson, the teacher should not tell the pupils the things they are to find, but he should lead them to observe with accuracy, and to express the results of their observation in proper language. The teacher's work is rather to guide by suggestion, so that the pupil may not go too far astray in his efforts to observe.

*The Limits of Object-Teaching* can now be readily

seen. In the objective course they constitute the first steps, and in the subjective course they are useful in the ultimate analysis necessary to the verification of laws and to the application of principles. Subsensuous knowledge, or that which is below the senses, and obtained through them, is derived from objects; but supersensuous knowledge, or that which is above the senses, and is the result of reflection, is aided only indirectly by object-lessons.

The final result of mental discipline is the attainment of supersensuous knowledge, and the ability to deal with abstract relations and principles. This consummation of education is equally hindered by a neglect of object-lessons, so that culture rests upon a narrow and insufficient basis of fact, and by a continuation of exclusive object-lessons too long, so that the mind is kept under the domain of the senses, and independent thought is rendered nearly impossible. In the latter case, such lessons become obstacles rather than aids to the highest attainments.

*Additional Caution.*—In the study of objects, and especially in the branches of natural history, there is a tendency to become so much interested in the objects themselves, as to neglect the lessons to be derived from such objects. The man who yields to this tendency degenerates from a possible naturalist to a mere collector. His work is often as unmeaning as that of the miser in hoarding money. The collection which is really valuable only as a means of culture, to him is the end of culture, and he remains in a state of mental vassalage to the specimens he has gathered. One good, however, may result from his work: The cabinet, once formed, may, in wiser hands, be a valuable aid in attaining the ends of a true education.

*Conclusion.*—When education is more thoroughly understood, both in regard to its aims and its methods, it is evident that natural science will occupy relatively a much higher place than now. From the beginning of school-life, the facts and elements of science will probably be taken as the basis of education. When this general result is reached, object-lessons will fall into their proper place as indispensable in the first steps of scientific research. In the pursuit of natural history the larger share of the work will consist of systematized object-lessons. But at the same time, in all probability, the peculiar form which these lessons have now generally taken, as altogether disconnected from the regular studies of the school, will be materially modified or entirely abandoned. When science is taught in a regular and systematic manner, fragments of science will no longer be necessary.

# CHAPTER VI.

### *RELATIVE VALUE OF THE DIFFERENT BRANCHES OF INSTRUCTION.*

THE END OF EDUCATION.—In considering the nature of education, Herbert Spencer says: "How to live? that is the essential question for us. Not how to live in the mere material sense only, but in the widest sense. The general problem which comprehends every special problem is the right ruling of conduct in all directions and under all circumstances: In what way to treat the body; in what way to treat the mind; in what way to behave as a citizen; in what way to utilize all those sources of happiness which Nature supplies; how to use all our faculties to the greatest advantage to ourselves and others; how to live completely. And this being the great thing needful to learn, by consequence is the great thing which education has to teach. To prepare us for complete living, is the function which education has to discharge; and the only rational mode of judging of any educational course is to judge in what degree it discharges such functions."

*Practical Questions.*—Admitting that it is desirable that education, to the extent of its influence, should contribute to good conduct and completeness of living, the questions that are forced upon us are: What course of study will best accomplish these ends? and what is the order in which the several branches of education should be presented? Ought we to accept the prevailing customs in these regards—customs inherited from remote generations—or should we submit each branch and each step in study to the test which this high ideal of the nature of educational work imposes?

*The Old and the New.*—It is always well to hold to customs and institutions of the past until it is clearly seen that a change will be for human benefit. The past imposes authority upon us to this extent, that we are to take for granted that any custom had its origin in human needs, and has been of use in promoting human welfare. This follows from the fact of its being. The good of society demands that this authority be obeyed and this custom or institution be conserved, until intelligence has so far advanced as to show that the interests of humanity demand a change, either in a readjustment of details, or in a reorganization of fundamental principles.

*Responsibility for Change.*—The burden of proof in regard to the desirability and necessity of a change rests entirely upon those demanding it; and this proof, to be perfect, should include two elements: one destructive, showing the imperfections and shortcomings of the old; and the other constructive, replacing the old by something manifestly higher and better. By the conflict between these antagonistic forces, the poise of society is maintained, and a slow but sure advance is made toward a higher state of civilization.

*Conditions of Change.*—In this perpetually recurring controversy two attitudes are obstructive to human welfare: the one obstinately clinging to the old social forms, which, from changed conditions and circumstances, have outlived their usefulness; and the other so eagerly and unintelligently iconoclastic as to wage war upon present institutions, before any rational and adequate system has been devised to take their place. The triumph of the one would arrest human progress, of the other would destroy social order.

The principles which should govern change, true in general, are true in regard to education. The past has transmitted to the present a course of study and a system of methods; and in proposing a change, the obligation is imposed upon us of showing the errors of present practices, and of presenting a system better adapted to the needs and circumstances of to-day.

*Real and Apparent Knowledge.*—At this point it is not intended to attempt anything like a scientific classification of human knowledge, but only such a general division as will be of use in solving the problem immediately before us.

In regard to education, the branches readily divide themselves into two classes: those that treat directly of the facts and laws of matter and mind, and those which are used to aid in the understanding and development of the main branches. These may be regarded respectively as knowledge, and the tools by which knowledge is obtained. Some of the studies pursued in school are of a double nature, combining both matter and form.

*Relations of Language.*—Language is useful for the

expression and preservation of knowledge; but in its use it is simply a tool of knowledge, and not knowledge itself. The means by which language is mastered in its use, including spelling, reading, and writing; and language itself, when actively employed in the prosecution of other branches of instruction, all occupy this subordinate position as tools, useful in proportion as they serve to disclose the treasures of real knowledge. When language, however, is studied in its structure, its history, and its relation to the development of man, it becomes a branch of real knowledge.

*Relations of Mathematics.*—Our first knowledge of objects relates to qualities alone; but before this knowledge is made exact, so as to merit the name of science, quantitative relations must be observed and measured. From the observation of these quantitative relations, the first ideas of number and definite extension seem to have arisen; and these ideas, abstracted from the objects which gave them birth, and reduced to order, form the elements of mathematics. The mathematical branches, so formed, are indispensable in measuring the quantitative relations of the concrete sciences, and in this sense they are simply tools of knowledge. When mathematics is studied to discover the laws of relations, which it discloses independent of the concrete, it furnishes real knowledge, and has a distinct place as such, in a course of study.

Macaulay says: " Bacon, assuming the well-being of the race to be the end of knowledge, pronounced that mathematical science could claim no higher rank than that of an appendage or an auxiliary to other sciences. Mathematical science, he says, is the handmaid of natural philosophy, and she ought to demean herself as such; and he declares he cannot conceive by what illchance it has happened that she presumes to claim precedence over her mistress."

*Direct and Incidental Acquirement.*—Experience demonstrates that the use of tools is most quickly learned by engaging in real work. The end to be accomplished in education is the development of the individual through the attainment of real knowledge. To this end the main effort of the pupil should be directed. In the endeavor to come into possession of this real knowledge, the pupil incidentally becomes familiar with the tools necessary to serve his purpose. The branches of real knowledge are mastered by steadily fixing the primary attention upon the thoughts which they contain; while, at the same time, the use of language, both in writing and speaking, and the elements of arithmetic and geometry, may be best acquired incidentally through the action of secondary attention.

*Kind of Knowledge Required.*—The necessities of the mind demand real knowledge to arouse its activities and to promote its growth and well-being. Language and mathematics can no more satisfy the cravings of the mind than the knife and fork and balance for weighing meat can satisfy the stomach in its cravings for food. However useful these branches and articles may be respectively in preparing knowledge and food, the one can never be knowledge nor the other food. This parallel does not hold in the advanced course of instruction, when both language and mathematics are studied for intrinsic principles, and in their general relations to human progress.

*Branches of Real Knowledge.*—The branches which furnish the real knowledge demanded by the mind are readily subdivided into two classes: those that treat of Nature below man, and those that treat of man and his works. These are roughly indicated as Science and Philosophy, or as the Natural Sciences and the Humanities. Properly speaking, the term science would apply to the whole body of knowledge in any department of human investigation which is reduced to systematic order; while philosophy would apply to the laws of relations, and the causes of phenomena and being which science unfolds.

THE BRANCHES AS RELATED TO DEVELOPMENT.—We have next to consider the value of the different branches in regard to the two great ends of education: the development of the powers, and practical use. For both these purposes real knowledge is demanded, and this knowledge should be presented in definite order. The purposes of study may be defeated by mistaking apparent for real knowledge, by presenting subjects at the wrong time, or by failing to recognize the order of dependence. We call attention, first, to the value of the branches in their relations to the powers of the mind.

*The Natural Sciences as Promoting Development.*—From objects are obtained the qualities, facts, and ideas which are indispensable in the development of the perceptive powers. The natural sciences furnish material for this purpose that is fundamental, that is easily accessible, and that is full of interest. Without the materials which external Nature furnishes, the perceptive powers cannot be brought into the highest state of activity, and the mind will lack that primary knowledge necessary for the normal operation of the higher faculties.

*The Discipline of Memory.*—As the office of memory is to record and preserve the results of the activities of the observing and reflective powers, it follows that those branches best calculated to stimulate these powers will also be best for the development of memory. We have already seen that the highest condition or form of memory is that founded upon the laws of association. The natural sciences when rightly presented tend to bring this principle of association into active exercise.

An idea is first gained, and then is associated directly with the name or word that expresses it, so that the two are henceforth one. These ideas are again associated by their likenesses and unlikenesses on successively higher planes, until the whole mass of knowledge is retained by means of its relations.

*The Humanities as Promoting Development.*—The humanities present facts and relations more complex than the facts and relations derived from the natural sciences, and hence come later in order. They serve, however, to carry on the development of perception and memory to a still more advanced state.

*Discipline of the Reflective Faculties.*—The higher faculties of the mind, including the imagination, reason, and judgment, are brought into most active exercise by those very facts which are found most valuable in developing perception and memory. From the facts which we perceive—their connection and dependence—we make inferences and draw conclusions; and the value of these inferences and conclusions will depend upon the accuracy with which we have observed, and the faithfulness with which these observations have been recorded.

*General Effect of Real Knowledge.*—Study of this kind tends to form a habit of acquisitiveness; a habit of collecting all the facts bearing upon given cases; of carefully examining and combining these facts or data; of drawing such inferences only as the data will warrant; and of verifying the inferences by renewed observations and experiments. These habits are such as inevitably lead to the highest results in every department of investigation, and they are necessary to the acquisition of truth in every direction.

*The Discipline of Conduct.*—In addition to the beneficial results to every power of the mind, the habits of thought formed by the careful study of real subjects, beginning with the natural sciences, directly tend to right conduct in life. In every step of progress the pupil learns the necessity of ridding his mind of bias, and of accepting that which is shown to be true. In this way a love of truth is constantly engendered; and in proportion to the love for truth will be the love for right, and the disposition to act rightly. Carried into the field of morals, these methods of thought must result in making truth supreme; in stimulating action in obedience to the dictates of truth; and in carrying into practice the principles of justice which are founded upon truth.

THE BRANCHES AS RELATED TO USES.—Besides its office of affording nurture to the mind and of giving it discipline, knowledge is indispensable to human well-being in every sphere of life.

Physical needs must be perpetually supplied, or the body dies. Children must have intelligent care, or they perish. The functions of industry and citizenship must be intelligently performed, or society relapses into a state of barbarism. Researches must be constantly made into the secrets of Nature, or civilization will cease to advance, and become stagnant.

*Uses of Natural Science.*—The natural sciences furnish the knowledge which is indispensable for these purposes, and which is the most fundamental of all. The scope of these sciences is broad. They make us acquainted : *first*, with the inorganic world ; *secondly*, with the two grand divisions of the organic world ; and *thirdly*, with the forces which control the action of matter in masses and in atoms. They make us acquainted with our physical environment, with the relations of these surroundings to ourselves, and with all the conditions necessary to be observed for the preservation of our own existence.

A neglect of the truths which they teach entails upon us disease, suffering, and death. An intelligent comprehension of these truths enables us to avoid, in a large measure, the causes of disease, to diminish suffering, and to prevent the premature termination of life. These truths are so fundamental that they affect every person during every moment of his existence. No other sort of intelligence can supersede this, as there can be no escape from the evil consequences which ignorance in this direction inflicts.

*Natural Science and Industry.*—The natural sciences lie at the foundation of all our industries and physical improvements. In the crude industries devised to supply primitive human needs, the physical sciences chiefly had their origin. Man step by step gathered all the facts which the industries supplied, observed relations, and inferred causes and laws. Reacting upon the industries, the sciences apply laws and principles to complicated cases, and produce results entirely unattainable in a more primitive society, but indispensable to present existence.

*Examples.*—A large share of our food is produced by agricultural processes. Unless agriculture is intelligently pursued, a considerable proportion of the present population of the earth would perish. But the successful pursuit of agriculture demands a knowledge of the soils, their composition and changes, the principles and methods of restoring the vast waste of constant cropping, and this implies a knowledge of mineralogy and chemistry. There is also demanded a knowledge of vegetable growth, which involves botany; of noxious and beneficial insects, and of the useful animals that subsist upon vegetation, which involves the various branches of zoölogy. Upon these sciences also depend the successful production of cotton, flax, and silk, and their manufacture into cloth and clothing; the various other manufactures necessary to supply human needs; the construction of houses so as to afford protection from the elements; the arrangements for artificial heating and ventilation; the construction of domestic utensils, and of weapons both offensive and defensive, and the creation of all those comforts and conveniences essential to the highest enjoyment of life.

Joined with mathematics, these sciences have enabled us to construct roads, railroads, bridges, and canals; to tunnel mountains; to furnish large cities with light, and never-failing supplies of water; to drain marshes and construct sewers; and, in a large measure, to comprehend sanitary laws, and provide the appliances necessary to secure perfect obedience to these laws.

*Ubiquity of the Elements of Natural Science.*—The facts of Nature which form the elements of the natural sciences are everywhere around us, and are forcing themselves upon our notice. They come thronging in through the avenues of sense on every side, demanding recognition. They will be recognized, and will perform their beneficent work, unless the attention is resolutely and systematically turned away from them and engrossed in other thoughts. This can only happen under a vicious system of education, where prominence is given to apparent rather than to real knowledge. Should we succeed, however, in shutting out the ideas which are appealing to our senses, we are made to suffer in actual pain, in the thwarting of desires, or in the loss of privileges or power.

The elements of the natural sciences are so closely connected with physical well-being that they more powerfully affect the mind in early life, and hence are adapted to awaken a deeper interest than any other branches of study. This interest renders acquisition easier, and gives to the mind a greater store of knowledge with the same degree of effort.

*Uses of the Humanities.*—The humanities, treating of man and his work, come in to carry forward the work of education toward completion. These branches include the division of man into races; the distribution of races upon the earth; the relation of man to his environment; the achievements of man in subduing Nature, and in controlling natural forces; and the changes which man has wrought upon the earth. They also include an examination of the nature and operations of mind, and the products of mind in their threefold manifestation—intellectual, moral, and æsthetic.

*Conditions of their Successful Use.*—The humanities, however, to be of use in general culture, in industrial pursuits, or in business operations, must present real knowledge, and not merely serve as tools for getting real knowledge. In respect to methods of study, they must also conform to the methods pursued in natural history and in other objective studies, where facts are first acquired and the process is continued through the regular chain of deductive operations until the law is discovered.

To any thorough understanding of the humanities, a knowledge of the facts and laws of the material world are indispensable. Thought and action everywhere are found to be so dependent upon outward circumstances and considerations that they cannot be understood until the forces that modify them are first comprehended. For example, the first steps in civilization are possible only in a region where the soil is fertile, the climate moderate, and where mountains or other natural barriers afford protection and isolation. The migration of races and the march of armies, which have been instrumental in spreading civilization, have been determined by the direction of mountain ranges, and the position of other natural obstacles.

The character of every nation has been, to a considerable extent, determined by the circumstances which have surrounded it, and these circumstances in turn have largely depended upon material conditions. The events of history can never be understood unless the physical conditions of the regions where they occur are first well understood. Even the literature and art of a people are found to be fashioned very much by the physical surroundings amid which they had their origin.

SPECIAL STUDIES.—The special studies under the head of the Humanities, which are of the greatest importance in the work of education, are history, language and literature, mental and moral philosophy, and sociology. Each of these contributes real knowledge to the pupil's development; the truths of each are necessary to his highest welfare; and from each laws are derived, essential as a guide to individual conduct, and to the general progress of the race.

*Importance of History.*—Mental and moral philosophy have received attention elsewhere. History will next be considered in its threefold aspect of chronology, philology, and archæology.

*Chronology.*—The study of chronology makes us acquainted with the achievements of the nations and races which at present inhabit the earth, and of those that have passed away, as far as recorded. Its field is history as preserved in literature and tradition. It shows the progress of man from a low mental and moral state to his present condition, not by an uninterrupted advance, but by a complicated series of progressions and retrogressions, difficult to trace and analyze. With the lapse of sufficient time, however, the direction of the change is manifest, and is seen to be growth.

The facts which chronology furnishes, supplemented by those derived from the other sciences which bear upon the subject, bring into light the sequences of events, and show that national triumphs and disasters have their roots in moral causes. In this chronological survey, we can see enough of the past of man to know what elements enter into human affairs, and we are able to distinguish the permanent from the transient, and to order both individual and national lives progressively more in accordance with the laws of the universe.

*Philology.*—When recorded history fails, investigation extends to a more distant past by means of philology. In the direction of historic research the pursuit of language receives its richest rewards. Studied not for the purpose of getting additional means of expressing knowledge, but for obtaining knowledge itself, it furnishes some of the most important links in the chain of evidence relating to the great problems of man's origin, unity, and destiny. In the structure of words are recorded the first dim perceptions of mind, looking out upon the unknown, and the successive steps toward an intelligent comprehension of the facts, forces, and relations of the universe. These words need to be studied with as minute a care as the specimens of natural history; both the living words and the fossil remains of human speech as appearing in the form of obsolete words and dead languages. The study of these specimens, living and dead, equally repay the investigator in furnishing material for broader generalizations, and in leading to a better understanding of the laws which control mind and its products.

*Archæology.*—The study of the monuments, utensils, and weapons made by man carries the mind back still farther into antiquity, back beyond chronology, beyond philology, and beyond every evidence of man's existence, except that which is afforded by the most imperishable materials upon which the labor of man has been spent. From our homes and from modern cities, furnished with all the materials of present civilization, we travel over the familiar ground of chronology, finding cities, and temples, and pyramids; and beneath the crumbling ruins of great cities described in ancient lore, we find the ruins of other cities of which even tradition is silent. Still going back, step by step, we find the evidences of human art continually becoming less complex; but at the same time we have not yet, by any method of research, gone back to a period when the inclined plane, the wedge, the lever, the wheel and axle, the pulley, and the screw were unknown. The same may be said of the spindle, distaff, loom, and needle.

*What is Gained.*—The study of these various phases of history puts man in possession of the past of humanity, back to the dawn of intelligence, and shows what elements enter into his individual being, and into the civilization of the race. This knowledge not only gratifies the natural curiosity in regard to the past, but is a necessity in putting man in the complete possession of his powers, and in enabling him to comprehend the tendencies of existence, so as to be able to adjust himself to its perpetually varying conditions.

This study, so difficult and profound, belongs to the advanced course of instruction, and is available only when a broad foundation of physical knowledge has been laid in the primary course. It supplements the physical sciences, and furnishes a field for thought and investigation full of the promise of fruit.

FOREIGN LANGUAGES.—The study of a foreign language may be pursued for either one of three legitimate purposes: The possession of additional means for acquiring and expressing knowledge; the knowledge found in the literature of the language; and the help which the language gives to philological research. As mental development is incident to all study pursued by proper methods, its consideration as the special object of linguistic study is not entertained.

*Elementary Study.*—All elementary study of a foreign language must be for the purpose of becoming acquainted with its structure and idioms, and with the meaning of its words. It furnishes the mind with no real knowledge, but simply puts it in possession of the implements by which knowledge may be acquired. As a means, this study is valuable; as an end, comparatively valueless. Carried to the point of mastery, it furnishes means of communication which may be used for valuable purposes; stopping short of this point, the time spent in its pursuit would bear much better fruit if given to the study of the vernacular, perfecting the use of one tongue, rather than obtaining a smattering of many.

*Foreign Literature.*—The study of a foreign language, when pursued for the purpose of gaining an acquaintance with the literature which the language contains, produces fruit in the form of development and culture. Such study belongs to the advanced course. To a critical appreciation of the finest literary productions of a people, an acquaintance with the language is doubtless a necessity; but science and philosophy can be obtained equally well from translations, and even the purely literary works can be better appreciated through a good translation, than by their study in the original, when their language is imperfectly mastered. In home dress, English scholars may come in possession of the best scientific thought of the world wherever it may originate. In poetry, and in the prose where form is an essential element, there will be loss in translation; but this loss may be largely compensated by the study of the English masters in these departments of literature.

*Comparative Philology.*—Linguistic study, pursued for the purpose of throwing light upon human history, and of discovering the laws and evolution of language itself, belongs to the higher and professional courses of instruction. It does not constitute the basis of culture, but rather it completes the superstructure in one direction.

THE ANCIENT LANGUAGES.—It is not designed here to enter into the controversies that have risen respecting the relative advantages of the ancient languages on the one hand, and of mathematics and the natural sciences on the other; but the scope of this discussion demands that the claims of the former, as the exclusive basis of culture, should receive examination.

*Advantages Claimed.*—The advantages claimed for the study of the Latin and Greek languages are: That there can be no complete or broad learning except through these branches, which have been honored by the use of centuries in all the great schools of instruction, and have constituted a prominent agency in the culture of educated men for many generations; that a broad culture must embrace an acquaintance with the life and thought of antiquity; that, by requiring patient and prolonged attention, they confer a severe mental discipline; that the act of translating into the vernacular cultivates discrimination in the use of language; that a familiar acquaintance with the ancient classics is necessary to an exact knowledge of all modern languages.

*Difficulties Encountered.*—Admitting that a thorough acquaintance with the Greek and Latin languages and literature may be necessary to the widest learning, it may be objected, to their general use as branches of elementary study, that it is utterly impracticable in our schools to carry the study of these languages to such a point of thoroughness as will at all realize the results aimed at.

A mere smattering of a language will not bestow the ability to enter into an acquaintance with its literature. This objection would seem to offset all the advantages named except two: the mental discipline resulting from the close attention required in the study of these languages, and the power of discrimination cultivated by the work of translation.

*Mental Discipline.*—It must be admitted that the responsibility rests upon the true educator of selecting such studies for pupils as will give the highest development with the least possible waste. The question is not whether the classic languages are capable of conferring upon the student certain beneficial results, but whether these results are attainable, and whether these languages will produce them more economically than certain other branches.

So far as mental discipline is concerned, including the habits of observation, of quick and accurate perception, of severe attention, of close and patient reasoning, it may be doubted whether any branches are capable of more effective service than the natural sciences and mathematics. And in regard to the cultivation of spontaneous mental energy, and a habit of original discovery, it will scarcely be denied that the natural sciences stand supreme.

In acquiring the power of nice discrimination in the use of language, there can be no doubt that the pupil will be benefited by a careful drill in translating a foreign language into his own tongue. But the question still remains, whether this result may not be accomplished by the study of modern languages; and whether a sufficient mastery of language may not be obtained for understanding and expressing all the thoughts ever born into the world, and even for giving the nicest and most delicate shades of meaning, by the study of our own vernacular. The language of Shakespeare, Milton, and Blackstone has powers and capacities which render it inferior to no tongue ever spoken by man.

*Schiller's Opinion.*—Apropos to the value of translating for the purpose of gaining power in the vernacular, the German poet Schiller said to a friend, who asked him whether he read Shakespeare in English: " My business in life is to write German; and I am convinced that a person cannot read much in a foreign language without losing that delicate tact in the perception of the power of words which is essential to good writing."

SUMMARY IN REGARD TO LANGUAGE. — From the foregoing discussion in regard to language we derive conclusions as follows:

*First:* That language in its use, to a wide extent, is acquired incidentally, and that this acquisition begins at an early period of infancy, and continues through life.

*Second:* That the study of language directly, whether in the form of grammar or of comparative philology, involves principles closely allied to mental philosophy, and hence belongs to the advanced course of instruction.

*Third:* That the study of the vernacular leads most directly to the mastery of language, and hence should be made the basis of all linguistic study.

*Fourth:* That the pursuit of the classic languages belongs to the professional rather than to the general course, and that classic study possesses no just claims to be considered the basis of modern education, or the exclusive means for the attainment of culture.

*Fifth:* That to reverse the process here pointed out, and to make the study of language the basis of instruction, is to violate the laws of mental growth, to fill the mind with words instead of ideas, and to form habits of expending so much force in verbal criticism as to overlook the weightier matter of the character and truth of the statement which the language contains.

*Sixth:* That literature, the highest product of language, should receive continued attention throughout the whole school course.

General Summary.—The conclusions in regard to the relative value of the different branches of instruction may be briefly stated as follows:

*First:* That real knowledge is demanded for both mental development and practical use; that the branches most valuable for mental development are those that enter most extensively into the affairs of life; that the order to be pursued in promoting the normal growth of the mind exactly conforms to the order of the presentation of the sciences founded upon dependence; and that the methods found to be most efficacious in arousing the faculties are the best calculated to unfold the truths of science.

*Second:* That the kind of knowledge best adapted to the promotion of the two great ends of education is that which lies nearest to us, which forces itself most strongly upon our notice, and which excites the greatest interest in the mind when attention has been directed to it. From that which is nearest and can be most easily known, the mind passes outward to the more remote, abstract, and unknown.

*Third:* That in the true course of study the natural sciences will serve as a basis; that language for expression will accompany every step in acquisition; that the mathematics will be coördinated with the concrete sciences; that the humanities will come in to complete the course; and that language as a science will be relegated to the advanced course.

# CHAPTER VII.

### *PESTALOZZI.*

SCHOOLS OF THE OLDEN TIME.—Up to the time of the Reformation the common people of Europe were in a state of abject ignorance in regard to the elements generally considered as belonging to education. Reading and writing were accomplishments monopolized by the higher classes, and by no means universal even among them. The higher education was in the control of the priesthood, and was administered almost exclusively in the interest of the Church. Common schools, in which the whole body of the people had a rightful participation, were not only unknown, but an idea so revolutionary to the existing order of society had scarcely ever entered the consciousness of the most advanced thinkers.

*Effect of Printing upon Education.*—The invention of printing, and the circumstances that followed the great protest against authority, resulted in a wide demand for schools in which reading should be taught. By slow degrees such schools were established, and in the most enlightened parts of Europe they became quite common.

*Care of the Schools.*—These schools naturally fell into the care of the priesthood, in both Catholic and

Protestant countries, in part from the force of habit, and in part because the priests constituted the only class who had sufficient education to manage them. The course of instruction in these schools embraced the alphabet, the elements of reading, the catechism, the memorizing of a certain number of maxims and rules, and sometimes writing. The whole of this instruction was of the most mechanical kind, and no attempt was made to develop the understanding of the pupil, or to give him that knowledge which would be of practical use in his future work.

*Teachers Employed.*—The teachers of these schools, apart from the priests, were usually selected not on account of their fitness for teaching, but because they were fit for nothing else. Soldiers who had lost a limb in battle, persons disabled by accident, and superannuated old men and women who were likely to become a public burden as paupers, were often chosen for teachers. In this manner ignorance came to the aid of routine, and reduced the value of instruction to its minimum.

*Value of Learning to Read.*—To a peasantry in a state of vassalage, who have no interest in the soil they till, whose labor is at the mercy of others, and who in consequence often suffer for the common necessaries of life, the mere ability to read is the veriest mockery. The training of the schools afforded no such intelligence as leads to the improvement of one's condition; and the ability to understand the printed page was of little value where there were no books to read and no leisure to spend in reading. Such an acquisition is poor comfort to a person destitute of clothing, and suffering from hunger.

Schools for the common people, wherever established in Europe, were substantially in the condition described, until about the commencement of the present century. The ruling classes seemed to regard the common people as proper materials for soldiers to extend conquests, or for subjects to be taxed; and the last idea that could enter their minds was that these people were human beings, with all the rights and inborn capacities of other human beings, and that, therefore, they were entitled to the best education which the age could give.

*Ideal Schools.*—Rousseau, the French philosopher, in some of his speculations concerning man and his destiny, gave an outline of an ideal state of society, where intelligence and justice should take the place of ignorance and selfishness. Prominent among the philanthropic schemes of this dreamy philosopher was a system of universal education, by which every one could obtain that knowledge which would be of most worth to him in bettering his own condition, and in contributing to the general welfare of society.

PESTALOZZI'S CAREER.—Johann Heinrich Pestalozzi was then a young man, residing in his native city Zürich, in Switzerland. His attention was attracted to Rousseau's writings, and they produced a deep impression upon his mind. He had become painfully aware of the ignorance and degradation of the common people of his native country, and the speculations of Rousseau seemed to give him the key to a method by which their condition might be improved. The circumstances of his own life had made him extremely sensitive to the injustice and absurdity of the divisions of society into castes, which gave to some special privileges, and withheld these same privileges from others. The impelling force that influenced his subsequent action was more a genuine hatred of tyranny and a belief in democracy than any consideration concerning the nature and method of education.

*Philanthropic Views.*—His ideas of education were forced upon him in his endeavors to raise the condition of the common people, and these ideas came not in the shape of a perfected theory, but rather as the result of experiments born of the necessities and conditions of the hour. His special work grew out of philanthropy rather than philosophy; but on this account, so far as it conforms to philosophic principle, it is all the more valuable.

*The Ideal reduced to Practice.*—The educational problem that presented itself to the mind of Pestalozzi was, whether the ideal of Rousseau might not be made real. After deliberating upon the question, he resolved to make the experiment. He first ventured to write and publish short essays upon the subject. Afterward, he embodied his views upon home education in a story entitled "Leonard and Gertrude." This book created a great sensation throughout Switzerland and Germany, and the author at once found himself famous as a literary man.

*Experiments at Neuhof.*—He also endeavored to carry his theories of education into practice by establishing a school at his farm at Neuhof. At this school he received juvenile delinquents from the city of Berne, where he undertook to eradicate their vicious propensities by a course of instruction and moral training. This experiment was the forerunner of the modern reform-school, now constituting a part of the educational system in nearly all civilized countries.

The scheme proved a failure, partly from his want of organizing and administrative ability, partly from pecuniary mismanagement, and partly from his want of experience as a teacher. The failure of his experiment left him nearly bankrupt; and at the age of fifty-three he found himself without profession, without money, and without employment. Judged by the ordinary standards of success, his life so far was a failure.

*Condition of the Country.*—During the wars that followed the French Revolution, Switzerland was the battle-field of the powerful surrounding nations. With little or no interest in the results of the conflicts, she was made to suffer more than either of the contending parties. Her harvests were plundered, her houses invaded, and, in some of the cantons, the larger part of the male population was carried away by the invaders. Women and children were left with no means of sustenance, and without shelter for their heads.

*School at Stanz.*—In 1798, the little canton of Nidwalden, at the southern extremity of Lake Luzerne, incurred the enmity of the French, and, in consequence, was invaded by a French army; the whole country was made desolate, and every village except the little hamlet of Stanz was burned. The sufferings of the houseless women and children were very great, and measures of relief were immediately instituted in the more prosperous cantons. Here was an opportunity for Pestalozzi, who at once volunteered to go to Stanz and take charge of the children who might be collected there—the philanthropic people of Berne furnishing the means necessary for their subsistence.

*Condition of the School.*—An old deserted convent was taken for the use of the school, and here Pestalozzi found one hundred homeless and almost naked children waiting his arrival. Straightway, with the means at his command, he prepared a kitchen, dining-room, and schoolroom. A large upper room was changed into a dormitory, where pupils and teachers slept together. With no means to buy books or apparatus of any kind, and in a room bare of everything save the rough benches, Pestalozzi commenced his work as a teacher. Necessity, with him, literally became the mother of invention. For want of books, the lessons were necessarily oral; and to gratify the awakened curiosity of the children, recourse was had to everything that could excite interest or afford instruction.

*Things and Representatives.*—During his first experience in teaching, it is related of Pestalozzi that, among other agencies, he made extensive use of pictures. One day he had occasion to refer to a ladder, but the picture required for illustration was mislaid, and could not be found. Seeing the perplexity of the teacher, one of the boys suggested that there was a ladder near the door which might be used in place of the picture. From this suggestion the idea for the first time dawned upon the mind of Pestalozzi that the things themselves were better than any representatives of them—when lo! object-teaching was born into the world.

*Intellectual Success.*—The success of the school at Stanz was so marked as to excite attention and admiration. It was found that the children were coming rapidly to understand *things*, and that the attention which they bestowed upon objects accelerated rather than retarded their progress in reading and writing. They were also constantly interested in their work; and study, which before had been an onerous task, was transformed into a delightful recreation.

*Moral Success.*—The healthy intellectual stimulus afforded, together with the peculiar circumstances and conditions of the school, gave a decided impetus, also, to moral instruction; and Pestalozzi found it a comparatively easy task to inculcate those principles of justice and benevolence which he considered the final outcome of all true education. It is related that when Altdorf, a village in a neighboring canton, was consumed by fire, and a large number of children were rendered houseless, Pestalozzi laid the case before the school, when the pupils, with one voice, requested him to take charge of these children also, notwithstanding the fact that, by so doing, they themselves would be obliged to put up with insufficient rations and limited accommodations.

*School at Burgdorf.*—About one year after the establishment of the school at Stanz, the canton was reoccupied by the French army, and the school was turned out, and consequently broken up, to make room for the soldiers. Immediately Pestalozzi applied for employment as a teacher, and was sent to Burgdorf as an assistant in a school conducted upon the old routine system. His methods, however, were so revolutionary, that the principal of the school straightway took measures to have him dismissed. He next took a position in one of the lowest of the primary schools, at that time conducted by an old dame. Here his success was so striking as to command the attention of the authorities, and, as a result, secured for him a place better fitted to his powers. In connection with able associates, he next opened a school in the deserted castle at Burgdorf, when, for the first time, he had an opportunity for a thorough test of his educational theories. This school continued for two years, and obtained great celebrity, both in Switzerland and Germany.

*School at Yverdon.*—Owing to political changes, however, he was obliged to give up his castle, and for a time the school was suspended. In 1803 it was reëstablished at Yverdon, on Lake Neufchâtel, where it continued twenty-two years, closing in 1825, two years before the death of its founder. The novelty of the teaching at Burgdorf and Yverdon soon attracted the attention of the principal educators of Switzerland, and the school became more famous than any other school of its time. Special students, appointed by different governments, and volunteers from every country in Europe, flocked to Yverdon to become acquainted with the new methods; and by these students the principles of Pestalozzi were carried back to their respective countries, and extensively put into practice. These principles at once obtained a stronger foothold in Germany than elsewhere; but, to a greater or less extent, they modified the educational systems of the whole civilized world.

PESTALOZZIAN PRINCIPLES.—As Pestalozzi has left no written code or authoritative *résumé* of his principles, we must look for them in the spirit of his work, and in such fragmentary statements as we find scattered throughout his writings.

*Order in Mental Growth.*—The first and most fundamental principle in all his work is, that the mental powers are unfolded in definite order, and that true instruction must be that which is intelligently adapted to each stage of mental growth, and directly tends to promote the next step of development. This principle, almost utterly ignored up to the time of Pestalozzi, is now generally admitted by educators, and is progressively becoming more and more the corner-stone of education.

*Home-Education.*—Among the means necessary for elevating the common people in intelligence and morality, one of the first that forced itself upon the attention of Pestalozzi was the importance and necessity of a thorough home-education. Indeed, in the development of his own ideas of education, this feature took precedence of all others. From actual observation, he saw, so frequently and so generally, that children at home were not only neglected in regard to their physical and moral needs, but that their naturally right instincts were perverted, and their whole nature demoralized, by bad examples and improper training, that he concluded that all effectual efforts at reform must begin at home.

*The Influence of Mothers.*—In all his earlier writings, his aim seemed to be to impress upon mothers the idea that they alone had power, through their influence at home, to work the needed reforms in society. He showed how susceptible children at an early age are to good influences, and in what manner these influences could be exercised to the best advantage. The mother has almost unlimited power over the child for the first few years of its existence, during which period habits are formed which go far to control action through life. It is all-important that, in this susceptible and formative period, all selfish propensities should be suppressed, and all good impulses stimulated. Indeed, neglect or misdirection at this period can never be compensated by subsequent education. Efforts to change the conduct of adults, who have grown up in ignorance and with slovenly and vicious habits, are usually entirely wasted, or the results produced are very insignificant when compared with the efforts put forth.

*Mistakes in Application.*—While this philosophy in regard to the importance of home-education and the influence of mothers was correct, Pestalozzi soon found that he had made a mistake in its application. True home-education can only be given by mothers who have themselves been truly educated. While the motherly instinct may be relied upon as sufficient to supply the child with the most common of the physical necessities, in all mental and moral work the mother must be guided by an enlarged intelligence. The love for the child will supply the motive, but this love must be supplemented by a knowledge of what constitutes the highest welfare of the child, and what means are best adapted to secure this welfare. To expect such results from mothers who themselves are neglected and misdirected at home, and who have no opportunity to correct their early impressions by education, would be absurd. "Do men gather grapes of thorns, or figs of thistles?"

*Education of Mothers.*—The third great principle. which may be considered as Pestalozzian is, that mothers should be educated. In consequence of the momentous results involved, this education should be as extended and complete as possible. Since the work of the mother is to shape the future destiny of the child, the whole well-being of society depends upon the intelligence with which this work is executed. The work involves principles of the most complex character pertaining to mental phenomena and to human relations; and the education of the mother must of necessity be incomplete unless it includes the facts upon which these principles rest. This view of the nature of woman's work, and of the preparatory culture necessary to the highest performance of that work, sets aside at once and forever all those contracted views of woman's sphere and education which are so frequently urged with an air of great profundity and wisdom.

*Study of Children.*—The next important principle of Pestalozzi is, that the teacher should make the child the subject of profound and careful study. While the general principles of mental philosophy derived from the aggregate study of mind will serve as a guide to general courses of instruction, a special study of the peculiarities of each child is necessary as a guide to the intelligent adaptation of general means to particular cases. Some of the most important changes now going on in education may be directly traced to the application of this principle.

*Training of Imbeciles.*—In no other department of instruction is the necessity of the study of each individual so apparent as in the education of imbeciles. The minds of these unfortunates differ from those of ordinary children chiefly in being more sluggish in action. All the ordinary appliances of education fail to arouse the dormant powers into activity. By a careful series of experiments, and by patient investigation which has continued through years, it has been found that the agencies necessary to be used in these cases differ from ordinary instruction, principally in the length of each step, and in the number of times each idea must be repeated. The results of these experiments have shown that imbeciles usually are susceptible of improvement; and they have also determined, with a degree of accuracy before unknown, the successive steps necessary in all primary instruction.

*Experience the Basis.*—The fifth principle is, that all school-work should be founded upon the actual experience of the child. To this end the exercises of the schoolroom should conform as much as possible to matters which interest the child out of school, and all instruction given should start from that which is already possessed. Much of the earliest instruction of the school will be to enlarge this experience by making vague notions more definite, and by showing relations between things which were before undiscovered. These exercises are also necessary to a thorough understanding of the subject—a result which Pestalozzi considered of cardinal importance.

*Object-Teaching.*—In all the works of the great reformer there is nothing more distinctly shown than that the systematic study of things should precede that of books. In popular estimation this is the most distinctive Pestalozzian principle of all. That the observing powers should be trained to perceive by exercise upon real objects, and that the office of books is to supplement the knowledge gained by personal experience, may be gathered not only from the writings of this author, but from the manner in which the schools at Burgdorf and Yverdon were conducted, and from the exercises of all the schools which have since been founded upon these models.

In another chapter we have shown the necessity of object-teaching, and the place such teaching should occupy in a school course.

*Practical Objections.*—Pestalozzi and his followers have been censured for having made too much of personal experience, and of having given too much prominence to object-teaching. There is, probably, an element of truth in this criticism, but the mistake was almost a necessary consequence of the circumstances of the case, and was but the exaggeration of a step in the right direction. From the system which ignored experience and made little or no account of understanding the subject, the reaction in favor of rational methods was violent. The rote-system was exploded; and as this system was founded upon books exclusively, it was but natural that the books should have been regarded as part of the discarded system, and that they should have been undervalued in the revision of the course of instruction which followed. To personal experience, which is indispensable as forming the basis of all knowledge, was assigned too high a place, and too little importance was attached to the knowledge which comes from the experience of others. These mistakes, incidental to all improvements in educational processes, are corrected by larger experiences, while the good resulting from the change remains as a permanent acquisition to the means of promoting human welfare.

*Conduct and Character.*—One of the ideas of education Pestalozzi made most prominent was, that all exercises should tend to promote good conduct on the part of the pupil, and that education was a failure unless it culminated in the formation of habits of good conduct. Intelligence he deemed valuable chiefly as it promoted morality. In his writings and practice he constantly enforced these ideas. The manner of conducting school exercises so as to lead to good conduct—a method directly resulting from Pestalozzi's principles—will be considered in the chapter upon Moral Teaching.

*Growth of the System.*—Many of the experiments instituted by Pestalozzi and his disciples, to put these principles in practice, have proved failures. The whole system is so exactly opposite to the old, in its aim and methods, that it has been difficult at once to determine the means that shall best express and exemplify the new ideas. Teachers educated under the old methods find it exceedingly hard to overcome their former habits; and although they may be convinced in theory, their practice changes slowly. But by almost imperceptible degrees the new ideas obtain a foothold and are consolidated into system, resulting finally in a complete revolution, which will substitute intelligent investigation for mechanical routine in every field of human thought and endeavor.

# CHAPTER VIII.

### *FROEBEL AND THE KINDERGARTEN.*

FRUIT OF PESTALOZZI'S PRINCIPLES.—The impulse which the works and experiments of Pestalozzi gave to education did not expend itself in mere imitation. The principles enunciated needed verification, and, in the broad field of education, they were to be applied in numberless ways, of which their author was probably entirely unconscious. This necessity gave rise to new experiments, and in some cases led to new and important discoveries.

*Education through Work.*—Among the ideas first promulgated by Pestalozzi was that a very considerable portion of true education might be obtained through work, and that kind of work which constitutes the ordinary vocation of the individual. In his first experiments at Neuhof with his juvenile criminals, he endeavored to carry this idea into practical execution, but without success. In his subsequent experiments, from the condition and circumstances of his school, this idea was subordinated to others which were forced upon his attention, and was never fully developed.

*Agricultural Schools.*—Von Fellenberg, a contemporary and friend of Pestalozzi, deeply impressed with this idea, instituted a series of experiments which resulted in his establishing a school of agriculture, where the work of the farm was performed by the students while attending to their studies. The work itself was found to be one of the most efficient of the means of improvement, and the pupils left the school not only fully instructed in the various branches of study, but with a minute and comprehensive knowledge of one or more of the industrial occupations, and, above all, with muscles trained to the performance of the work necessary to be done in the wide field of industry.

The success of Von Fellenberg in his little Swiss farm was so complete, that his plans were extensively copied in France and Germany, and afterward in the other countries of Europe, and in the United States. The agricultural schools now supported by most of the civilized nations are the direct offspring of Von Fellenberg's experiments; and the technical and trade schools have indirectly proceeded from the same source.

*Limitation of these Schools.*—In these agricultural, technical, and trade schools, the principle of thought-expression through muscular action was made practical, but the work was confined chiefly to the higher schools. The German trade schools take pupils at the age of fourteen, or after they have mastered the seven years' primary course. Most of the technical schools did not receive pupils until some years later.

THE WORK OF FROEBEL.—It was left to Froebel, an eminent German teacher, to apply the same principle to the training of children. From personal observation and study, he became thoroughly convinced that one of the principal causes of evil conduct was the wrong direction or bias given to the mind of the child in its earliest years. By a vicious system of home instruction, afterwards supplemented by an equally mischievous system of school-training, he saw that natural and innocent instincts and inclinations were constantly thwarted, and the mind forced out of the path which Nature pointed out as the most direct course to excellence, and into the way sanctioned by fashion, custom, or caprice. As a result of this false education, he saw natural activities smothered at their birth, and possibilities of useful life materially diminished.

*Philanthropic Motives.*—As in the case of Pestalozzi, the study and experiments of Froebel seemed to spring from an intense desire to benefit the human race, and from the conviction that measures of reform must commence while the mind is in its most plastic state. He had but little faith in measures designed to improve and reform those who had grown to maturity in ignorance, and with whom ill-conduct had become a rigid habit.

Froebel accepted the principles laid down by Pestalozzi without hesitation. These principles, he saw, were designed to bring instruction into harmony with Nature, and he set about devising means by which such harmony could be fully realized. He confined his experiments largely to young children, and for their instruction he devised the methods now known as the kindergarten system.

*Development of the Kindergarten.*—The word kindergarten literally means a place where children are cultivated. Froebel's plan was to collect a number of young children and place them in such conditions that their own free and spontaneous acts would, in a large measure, contribute to their full development. The teacher's work was simply direction—taking care that the natural activities of the child always had an opportunity for free expression, and in the proper direction.

Froebel's success was so great, that a large number of teachers became converted to his methods, and kindergartens were established not only throughout Germany, but they have been introduced extensively into most of the civilized countries of the world.

*Obscurity of Expression.*—Like many other reformers and originators of great schemes, Froebel was far from being clear in the enunciation of the principles upon which his work was founded. His insight into the nature of children, and his ability to provide the appliances necessary for each step of their advancement, were far in advance of his ability to formulate his work upon a philosophic basis and give it full expression. He seemed also to have imbibed, at an early period, certain mystical metaphysical notions, which gave a bias to his thinking, and caused him to clothe his thoughts in obscure phraseology.

KINDERGARTEN PRINCIPLES.—From the spirit of his work, and from the practices common to kindergartens generally, we find that the following principles serve as a guide to this system of instruction:

*Inherited Powers and Tendencies.*—Every child is born with capacities and traits which are inherited from its ancestry. These traits give general direction to thought and conduct, but they may be materially changed by education. A naturally good disposition may be ruined by a false system of education, while evil traits may be nearly, or quite, overcome by a judicious education. The education of one generation appears as an inherited tendency in the next.

This principle completely overthrows that philosophy which insists that the mind is a blank paper upon which the educator may write what he pleases; and it is equally fatal to the opposite philosophy, that education can do little or nothing toward changing natural tendencies. Froebel shows that the truth lies between these extremes, and that human progress depends upon the fact that inherited traits may be changed by education, and that the results of this education may, in turn, be transmitted by inheritance. Examples of the inheritance of qualities are seen in the history of every nation, and of nearly every family. The successive generations of the Hebrews were always noted for their deep religious fervor, the Greeks for their love of beauty, and the Romans for their power of social organization. Personal peculiarities, in like manner, are transmitted in families. Through successive generations in the same family line, we find a general love of learning; in another, a love of gain; and in still another, a general indolence, which prevents either physical or mental improvement. In intellectual families, the form of scholarship may, in like manner, be transmitted—one showing a taste for the classics, another for natural history and kindred branches.

*Education should Commence Early.*—Education should begin at the earliest period of conscious existence.

Everything that can make an impression upon the senses of the child, whether in the form of visible objects or tones of voice, becomes of importance as educational influences. The mother at home, and the teacher at school, should so arrange these objects that the impressions conveyed will exactly respond to the power of the child most active at the time, and in such a way that each in its time will excite the deepest interest and leave the most permanent impression.

Early impressions are most durable, and many a man has tried in vain to overcome evil habits contracted in childhood. This is especially true in regard to habits of speech. Again, by a proper attention to the character and order of the impressions made upon the mind of the child, a large amount of knowledge can be gained incidentally and unconsciously, thereby saving the time and effort which would be needed in acquiring the same knowledge at a later period. This early education, however, is possible only through the efforts of thoroughly educated mothers, and all that teachers can do is to supplement the instruction commenced in the nursery.

In regard to this subject, Herbert Spencer says: "Whoever has watched with any discernment the wide-eyed gaze of the infant at surrounding objects, knows very well that education does begin thus early, whether we intend it or not; and that these fingerings and suckings of everything it can lay hold of, these open-mouthed listenings to every sound, are the first steps in the series which ends in the discovery of unseen planets, the invention of calculating engines, the production of great paintings, or the composition of symphonies and operas. The activity of the faculties from the first being spontaneous and inevitable, the question is, whether we shall supply in due variety the materials on which they may exercise themselves; and to the question so put, none but an affirmative answer can be given."

*Education based on Self-Activity.*—The education of children should be based upon *self-activity*. The needs of every child give rise to desires, and the desires to activities of some kind. A philosophic system of education will look through these activities to the needs which they represent, and will so direct them that, while they excite present interest and gratify present desire, they will also contribute to intellectual and moral growth and to the future and permanent well-being of the child.

The lowest manifestations of activity are those of mere physical motion; but these are necessary to secure that control over the muscles which is requisite to self-support and self-protection, and which must precede intellectual growth. The curiosity of children, manifested in their desire to handle objects, to open boxes and drawers, and to break playthings, is but an indication of their endeavor to convert vague and unsatisfactory notions into distinct ideas. Von Fellenberg says: "Experience has taught me that indolence in young persons is so directly opposite to their natural disposition to activity, that, unless it is the consequence of a bad education, it is almost immediately connected with some constitutional defect."

*Spontaneous Activity, or Play.*—The child must be left free to show its activities and express its desires. This freedom is best manifested in *play*, which is free activity gratifying desires, and, when not perverted, the instinctive and unconscious manner in which well-being is promoted. It also includes the first deeds of the child, in endeavoring to supply its own needs and to give pleasure to others.

Play, which has been defined as the poetry of childhood, may always be considered as an activity which, in some way, ministers to needs, and it is a guide to the teacher in determining what are the needs that require the most attention at the time. It is also a potent force to be used in the work of education. But, to this end, the plays must be so arranged and systematized that the child will always find the variety of nature, and each play in its turn will be instrumental in furnishing him with new ideas, and leading him to higher activities.

*School Exercises should give Pleasure.*—Whatever gives pleasure to children generally and at all times, always serves to promote their development in some way. This statement is not only the enunciation of a great truth, but one entirely antagonistic to the old system of education, which held that study was valuable in proportion as it was distasteful, and that culture was to be sought in thwarting, rather than in gratifying, natural inclinations.

The converse of this proposition is also true. Whatever is distasteful to children generally, and whatever is performed as mere task-work, is of but little worth in promoting the true development of the child. Much of the work which forms the staple of school instruction at the present day is of this character. Reading-lessons that children cannot comprehend; the memorizing of the words of a text-book; the beginning of a subject by learning definitions instead of facts; the premature study of grammar; the reasoning processes of mental arithmetic at too early a period; the spelling and defining of words largely in advance of their use—all illustrate this distasteful work, and all are examples of waste both of time and effort.

*Caution.*—This proposition, however, must not be taken as meaning that all desires of children are to be gratified, or that such desires are always prompted by real needs. A great variety of unnecessary desires may arise from inheritance, or from false impressions made very early in life. It is only when wide investigations are made, extending over considerable time, that teachers can distinguish unerringly between the manifestations of spurious and real needs.

*Physical and Mental Activity combined.*—Education, as much as possible, should connect every step of instruction with some kind of bodily activity. As the hand is the chief instrument of work, it should be specially trained to perform quickly and accurately all the motions needed in the ordinary affairs of life. This training of the hand to do, while training the mind to think, is one of the most distinctive features of the kindergarten system. Indeed, it is beginning to be apparent that the most effective way to produce the thinking is through work actually performed by the hand— the case being analogous to that of getting the use of tools by the performance of real work with the tools, rather than by the study of the tools themselves. In another respect, this training of the hand is of immense benefit in mental development. The mind thinks, and the will executes. As the mind makes use of the brain for thinking, the brain must be trained to perform its function in the most effective manner possible; and as the will makes extensive use of the hand in executing, the hand must be trained to execute the mandate of the will in the most effective manner possible.

The effect of this training of the hand is, first, to make the mental impressions deeper and more lasting; secondly, to greatly increase the interest of every subject by the discovery of relations which would otherwise be undiscovered; and thirdly, by bringing the hand under such perfect control, that in all subsequent time it will be immediately and effectually responsive to the will.

The means taken for this training are the successive use of objects, which the pupil not only sees but handles; the use of blocks in building, accompanied by instruction in regard to the methods of building; play in sand, and modeling in clay with purpose in view; drawing, both inventive and imitative; and the gradual use of mechanical tools that are needed in the various occupations.

*Harmonious Development of all the Powers.*—The next fundamental principle of Froebel is, that the whole nature of the child needs instruction and training from the very first. While he fully recognizes the importance of order and time in educational processes, he claims that a symmetrical and harmonious development of all the powers demands that each one shall receive attention in proportion to its present activity, and in such a manner as to promote its normal growth.

*The Schools demanded by these Principles.*—The system of education which is devised to carry this principle into practice must provide for physical growth and well-being, by the careful training of every muscle in the body, and the special training of the hand; for the gradual development of the mental faculties in the order pointed out by Pestalozzi; for moral culture, by all possible incentives to well-doing; and for æsthetic culture, which shall develop taste and lead to an appreciation and creation of the beautiful. The final outcome of this fourfold system is the full possession of physical health and strength, and a distinct recognition of the true, the good, and the beautiful, as guiding our actions and as completing our lives.

PRACTICAL KINDERGARTEN WORK.—Kindergarten instruction should commence at the age of three years. The children are brought together in a pleasant room, where are collected the appliances necessary for all their varied plays. Care should be taken that the objects are not in such profusion as to distract attention and produce uneasiness. In Froebel's opinion, nothing can be more fatal to intellectual stimulus than the great quantity of toy-rubbish with which children are often supplied.

*The kind of play* in which each pupil engages is determined by his own inclination, somewhat guided by the teacher.

*The method of play* is suggested by the teacher, and the play is so controlled that it teaches an important lesson. In this way, literally, all play becomes work, and all work becomes play.

*Original Work.*—The work is so conducted, also, that the teacher tells but little, leaving the pupil to discover the needed truth, and so leading to the development of creative energy. This last result is obtained largely through the process of inventive drawing, and the hand-work in which the child is constantly engaged.

*Singing.*—In the kindergarten, singing is one of the conspicuous agencies used in the promotion of æsthetic culture, the rhythm of sound and motion being considered of prime importance. The songs selected, both in regard to their words and their music, are simple, and such as the experience of the world has shown to be of interest to children. The delight of children in the melodies of Mother Goose affords a key to the nature of the songs which are best adapted to the kindergarten methods.

*"Playing in the Dirt."*—The love which children have for playing in the sand is turned to good account in the kindergarten in the teaching of form and of quantity; and their love for making "little dirt-pies" is directed to systematic modeling in clay. There is no manifestation of childish interest that is not or may not be made profitable in devising systems of instruction.

*The Law of Order.*—In the world of mind and matter Froebel saw the evidences of infinite order, which must be obeyed in all processes of instruction. In the language of one of his most distinguished disciples, " he made the eternal archetypes of Nature the playthings of childhood, and the mutual relations and combinations which Nature employs in her secret workshop, the child's laws and rules of play."

*Study of the System.*—The study of the details of the kindergarten system cannot fail of being a benefit to every teacher. Although the work as a whole may not be adapted to the condition and circumstances of the community where he is engaged, the full elucidation of the methods employed are suggestive of a thousand expedients calculated to interest and improve almost any grade of schools. By the study of these methods, also, the principles upon which they are founded are much more readily understood and appreciated. This desirable information will be found in any of the kindergarten manuals which are published in various parts of the country.

*The Kindergarten at St. Louis.*—The kindergarten system has been more thoroughly tried at St. Louis than elsewhere in this country. Under the intelligent direction of Mr. William T. Harris, the philosophic superintendent of the city schools, the experiment has been made of connecting kindergarten instruction with the public schools. This experiment raised many questions concerning the system itself, and the modifications it needs to adapt itself to the necessities of American schools. From a late report of Mr. Harris we make the following extract:

*Necessity of Study and Experiment.*—" While it is probable that the kindergarten may require modifications to adapt it to American educational needs, it is not at all certain wherein or how much, until its aims and methods have been studied, and practical experiments have been instituted. It may be that only slight changes are required to adapt it to our system—changes relating to arrangements of furniture, length of session, age of admission, etc. It may be that modifications of the inner nature of the system—its psychological idea—may be required to adapt it to American wants. Experiment will doubtless evolve, one after the other, the practical and theoretical problems, and discover the best solutions.

*Scope of Education.*—" It is conceded that education includes very much more than the province of the school. The stage of nurture includes first the physical care of the child and the training of body; next the formation of habits in harmony with the customs and usages of civilized life. His eating and drinking, and other personal habits, must be those of humanity, and not those of natural impulse—those of animals. From the first the child begins to use his senses as instruments for obtaining knowledge. His growing power is watched anxiously by the family, and his efforts are stimulated and encouraged. He acquires, in this way, a most important stock of theoretical ideas, as well as command of the use of his senses and of language, the most important of all instruments, before he comes under the influence of the school.

*Scope of the Kindergarten.*—" The kindergarten proposes to invade this realm of nurture; to systemize it, from the cradle onward to the school. The mother shall substitute conscious, rational action for whim and caprice in the management of her child, and shall watch over the orderly development of the faculties of her child, as a scientific gardener watches over the development of plants in his garden. Froebel proposed to have this realm of nurture transformed into systematic culture, embracing provinces—physical, mental, and moral. He proposed to do this in such a way as to preserve all the sweetness of childhood, and to stimulate and encourage its spontaneity.

*Delicate Adjustments.*—" Here was the great point in Froebel's success. He overcame seeming impossibilities, by adopting a method which could be put in practice without injury to the spontaneity of childhood, while it really disciplined the child's will into rational forms. This delicate point is at once the greatest merit of Froebel, and the ground of the greatest danger for those who attempt to carry it out in practice. It is still more dangerous for those who attempt to modify Froebel and naturalize it in other countries. Lacking a full insight into the problem, and consequently misunderstanding Froebel's intentions, in the order and make-up of his gifts, it frequently happens that modifications are proposed which utterly lack the delicate adjustment of Froebel. If carried out, they would permanently injure the development of individuality in the child, and produce a stunted character. Froebel himself goes almost to the edge of this matter: it is easy to go over the edge.

*Philosophy Involved.*—"Momentous questions must be settled in psychology before one can fully appreciate how wisely Froebel has planned, or how dangerous it is for his followers to depart from his footsteps without a full insight into the subject. There are deeper grounds than mere national ones, important though the latter may be. There is human nature in general, and the law of its unfolding—common to all civilized nations. What is common to civilized nations, however, is not shared by half-civilized nations, for they interfere with the development of individuality at a far earlier stage than civilized nations do, and purposely dwarf its growth. Civilized nations differ as to limits imposed; but all peoples who have set a constitutional limit to the caprice of their chief executive, allow individuality to develop to that degree that it discriminates its rational from its arbitrary phase.

*Questions to be Settled.*—" Should caprice be tolerated in any phase of the development of childhood? Ought it not to be annihilated as soon as it appears? Is it wise to rationalize the activity of childhood as soon as it begins? Is there not a danger in any systematic training of the child, that his will-power may become weakened by subordinating it to prescribed rules before it gets developed sufficiently? Moreover, that question of too much stimulus at an early age is a serious one. We all know that the children brought up in the city are over-excited from infancy by the multitude of objects continually presented to their senses. In the country it is far otherwise. The difference between city-developed individuality and that of the country is very great as to depth and toughness. The alertness of the city intellect is purchased at a sacrifice of other qualities which are essential to fully-developed character. Questions like these deserve careful consideration."

## CHAPTER IX.

*AGASSIZ; AND SCIENCE IN ITS RELATIONS TO EDUCATION.*

THE SCOPE AND END OF SCIENCE.—In an article upon the "Culture demanded by Modern Life," Prof. Youmans says: "Science, in its true and largest meaning, is the right interpretation of Nature—a comprehension of the workings of law wherever law prevails. It matters nothing whether the subjects are stones or stars, human souls, or complications of social relations; the most perfect of each constitutes its special science, and the comprehensive view of the relations which each sustains to all realizes the highest idea of science."

This definition at once elevates science out of the domain of mere materialism, and makes it comprehend every department of human thought. The "right interpretation of Nature" means the pursuit of truth in every field of research. It is not the subject-matter, but the positive knowledge of the subject, including both facts and inferences, that constitutes the science. The highest science is that which starts from the laws established by the special sciences, coördinates them all, and, by a process of higher inferences, arrives at the highest and most comprehensive laws.

*Philosophy and Utility.*—In the ancient philosophies, a broad distinction was made between the products of reflection, or speculative thought, and those subjects which consider the common and daily needs of men. The former alone were thought worthy of attention, and scholars were encouraged to pursue truth and virtue for their own sake. The methods of these philosophies were also, to a great extent, those of speculation rather than investigation, and the value of the physical sciences was quite underrated. This sentiment in regard to the nature of philosophic research continued down to periods comparatively modern. Bacon was the first philosopher to take distinct issue with this idea, and to proclaim that the true object of philosophic inquiry was "fruit," in the promotion of human welfare, and that the true method was the investigation and interpretation of Nature.

The spirit of the old philosophies, to some extent, still survives, and scientific men of the present day exhort enthusiastic students "to pursue science for its own sake," and they frequently brand the idea of use as a mere "bread-and-butter consideration," beneath the notice of the true votary of science.

*Prof. Tyndall's Opinion.*—Prof. Tyndall, in his farewell speech at New York, uses the following language in regard to this question: "In the pursuit of science, the first worker is the investigator of natural truth, whose vocation it is to pursue that truth, and extend the field of discovery for the truth's own sake, and without reference to practical ends." Again he says: "Keep your sympathetic eye on the originator of knowledge. Give him the freedom necessary for his researches, not demanding of him so-called practical results. Above all things, avoid that question which ignorance so often addresses to genius: 'What is the use of your work?'" These extracts show the persistence of philosophic notions, even after the systems of thought to which they were attached have been entirely superseded.

*Another View.*—Many of the most far-seeing thinkers of modern times do not share in this opinion of the ignoble nature, or secondary importance, of utility. They claim that the question "What use?" is entirely legitimate when applied to any pursuit in which mankind can engage, and that the answer to this question, showing that the pursuit is useful or otherwise, is an infallible guide in determining whether it should be undertaken or not. The term "use," however, would not be restricted to any mere material consideration, but would be made to include all possible human needs, physical and spiritual. In this broad sense, *use* becomes the most powerful incentive to labor and investigation. A desire to reap personal advantage, or to benefit one's own family or kindred, or the broader philanthropy which considers the welfare of the whole human family, is a much stronger motive for action in any direction, than one which takes hold of the intellect but fails to reach the emotions.

*Prof. Huxley's Opinion.*—In a lecture upon "Biology," Prof. Huxley says: "I judge of the value of human pursuits by their bearing upon human interests; in other words, by their utility. Now, in an Englishman's mouth, it generally means that by which we get pudding, or praise, or both. I have no doubt that is one meaning of the word utility, but it by no means includes all I mean by utility. I think that knowledge of every kind is useful in proportion as it tends to give people right ideas, which are essential to the foundation of right practice, and to remove wrong ideas, which are the no less essential foundation and fertile mothers of every description of error in practice. And, upon the whole, inasmuch as this world is, after all, whatever practical people may say, absolutely governed by ideas, and very often by the wildest and most hypothetical ideas, it is a matter of the greatest importance that our theories of things, and even of things that seem a long way apart from our daily lives, should be, as far as possible, true, and, as far as possible, removed from error. It is not only in the coarser, practical sense of the word 'utility,' but in this higher and broader sense, that I measure the value of a study."

*Antagonisms Harmonized.*—There seems to be no need of essential antagonism between those who would urge the importance of original investigation and those who demand that "fruit" to human welfare shall be the result of all investigation. From history we derive two essential facts bearing upon the subject. In the Middle Ages, when intellectual operations were purely speculative, ignoring alike Nature and human needs, the speculations themselves were valueless as reaching results in any of the realms of truth; and the vital force spent upon them was, in a great measure, wasted. On the other hand, since the time of Bacon, scientific investigation has been pursued in the spirit of utility, and there have resulted, not only increased comforts and happiness to man, but higher philosophic results in the regions of pure intellect and morals than the world has ever before seen. Intellectual speculation, divorced from humanity, results in visionary dreaming and in the destruction of intellectual power. Intellectual investigation, in the interests of humanity, reaches the loftiest heights of pure thought, and indefinitely increases intellectual power.

From the facts of history, the broad inference has been made that every discovery in the fields of physical, intellectual, or moral activity has been of use in establishing a law, and the discovery of every law has directly benefited man. No matter how useless the new truths appeared at the moment of discovery, in the end they were found useful as contributing in some way to human welfare.

*Incentive to Investigation.*—This generalization becomes an incentive and an inspiration to active scientific workers. With the most implicit faith that any discoveries which he can make will be of use to the human race, the student of science can now devote himself to any branch of scientific research to which his taste may incline him. His answer to the question "What use?" is ever ready in general terms, if not in specific details; and there is no reason for either misrepresenting the nature of utility, nor for ignoring it altogether. The great incentive to endeavor still remains; and although he may never experience the direct benefit of his discoveries, in the certainty of their final utility, he may abandon himself to the pleasure of their pursuit, content to leave the richest fruit of his work to be gathered by those who come after him.

It is seen from the foregoing that the true scientific

spirit constantly considers human welfare, and in this way indirectly promotes moral action. It seeks to find that which is true, in order to establish that which is good. The discovery of every new law, in the infinite order of the universe, becomes at once a new power to be used for human advancement, and a new incentive to human action. We have next to consider the methods which science uses most directly and effectually to accomplish its work.

*Methods of Science.*—The general method, as contained in the direction to investigate Nature closely and accurately, was laid down by Bacon. The successive steps in this investigation as now practised by scientific men are stated as follows by Prof. Huxley:

*First: Observation of Facts*, including that artificial observation called experiment.

*Secondly:* The process of tying up similar facts in bundles, ticketed ready for use, which is called *comparison* and *classification;* the results of the process—the ticketed bundles—being named *general propositions.*

*Thirdly: Deduction*, which takes us from the general proposition to facts again, teaches us to anticipate from the ticket what is in the bundle.

*Fourthly: Verification*, which is the process of ascertaining whether in point of fact our anticipation is a correct one.

*Scientific Methods in Teaching.*—It will be seen that the steps in this scientific method are substantially those which have previously been described in the chapters on Objective and Subjective Teaching. The experience of scientific men has shown that this is not only the most direct method of making new discoveries, but it is the only method by which positive and certain knowledge can be obtained, and made a permanent possession of the mind. The experience of teachers has also shown that these methods are the best and most direct for accomplishing the objects of education—the acquisition of useful knowledge, and the development of the mental faculties. The man of science and the educator, though starting from different points and traversing different routes, have arrived at the same results, the conclusions of the one strengthening and corroborating those of the other.

*Defects in Teaching which Science Remedies.*—In the work of Pestalozzi, the subject-matter of the lessons given in the classes was of a fragmentary character; and although it aroused the attention and trained the observing powers, it often failed to show the relations of one lesson to another, and to give that connected chain of thought necessary to scientific reasoning.

In the schools founded upon the Pestalozzian principles, the same state of things is usually observed, the objects being chosen solely for their use in impressing the direct lesson of the hour, without considering the relation of the object to the other objects or facts in the same field of investigation or department of thought.

*Waking up Mind.*—In the "Theory and Practice of Teaching"—one of the most valuable of all the contributions which this country has yet made to the literature of teaching—the author, David P. Page, gives a most interesting sketch of a lesson upon an ear of corn, under the suggestive title of "Waking up Mind." This work was published in 1847, and the lesson in question was one of the first expositions of the nature and value of object-lessons ever made in this country. But Mr. Page died before he could see the fruits which were to come by following out the principles involved in his model lesson. He probably little thought that the suggestion, which he regarded valuable only as breaking the monotony and tedium of the ordinary schoolroom routine, was destined to very nearly supersede that routine in primary schools; and that all the work given to pupils would eventually be so arranged that each lesson would result in "waking up mind."

*Growth of the Scientific Principle.*—The method so graphically described by Mr. Page has been largely adopted since the date of his writing, under the name of object-teaching, and its principles and limitations are now quite clearly understood. Meanwhile, science has become more and more systematic, and at last it is seen that the methods of science and the methods of education are identical. Science dealing with knowledge, and education dealing with development, move along the same routes; and the apparent antagonism between the practical and the theoretical disappears.

Many of the most prominent among the scientific men of the present century have taken deep interest in educational work, both for its special bearings upon science, and for its effects upon humanity at large. In the general change of educational methods they have recognized the evidences of real progress; and there has come to be a quite prevalent opinion that these changes should go on until our school courses include the subject-matter as well as the methods of science.

*Agassiz's Work.*—Among those men of science who became specially interested in schools, none occupied a higher place than Prof. Louis Agassiz, the great naturalist. During the whole of his long and most honorable career as a man of science, while intent upon his special work, he ever sought to raise education out of its narrow formalism, and to infuse into it something of the spirit which animates the devotee of science. During the last years of his life, the educational value of science seemed to occupy his attention more and more; and he so devoted his energies to this work, that he may be justly regarded as the great leader in the new educational reform.

EARLY LIFE.—The early life of Agassiz eminently fitted him for this position. He was born upon the banks of Lake Neufchâtel, in the northwest part of Switzerland. His early youth was passed amid the most noble and beautiful scenery in Europe. In his work on Pestalozzi, Prof. Krusi gives the following description of this lake and its vicinity:

"To the west, the Jura Mountains extend in an unbroken chain, delightfully varied by pastures, forests. deep ravines, and masses of bare rock. From the summits of these mountains the traveler looks down upon the tranquil lake beneath; while to the south lies the wide valley, with all its variegated richness, bounded by the snow-clad Alps, from the centre of which towers the majestic summit of Mont Blanc. The valley is traversed by the river Orbe, which, fed from an invisible lake above, rises suddenly from beneath a high rock, and lower down falls over a precipice."

*Love of Nature.*—With such attractions around him, the peculiarly impressible mind of young Agassiz could scarcely fail of becoming enthusiastically in love with

Nature. Much of his time in early youth was spent upon the lake, or among the hills, not for the purposes of mere recreation, but for study. The fish he caught were lessons rather than food; and at the age of eleven years, when he was sent to school, he was familiar with the names, appearance, and habits of all the finny tribe of Lake Neufchâtel.

*Vacation Studies.*—During his vacations he pursued, with intense enthusiasm, the other departments of natural history, and traversed fields and forests to become minutely and thoroughly acquainted with their various inhabitants. This devotion to the study of Nature served to increase rather than diminish his love for books, and in all the schools he attended he stood among the foremost in his class. The knowledge of fishes which he obtained upon his fishing excursions while a boy, and which he greatly extended during his school vacations, was so accurate and exhaustive within the limits of his observation, that, while at the university, he was able to make many important corrections in the published works on this subject. At a little later period, a scientific expedition returned from Brazil with an immense amount of material for scientific study. The professor who had collected the fishes unfortunately died before his work was completed, and to Agassiz was committed the task of arranging, classifying, and describing, the specimens preserved. This work was performed with so much ability, that it placed him at once in the foremost rank of naturalists.

*Study of the Glaciers.*—His next great work was the examination of the glacial system of the Alps. These peculiar formations of ice, which extend downward from the general snow-line of the mountains thousands of feet, and in some cases along the slope of the mountains many miles, had attracted the attention of scientific men from early times, and many ingenious speculations had been made in regard to them. Agassiz became deeply interested in these inquiries; but instead of hazarding speculations concerning them, he set about a series of observations and experiments, which occupied many months, and occasioned several visits to the mountains. He was obliged, at times, to pass weeks together in a rude hut high up on the mountain, and on the very verge of the glacier. His efforts were rewarded by the most complete success; and, from the facts which he gathered, he was able to determine the nature of the glaciers, their origin, their rate of motion, and their effect upon the ground they traversed.

Enlarging the generalizations from the facts observed, he was competent to state the laws which governed the formation, motion, and continuance of glaciers so accurately, that all subsequent observations have only served to verify them; so that evidences of glacial action have been found in numerous places where before they had never been supposed to exist. Guided by the inferences and generalizations which he made, we are now able to look back upon a period in the earth's history when masses of ice, thousands of feet thick, extended from the northern polar regions far toward the equator, flowing slowly and irresistibly forward, disrupting mountains, and ploughing out deep furrows for streams and lakes, and finally dissolving under the heat of the semi-tropical zone. By the means of this generalization, a new light was shed upon geology and geography, and a new province of the unknown was brought within the domain of human intelligence.

SPIRIT OF HIS WORK.—The spirit cherished by Agassiz while young, animated him through life, and in all his work he was a most careful investigator, allowing no facts to escape him, while he was always reticent in regard to opinions until the whole case had been examined. These qualities and habits gave weight to his mature judgment, and he became a great power in the scientific world.

*The Old Methods Distrusted.*—Agassiz's experience in the schools early made him distrustful of the methods of education generally pursued. He was conscious that, for his own knowledge and mental power, he was more indebted to his solitary rambles than to his formal course of study. He further saw that, in the prevailing education, language largely took the place of thought; that more attention was given to the symbols of knowledge than to the knowledge itself; that much of the knowledge pretended to be given was so inaccurate and superficial as to be of little worth; that text-books and lexicons were invested with an inflexible authority fatal to independence of thought; and, in short, that the elaborate machinery of the schools failed to secure either accurate knowledge, vigorous thought, or right conduct.

*Reformation Begun.*—These errors, he saw, could be corrected only by a radical and fundamental change in the whole system of education, in which the scientific spirit and methods should play a prominent part. He commenced the work of reform with his characteristic caution and energy, calling attention to some of the prominent defects of education in his public lectures, and demonstrating the superiority of the new system by instructing classes of students in the Museum of Natural History which he established at Cambridge.

*The School at Penikese.*—His success was so great, that he resolved to try and reach the public schools by instruction offered to teachers. To this end, he set about the establishment of a class, to be held in the summer vacations of the schools, where teachers might obtain a knowledge of the scientific methods. His idea finally took shape in the establishment of the Anderson School of Natural History at Penikese Island, on the southeast coast of Massachusetts. At this point fifty pupils were in attendance the first year, under his immediate supervision. He was assisted in his undertaking by several of the most noted specialists in natural history. The instruction given was chiefly for the purpose of illustrating methods. Each pupil was set to the study of some specimen of zoölogy, in which study he was obliged to exercise his observing powers until he had seen, and was able to describe, the most noticeable points in the object. The facts derived from a large number of observations were then compared, and inferences made, which led to the establishment of general laws. The result of the experiment was in the highest degree satisfactory in regard to the nature and amount of the instruction given, and the enthusiasm inspired among the pupils.

*A New Era.* — The establishment of this school marks a new era in the history of education in this country. Teachers, fully imbued with its spirit, have carried its methods into their respective spheres of labor distributed throughout the country; and from their schools, as centres of influence, both the spirit and methods are rapidly spreading downward toward the elementary schools, where they will eventually become the common possession of all pupils in every grade of instruction. The new influence is demonstrated in a deeper interest manifested in study, in the fresh impulse given to scientific research, and in the greater ease with which pupils are aroused to intellectual life.

*Unfinished Plans.*—The life of "the master," as he was affectionately called by his pupils, was cut short at the very beginning of this most important enterprise of his life, and it is left to others to carry on to a successful termination the work which he began. Unfortunately, he left no authoritative statement in regard to either the methods or plans which he intended to pursue, and probably he had never consciously formulated them. After taking the initial steps in the right direction, he would have been guided by the same principles which must control all fruitful investigation, and welcomed such truth as would have been developed, each new truth extending the boundaries of experience, and serving as a guide to the next step in advance.

SUMMARY OF PRINCIPLES.—From direct statements made in the lectures of Agassiz, from fragmentary hints scattered through his writings, and from the general tenor and spirit of his works, we may regard the following principles as lying at the foundation of his theory of education, and as indicating the direction which effort must take in order to reduce this theory to practice.

*Training the Observing Powers.*—He was a thorough believer in the Pestalozzian principle, that the senses and the observing powers are to be cultivated and trained from the outset, and that the other mental powers are to be brought into activity in the order of their natural growth. Further than this, he believed that the successful operation of the higher faculties of the mind in solving the problems of thought, and in arriving at just conclusions, depends upon the faithfulness with which perception has been cultivated; and he seemed to have little faith in the value of that instruction which has no basis in experience.

*Importance of Hand-Work.*—In his practice he strongly supported the most distinctive feature of Froebel—the necessity of training the hand as well as the eye. In all his work he instructed his pupils to handle the specimens which they were studying, so as to become familiar with them under all circumstances. He also advocated the general introduction of drawing as one of the most essential of the studies which could be pursued in the common schools. He frequently remarked that, " in the study of natural history, the ability to draw the specimens under consideration is equivalent to the possession of a third eye." He regarded drawing, also, as one of the most important aids to mental development, and to the acquisition of knowledge in every grade of school.

*Science the Basis of Education.*—From his experience and observation he was convinced that the subject-matter of instruction, in general use in schools, is of but little practical importance in promoting the highest interests of humanity, thus defeating one of the fundamental aims of education. The recollections of his boyhood days gave him an intense sympathy with those who had a longing for real rather than apparent knowledge. He found in science, understood in its widest sense, the subject-matter which would serve the double purpose of education in the most effective manner.

Besides this, he found that the possession of real or scientific knowledge was of the greatest importance, not only in carrying on all the complicated relations of society, but in successfully competing for the prizes of the world. In agriculture, in manufactures, in the arts, and in business generally, success depends largely upon the possession of accurate knowledge in these several departments. In the struggle for existence, ignorance has no chance in competition with intelligence.

This accurate knowledge is of benefit in other respects. It bestows upon labor its largest returns, and gives to the laborer leisure for higher pursuits. It directs efforts to worthy and attainable ends, and points out the way of improvement. It prevents the loss involved in making anew experiments which time and again have resulted in failure; and it effectually warns against the continuance of courses of conduct which are destructive alike to human effort and human welfare.

*Knowledge Necessary for Discipline.*—In addition to the practical value of scientific knowledge, he regarded the methods of science as preëminently adapted to the culture of the mind. These methods lead not to speculative but to accurate results; and he had a profound distrust for that culture which ignores, or affects to despise, scientific knowledge. He would extend to every department of human thought the methods which had proved of so much value in his own field of natural history.

*Authority in Science and Education.*—Prof. Agassiz utterly repudiated authority in science or education. The fundamental condition of all excellence in mental work is absolute freedom of thought. Investigation is in direct antagonism to authority in any of its forms. Every human being must be free to investigate and to think, and to follow the results of investigation and thought whithersoever they may lead. The objective point of all study is truth. Any system that imposes authority upon the intellect, so far as it succeeds, stifles investigation, and takes away from the individual the power of judging between truth and falsehood.

Authority is also fatal to that confidence which every one should have in the results of his own mental processes. This confidence will be more or less absolute, depending upon the carefulness of previous study; but the interposition of authority leads to a distrust of inferences which are based on well-known facts, and in this way weakens both the intellect and the will.

*Thoroughness in Work and Study.*—In all the sayings and work of Agassiz he advocated and practised the greatest possible thoroughness. His maxims in this regard may be summed up as follows: "Observe carefully, and compare the results of different observations, before you state your conclusions as facts." "Be sure of all the facts that enter into the case before you generalize." "Verify the results of your generalization before you state it as a law or a principle." "Never be hasty in coming to decisions." "Be reticent as to the expression of opinions until the most thorough investigation has been made."

*Scientific Object-Lessons.*—The system which Agassiz put in practice in his school at Penikese, and which he advocated in his lectures, includes object-lessons; but from the very outset he would give these lessons in connected series, making each series lead directly into one of the sciences. By this means all the good results of object-lessons will be gained, with the additional advantages that both the methods used and the knowledge gained are of great worth in after-life.

The principles of teaching which Agassiz advocated and practised are now generally accepted and made the basis of instruction in scientific schools. Among scientific men there is a substantial agreement in regard to them. Laboratories for practical experiment and investigation on the part of the students are now a part of the equipment of all the technical and scientific schools, and they are rapidly becoming a necessity wherever science is taught.

*Corroborative Views.*—The following extract from a late speech of Prof. Huxley upon the study of biology shows how far he is in accord with the practices which proved so successful at Penikese: "Granting that biology is something worth studying, what is the best way of studying it? Here I must point out that, since biology is a physical science, the methods of studying it must be analogous to that which is followed in the other physical sciences. It has long been recognized that, if a man wishes to be a chemist, it is not only necessary that he should read chemical books and attend chemical lectures, but that he should actually himself perform the fundamental experiments in his laboratory, and know exactly what the words which he finds in his books and hears from his teachers mean. If he does not, he may read till the crack of doom, but he will never know much about chemistry. That is what every chemist will tell you, and the physicist will do the same for his branch of science. The great changes and improvements in physical and chemical scientific education, which have taken 'place of late, have all resulted from the combination of practical teaching with the reading of books and the hearing of lectures.

"The same thing is true in biology. Nobody will ever know anything about biology, except in a dilettant, 'paper-philosophic' way, who contents himself with reading books on botany, zoölogy, and the like; and the reason for this is simple and easy to understand. It is, that all language is merely symbolical of the things, of which it treats; the more complicated the things, the more bare is the symbol, and the more its verbal definition requires to be supplemented by the information derived directly from the handling, and the seeing, and the touching of the thing symbolized: that is really what is at the bottom of the whole matter. It is plain common sense, as all truth in the long run is, only common sense clarified.

"If you want a man to be a tea-merchant, you don't tell him to read books about China, or about tea, but you put him into a tea-merchant's office, where he has the handling, the smelling, and the tasting of tea. Without the sort of knowledge which can be gained in this practical way, his exploits as a tea-merchant will soon come to a bankrupt conclusion. The 'paper-philosophers' are under the delusion that physical science can be mastered as literary accomplishments are acquired, but unfortunately it is not so. You may read any quantity of books, and you may be almost as ignorant as you were at starting, if you don't have, at the back of your minds, the change for words in definite images, which can only be acquired through the operation of your observing faculties in the phenomena of Nature."

*Uses of Hypotheses.*—The question has lately arisen in scientific circles as to whether hypotheses and theories as such should be taught in our schools—one party claiming that school-instruction should be confined to demonstrated science, and the other maintaining that the relations of the facts can be much better understood by grouping them in accordance with a probable theory. In the discussion, one position taken by those in favor of excluding hypotheses is entirely untenable. It is assumed that demonstrated laws, or the results of scientific study, should be taught to pupils, and that such laws should be made the basis of their education.

A practice of this kind would be subversive of the highest good to be derived from educational processes. It would state scientific truths in dogmatic forms, and would require an unquestioned acceptance of them. It would present principles before the facts are known upon which the principles are based, and it would give formulas of words meaningless to those acquiring them. It would retain in the worst form the dogmatic and memorizing processes.

On the other hand, the teaching of hypotheses prematurely is open to similar objections. Presented before all the facts bearing upon the case are known, and before the evidences have been investigated, the hypothesis becomes a mere verbal formula. As an instrument of education, it fails to awaken the mind to any productive thought; and it frequently becomes a serious detriment to future investigation, from the mistaken notion that the matter is already understood.

*Value of Hypotheses.*—Science in-the-making makes use of hypotheses. When facts in a certain direction first become known, they are apparently disconnected. A hypothesis is the effort to construct a rational system that will show all the existing relations, and it is relatively good when it accounts for all the facts in the case without disregarding laws which have been established in other departments of thought. When new facts bearing upon the case are discovered that the hypothesis does not cover, then it must be changed or abandoned for a larger one. These provisional hypotheses are necessary to scientific advancement, and they are detrimental only when facts are distorted or suppressed for the purpose of maintaining them.

*Hypotheses in Education.*—It is very plain that the hypothesis which accounts for facts has no place in primary schools, or in any schools, until the facts are first known. It must be inferred from the facts, and the true office of the educator is to present facts in such connection that rational hypotheses must be inferred. The grounds for inference are well set forth in the following extract from an essay by Prof. Clifford:

" Suppose that we do not merely want to make a supposition, but to infer from facts before us what actually happened in any case. Then we must make the assumption that there is some sort of uniformity in Nature. Without this we cannot infer at all; for inference consists in transferring the experience which we have had under certain conditions, to events happening under like conditions of which we have not had experience. It is true that we cannot be absolutely sure of the uniformity of Nature, or that our present conception of it is right; but still, it is the only thing we have to go upon. Human knowledge is never absolutely and theoretically certain, but a great deal of it is certain, which is all we want."

Taking the uniformity of Nature for granted, the hypothesis may be inferred from the facts known—the process being one of comparison and generalization. All comprehensive generalizations, however, belong to the advanced course of instruction, as they appeal exclusively to the reason and judgment. A hypothesis given antecedent to study is an obstacle to improvement; but inferred as a resultant of study, it becomes an important aid to intellectual progress.

# CHAPTER X.

## *SYSTEMS OF EDUCATION COMPARED.*

INTRODUCTORY.— The examination of educational principles in the preceding pages has led, incidentally, to a notice of the methods of teaching which have been practised from time to time. These methods, so widely differing in kind, have all grown out of the different theories in regard to the ends to be sought in education, and the best means of accomplishing these ends. In the present chapter there is given a more extended summary of methods, with a brief examination of the principles upon which they are founded.

The methods to which special attention is directed may be grouped under four heads, viz. : " Memorizing," " The Study of Books," " The Study of Things," and " Experiment and Work." Each of these now has its special advocates, and each is loudly demanding recognition. The first two have the advantage of possession, and the last two of representing the new thought in education.

MEMORIZING.—Upon the establishment of regular systems of school instruction, the first efforts nearly always seem to be directed to making the people acquainted with the results of the experience of investigations and reflections of the sages of the past. This wisdom, usually expressed in the form of aphorisms and proverbs, is considered the best possible basis for education ; and committing the words to memory is regarded as the best, if not the only, means by which the wisdom may be obtained.

*Chinese Schools.*—In China this system came very early into practice, even before the time of Confucius, and has continued until the present day. Chinese schools are nearly as numerous as those of the most advanced civilized nations. They are regularly graded, from the primary schools in the little hamlets, to the Imperial University at Peking. Throughout these schools the instruction consists solely in memorizing the productions of the classic Chinese writers. This instruction is graded to meet the requirements of the different grades of schools, that of the primary schools including the easier and more common literary works, while that of the University embraces the writings of Confucius and the other most distinguished religious and moral teachers.

The examinations aim solely to test the fidelity of pupils in repeating the exact words in which the wise sayings of the sages are recorded ; and no effort is made to make them understand any portion of the doctrine which the words contain. Criticism is a thing unknown, as a doubt would be equivalent to sacrilege. The graduates of the schools are rewarded with official governmental positions, and every possible incentive is offered for success in school-work. Indeed, through the school only can any one obtain position or preferment. In no other country does the successful scholar so directly receive reward.

History demonstrates the results of the Chinese system. The memorizing of words, and the blind and implicit acceptance of authority, though rigorously pursued for centuries, have proved an inadequate basis of education. For a thousand years, the people who made the earliest advances in most of the arts and sciences have remained stationary, or have gone backward in the scale of civilization.

The very measures taken to perpetuate intelligence have been the most efficient means of arresting progress; and as long as the methods of instruction are unchanged, the most populous empire of the world must remain in a state of semi-barbarism.

*The Monkish System.*—Schools established during the Middle Ages were all in the charge of monks, and the staple of instruction was the memorizing of such texts and rules as would best promote the ends proposed. The Credo, Pater Noster, and the standard Latin hymns, committed to memory, with no idea of their meaning, constituted the main part of school duty. The effort of the monkish teachers was as much directed to the exclusion of such knowledge as did not directly support their views and authority, as it was to promulgate that of the opposite kind.

The school did little to banish ignorance from the people. Science was interdicted by the Church as opposed to religion. "For many centuries," says Hallam, "to sum up the account of ignorance in a word, it was rare for a layman, of whatever rank, to know how to sign his name."

As with the Chinese, the monkish system of education demanded a blind acceptance of authority, and it was nearly as fatal to human progress. For almost a thousand years the human intellect was kept in a state of vassalage. The improvement of the masses, which characterizes modern civilization, scarcely commenced until the shackles of monasticism were removed, through successful insurrection and revolution.

The baleful effects of the old education long continued after the system in which it had its origin passed away. Memorizing went on with a simple change in the objects upon which it was exercised, and authority was still invoked, although authority of a different kind.

*English Schools.*—In the English public schools, the memorizing process has always maintained a considerable foothold. The classic languages were made the basis of culture, and these languages were taught through the grammar. Pupils were required to commit to memory an almost endless number of paradigms, rules, and exceptions, and they were taught to obey implicitly the authority of grammar and dictionary. This exercise was varied by obliging the pupil to write Latin verses, in which the only excellence sought and required was that the words should be properly chosen in regard to quantity, so that the work would scan, no attention whatever being paid to the thought which the words expressed, and frequently it was not even required that the words should form correct sentences.

The prevalence of the mechanical method in English education may be inferred from the large number of endowed grammar-schools. According to both usage and law, the name *grammar*-school is made to signify a school in which the Greek and Latin languages are the only branches of instruction. Up to the time of the Reformation, the grammar-school was the only school in existence in England; and to this day, among endowed or public schools of all varieties, the grammar-school holds a position of preëminence.

GROUNDS OF DEFENSE.—In our own schools the memorizing process still lingers, and teachers require the pupil to recite the text *verbatim*. He may catch the thought contained in the words, or he may not; the text he must get. The grounds upon which this course is defended are as follows:

It fixes the attention upon the lesson, and thereby induces habits of attention; it trains the memory; it enables the teacher to judge whether study has been faithfully performed; it furnishes an excellent exercise in language, both in regard to the structure of sentences and the use of words; and even if the subject is too difficult to be understood, it may be well to have it lodged in the memory, ready for use when the mind is so far developed as to comprehend it.

Let us examine these reasons in detail.

"*Securing Attention.*"—The primary attention which should always be fixed on thoughts, by this process is fixed on the words, leaving the thought to take care of itself. This word-food does not conduce to mental growth. By thus using chaff in the place of substance, the mind is starved and stunted, and its future growth becomes impossible. It busies itself henceforth with trifling details, and loses its grasp of the subject as a whole.

"*Training the Memory.*"—We have already seen that the retentive powers are best cultivated by associating each new idea with something of its kind, so that it may be retained simply because of its relations, thus relieving the mind of the vast strain which would be put upon it without this association. The process in question tends to cultivate *arbitrary memory*. When this power is unnecessarily developed, it absorbs much of the vital force, cumbers the mind with unrelated and often useless matter, and effectually prevents the higher and better cultivation of the retentive powers through association.

"*Judgment of Study.*"—By means of genuine study, whether directed to objects or books, the mind gets possession of real knowledge. The true test of study is the possession of this knowledge. The mere recitation of the words of the book is no truthful standard by which to judge of real study. It may decide upon the faithfulness with which the words are reproduced, but no opinion can be formed in regard to the understanding of the thought until such thought is fully expressed in the language of the pupil.

"*Cultivation of Language.*"—The true mastery of language consists in the ability to use language with correctness and facility, and this ability comes from practice alone. Committing to memory the verbal construction of others can aid a pupil very little in acquiring the power to construct for himself. By relying upon the book for the language in which he clothes his thoughts, he is unfitted for original expression, just as the constant use of crutches would unfit him for the free and vigorous use of his limbs in walking.

"*Future Use.*"—The claim that it is well to fill the mind with the forms of knowledge, that cannot be understood or intelligently assimilated until some future time, is only paralleled in absurdity by the claim that the stomach of a child should be filled with food that can be digested only when he becomes an adult. This claim is equally absurd when examined from another point of view. The words remembered are not knowledge, and they can be transmuted into knowledge only when the thought which they express is fully understood. Even to a future understanding of the subject, the possession of the words would be rather a hinderance than a help, by fixing the attention upon form instead of sense.

We thus see that the practice of memorizing the text is utterly indefensible upon any ground of philosophy, and that it remains in our schools as an evidence of the persistence of evil practices, long after the occasion which gave them birth has passed away.

THE STUDY OF BOOKS.—After the revival of learning which followed the invention of printing, books, which before had been monopolized by the few, came into general use. In them was preserved all the wisdom of the ages which had passed. This wisdom was eagerly sought for, with an interest that was only intensified by the previous privation. In the process of time, the reaction against the monopoly of learning by the few was carried to an extreme, and books became almost objects of worship, and were at once made the basis of education.

*Ideas of what Constitutes an Educated Man.*—It

soon came to pass that an "educated man" meant one who had a plethoric knowledge of ancient lore, rather than one who had full possession of his faculties, and who could perform with ability all the duties of life. In popular estimation, the pedant who could repeat chapter and verse from old authors, or recite from the original of Homer or Horace, was a profound scholar, even though he had as little practical sense as Scott's Dominie Sampson. On the other hand, the man who had ability to construct a machine which would emancipate millions of men from an unprofitable toil, or one capable of managing the affairs of State, so as to preserve peace, secure the rights of all the people, and stimulate a nation to a higher state of civilization, was not an educated man, unless he could construct and scan Latin verse, and decide, off-hand, obscure points of Greek etymology.

*This Worship of Books* has continued until the present day, and has tended greatly to vitiate our whole system of instruction. In most of the schools in this country, instruction is very largely confined to recitations in certain text-books. The question in regard to proficiency is not whether the pupil understands arithmetic, but whether he has been through with Smith's or Jones's arithmetic. The lessons assigned are not definite topics to be studied and mastered, but a certain number of pages to recite; and, in the examination, the success or failure of the pupil usually has been determined by his ability to reproduce an author, and not by his ability to demonstrate the subject.

*Evils resulting from Abuse of Books.*—The first evil result of the abuse of books is that this process of study, having no basis in experience, gives to the student apparent rather than real knowledge; and, while it may satisfy his appetite for the moment, it contributes very little to mental development. The knowledge gained is apprehended rather than comprehended, and there is a constant tendency to accept words, without looking for the thought which the words represent.

The knowledge gained from books is, at best, second-hand; and although indispensable to a full education, yet the same material, gained at first-hand from actual investigation, not only will make a much deeper impression, but will lead to a closer examination and a more profound knowledge.

By relying exclusively upon books, the habit is formed of accepting authority without question—a habit fatal to the cultivation of self-reliance and mental progress. The first effort of the mind is to observe, and, next, to understand. The process of understanding includes the most careful examinations and comparisons at every step of progress; and this process is entirely subverted by the exclusive lesson-reciting method.

*The Place of Text-Books.*—We have already seen that the child's first knowledge comes from things, and through the senses. Before he enters school he has gained a large amount of knowledge from the external world. The first school-work should be to increase his power of observation, and to arrange the results in systematic order. When the objects of the fields and the streets, and the phenomena with which he is in daily contact, are well-nigh exhausted, recourse may be had to books, and the instruction carried on by this means from the known to the unknown. The lessons should be so arranged that the book-knowledge will be directly engrafted upon that gained from experience; and, just so far as books fail in this particular, they fall short of their highest usefulness.

*The Necessity of Text-Books.*—In the present condition of education text-books are indispensable. They are useful as the repositories of knowledge. They supplement the knowledge gained from experience. They arrange knowledge upon the different subjects of investigation, and present it in an unbroken series, and in the order of its logical relations. They furnish the basis by which classes are kept together. They lead the mind out into the great unknown, and store it with facts that cannot be directly known by observation. And, lastly, they furnish the crutches upon which multitudes of superficial and unqualified teachers are able to plod along in the unvarying routine of prescribed work.

*The Proper Use of Text-Books.*—Text-books, however, should be used as a means, and not as an end. They are valuable as embodying the knowledge necessary for school purposes, and for nothing else. The proper study of books is to look through the text to the thoughts conveyed; and study is profitable just in proportion to the accomplishment of this end. The facts and principles derived from books need the same careful examination and the same close scrutiny as those derived from the observation of Nature. The habits arising from this examination and scrutiny form one of the most important of all educational ends.

*Increased Demand for Text-Books.*—As the cause of education advances in the right direction, there will doubtless be a call for more rather than less books for our schools. Besides the regular treatises in the various branches of instruction, there will be a demand for larger and more complete works upon the sciences, so that every pupil will have an opportunity to know the exact state of human thought on the various topics that occupy his attention. At no distant day in the future, an unabridged dictionary and some complete encyclopædia of general knowledge will be considered a necessary part of the equipment of every school.

THE STUDY OF THINGS.—When investigation began to be made into the nature of the mind's action, it was found that the intelligent study of things took precedence of all other kinds of knowledge. We have already shown the relations of this kind of study to mental development, and we here have only to give a brief summary of the advantages to be gained by this course.

*Cultivation of Perception.*—In no way can the perceptive faculties be cultivated so surely as by the study of natural objects. Such objects range from the simple to the complex, and they are found in almost infinite variety. By the study of them the observing powers have an ample field for exercise, and the exact stimulant necessary to excite them to activity.

*Basis of Experience.*—The observation of objects and of the phenomena of Nature gives a basis of fact derived from actual experience which enables the pupil to understand his subsequent study from books. From his observation of elementary forms, he can understand descriptions which involve very complex combinations of forms; and from the observation of the facts concerning elevation, the flow of streams, and the changes of the weather, he can understand the physical features and climate of countries which he can never visit. Without primary experience, however, the descriptions of these regions, no matter how vivid they might be, to him would become a mass of unmeaning words.

*Materials of Thought.*—In regard to knowledge itself, this study of things furnishes the mind with the materials upon which thought can be expended. It gives a solid foundation for all future acquirements; and when carried out to its proper extent, this foundation is made broad, and entirely adequate for all purposes.

EXPERIMENT AND WORK.—The old education was regarded as the very antithesis of work. It was only after an experience of centuries that the idea began to be entertained that one part of education was to fit men for the performance of their daily duties; and not until early in the present century were there made any provisions in the schools for the special training of the working-classes.

*Technical Schools.*—The claims of work in the arrangement of national educational systems, though tardily and grudgingly recognized, have at length been admitted to some degree in most civilized countries. Agricultural schools on the general plan of Von Fellenberg are quite common; and in Germany liberal provisions are made for the support of trade schools, to immediately follow primary instruction, and for technical schools of a higher character. In France, also, technical education has received conspicuous encouragement.

*Superiority of Educated Workmen.*—At the Paris Exposition of 1867, the manufactured articles from the different countries were brought together and compared.

It was found that in nearly every department of industry, so far as both design and workmanship are concerned, the artisans of France and Germany surpassed those of England, though the latter had greatly the advantage in inherited aptitude and in individual experience. This result showed the superiority of educated over ignorant workmen, and it stimulated the English people to great exertions in the establishment of schools for the benefit of their manufacturing operatives. The same result has tended materially to extend technical schools everywhere.

*Work in the Kindergarten.*—In the kindergarten system, it has been shown that all kinds of bodily activity can be turned to good account in the process of educating children, and that these activities, beginning in spontaneous plays, may be made to glide insensibly into profitable work. This work gives mechanical skill, and at the same time becomes a means of harmonious development.

*The Next Step Demanded.*—The next important step forward in education is to arrange courses of study for schools that shall embody the kindergarten principle, and culminate in the skill which is now obtained only in the technical schools.

*Manual Training.*—To Samuel G. Love, Superintendent of the Jamestown (New York) public schools, is due the credit of the earliest experiments in manual training as an integral element of all grades of the schools under his control. In the autumn of 1874 he made a beginning by opening a printing office. A press, type, and fixtures, costing one hundred and twenty-five dollars, were purchased and set up in an unoccupied room on the fourth floor of the school building. The Board of Education, while it approved of manual trainning in theory, did not find a sufficient interest in the public mind to warrant it in appropriating funds for the experiment. Money to meet the expenses was supplied by a "fund" originated and realized from annual exhibitions given by the pupils. From two hundred and fifty to three hundred dollars were raised in this way each year. This "fund" was devoted to the various experiments in manual training, and incidentally to educating public opinion.

The kindergarten employments were next introduced. In 1881 a sewing class was put in operation. One of the basement corridors was enclosed by a glass partition and supplied with material for the work. The sewing was graded, and as soon as the pupils could do the work of a grade they were promoted. In 1877 work with tools began in the same quiet way. Some article being needed, a boy who had become discouraged or rebellious was asked to try his hand at making it, and by his own labor prove of use to the school and redeem his reputation. The work was usually done at the janitor's bench in the basement. The janitor was a good carpenter, and acted as a teacher in the beginning of the experiment. After a time another corridor of the basement was fitted up with a single workbench and supplied with tools. Two boys were sent there at a time, each to work half of the hour and to watch the other half, both under the direction of the janitor. In this gradual manner manual training was introduced into all the departments, and at the same time public opinion was educated. In the spring of 1882 the Board of Education raised a fund with which a shop was built, large enough to accommodate five benches and three lathes, with a loft for storing lumber. The shop was equipped with tools and fixtures to put it in complete running order. This done, it was placed in charge of two young men and under the general direction of the janitor; one of them gave instruction to classes every school hour of the day. In 1884 two wings were added to the High-School building, and in the basement two rooms were fitted up, one of which is used for a sewing-room and printing office, and the other for the shop. These rooms are twenty-eight by thirty-seven feet, are well lighted, are supplied with the needed tools, material, and instructors, and are kept open during all the school hours of the day, four days in the week. The old shop was fitted up for a kitchen, and every Friday during each term two classes of six each receive instruction in the art of cooking. This history is given at length here, to illustrate the difficulties in the path of the teacher when any departure is made from the old routine of text-book instruction.

Mr. Love issued a book entitled Industrial Education, in which, on page 21, he gives generous recognition to the author of "Principles and Practice of Teaching" of aid in solving the difficult problems of public-school administration. Their discussions of philosophy and methods during the years 1867, '68,' and '69, led them to the conclusion that manual training was essential to the harmonious development of the child. From that time forward they both used all the influence at their command to introduce it into the public schools. So profoundly was the author of this book impressed with the importance of the manual element in education that he made that the subject for every paper read before the New York State Teachers' Association at its annual meeting in 1880, at Canandaigua, of which he was president.

Much of the widespread interest in manual training is due to pioneer work done by Prof. Runkle. The Moscow exhibit at the Philadelphia Exposition was a revelation to him. He saw in it a sound and systematic method of teaching applied to the mechanic arts, and the vivid impression on his mind led to important results. On August 17, 1876, he submitted a report to the corporation of the Massachusetts Institute of Technology, of which he was president, upon the Russian system, and recommended its adoption. The corporation accepted his recommendation and proceeded at once to put it in operation by establishing "The School of Mechanic Arts." The systematic grading of the work, in accordance with its underlying principles, as in the Russian system, was seen to be a necessary preliminary to the introduction of manual training in public schools. Prof. Runkle was the first person in this country to definitely set forth the value and proper place of "the manual element in education." His active sympathy and wise counsel are ever at the service of all movements for the improvement of the public schools. In Brookline, Massachusetts, where he resides, the principles he has so long advocated are fully appreciated, and enter as an intrinsic element into the whole course of study.

Since 1876 the question in the minds of the more scientific thinkers has been, How can manual training be made a part of the system of public schools? Experiments have been carried forward in many cities and towns, some having adopted the Russian system, some the "sloyd" as adapted from the Swedish, while others have combined the two systems. Thus far the conclusions derived from experience, re-enforced by the researches of the psychologist, seem to point out the Russian system as the one best fitted for advanced classes. "Sloyd," as modified and adapted by years of experiment in the North Bennett Street Industrial School, Boston, founded and supported by Mrs. Quincy A. Shaw, is best suited to the intermediate grades. Mrs. Shaw is also maintaining a normal class for the instruction of teachers, women as well as men, in mechanical drawing and tool work (sloyd), Mr. Gustaf Larsson, principal.

Schools where truant children are cared for have also found manual training especially valuable in its moral influence by creating a sense of power, thus giving birth to a healthy self-respect, an essential element in the foundation of character.

Dr. Felix Adler began his experiments in 1880. The Workingman's School, founded and directed by him, has accepted object-teaching as originated by Pestalozzi, and has at that point taken a step further and connected manual training with it, in order to facilitate "a knowledge of the properties of things by causing the pupils to *make* those things." I quote from an address by Dr. Adler given at a Conference on Manual Training held at Boston, in 1891: "The old object method was to teach the child to observe, which is better than to teach the names of things; but manual training teaches them not only to observe but to create." In this address Dr. Adler ably sets forth "the relation of manual training to the moral instruction and the moral strengthening of the pupil," and in so doing grounds the claims of manual training upon the deepest and most urgent needs of our school system.

In giving this brief sketch of the history of manual training in this country, I have confined myself to the efforts of the pioneers. A volume would be needed to describe the work in its later stages.

*Hand and Brain Culture.*—The advantages to be derived from making hand-culture go along side by side with brain-culture may be summed up as follows:

*First:* By handling objects, a greater interest is excited and a deeper impression is made. As nearly as possible, all the senses are aroused to activity, and all are brought to bear upon one object and made to contribute to one result.

*Secondly:* The manipulation of materials necessary to work leads to a closer investigation in regard to both the qualities and the relations of objects, and changes vague notions into positive knowledge. It corrects those superficial ideas derived from the study of words alone, and prevents conclusions from narrow premises.

*Thirdly:* It trains the muscles to respond immediately to the will, and gives skill in the use of tools, and in handling materials. This training and skill may be used directly in the work which has furnished the practice, or it may be used in almost any other kind of hand labor.

*Fourthly:* In acquiring skill, the intellect is excited, and this excitement reacts upon the muscles, so that skill is more quickly attained. The muscular and the intellectual training thus mutually assist each other. If a due proportion is maintained between them, neither being carried to excess, it is evident that both may be acquired at the same time, and that the time spent in the acquisition will be less than that required for the development of either when the two are separated.

*Fifthly:* The dexterity acquired by the hand, in fashioning materials into implements, utensils, and ornaments, is a never-failing source of delight, and it furnishes pleasant and profitable occupation for hours, which would otherwise be passed in idleness or dissipation.

GENERAL SUMMARY.—The great problem which is now set for the solution of teachers is, how to harmonize the ideas contained in these separate, rival, and apparently antagonistic systems. That some important truth is embodied in each one, is probable from the fact that each has its strong advocates, and each has its measure of success. To eliminate the distinct principle involved in each, and to give to this principle its exact value, is, at the present time, exceedingly difficult.

Reversing the order in which these systems have been examined, we see, in the bodily activities, agencies and forces which may be used in educational work. These forces are natural, and therefore proper to be used; and the manner in which they are constantly obtruded upon our notice seems to demand of us a faithful recognition. The experiments made in this direction have more than corroborated the *à priori* conclusions in regard to the use of these forces; and work, as a part of the regular exercises of school, will, in time, undoubtedly become universal.

These activities must have materials upon which they can be spent, and these materials are the things that must be studied. These things will be selected in reference to the skill to be acquired in their manipulations, the practical value of the knowledge to be gained from them, and the character and fitness of the development which they afford.

The study of books comes in and supplements the knowledge gained from the study of things. Under the most favorable circumstances, by far the greater part of the knowledge which we possess must come from the investigation, experience, and reflection of others; and this knowledge must, to a large extent, be obtained from books. To exclude books from a school course would be to ignore the processes and results of civilization. Not only should books be used, but they should be more largely and generally used than at present; and the only change demanded is, that no attempt shall be made to get more out of them than they contain, or to make them do the work in education which can only come from experience in the study of things.

The proper cultivation of the memory is not only desirable, but indispensable. Mental development would be impossible if the mind did not have power to retain the knowledge it receives. In the study of Nature the memory has a wide and fruitful field for exercise; and when this study is supplemented by hand-labor, a much deeper and consequently more lasting impression is made. The relations of things, in the infinite variety of Nature, furnish the foundation for the most perfect development of associative memory; and should any mere verbal exercise be considered important, it may be found in committing to memory poetry, or poetic prose, in which noble sentiments and truths are embodied in beautiful forms.

# CHAPTER XI.

## *PHYSICAL CULTURE.*

INTRODUCTORY.—It has been well stated that "first of all, man is an animal, and that the first requisite of success in life is to be a good animal." In this statement the fact is recognized that, as regards vital processes, man is subject to the same laws as the lower animals, and that the perfection of his manhood depends upon bodily health and vigor. A failure to provide for physical culture, or to observe the conditions of physical well-being, will vitiate all educational processes, and render abortive all attempts to reach the highest intellectual and moral development.

*Opposing Theories.*—In the past, two theories have been held in regard to physical culture. The one is founded upon the notion that there is a natural and inevitable antagonism between the body and the spirit, and that the welfare of the latter is in inverse ratio to that of the former. The advocates of this theory hold that spiritual matters alone are worthy of the attention of intelligent beings, and that the highest spiritual good is promoted by thwarting natural desires, and by "mortifying the flesh." By them, a half-developed or diseased body is considered rather desirable than otherwise.

The second theory regards physical culture as the principal end of education. It places an undue estimate upon the highest muscular development, and it turns all the vital forces into this one channel of expenditure.

The reconciliation of these antagonistic views may be found in the higher intelligence which recognizes in the body the machinery through which the mind must act, and which sees that the perfection of mental action must depend upon the perfection of the machinery through which it manifests itself. This idea at once disposes of the old notion of antagonism, and furnishes the standard by which we judge, both of the importance and the limits of physical culture. It makes the possession and preservation of health the most fundamental of all educational ideas, and, at the same time, it shows that physical culture should be limited by the demands of intellectual and moral culture.

Recognizing the intimate relation of body and mind, the physical culture demanded by education should have for its objects the full growth and perfect nurture of the body, the preservation of health and of those conditions best calculated to promote intellectual and moral vigor, and the attainment of strength sufficient for all the ordinary exigencies of life. This definition excludes the idea that in our educational processes, the vital forces should ever be exhaustively turned in the direction of muscular development, or that the production of athletes is a legitimate object of the schools.

*Factors of Physical Culture.*—In the attainment of physical well-being, four distinct factors are to be considered in education : intelligence in regard to the laws of life; sensibility as to the observance of them; the disposition of educational appliances so as to conform to them; and the formation of habits which lead to an unconscious observance of them. In regard to the intelligence and sensibility, the teacher's work is mostly indirect, as he has to deal with actions largely beyond his control, and has to approach the subject through intellectual and moral channels. In the disposition of educational material, his work is principally advisory, as authority in these matters rests with school directors. The direct work of the teacher is confined to legitimate schoolroom exercises, which tend to the formation of proper habits to be observed through life.

*Scope of Instruction.*—The full text of instruction, necessary to the understanding of the vital processes, and how their vigor is to be maintained, is found only in the elaborate treatises upon physiology and hygiene. In the present work there is space only for a general analysis of the topics to be treated, and a few principles under each head, for the double purpose of showing the importance of the subject and of stimulating further inquiry in the same direction.

*Preparation on the part of Teachers.*—No teacher should enter upon his professional work until, from study and investigation, he is familiar with physiological and hygienic laws. Such knowledge is much more important, both to him and his pupils, than the details of arithmetic and grammar. Without this knowledge, he has no key to the solution of the problems which are of daily occurrence in school, and his mistakes and blunders are liable to be of so serious a nature as to vitiate his whole system of teaching. With this knowledge, he is able to give such instruction directly in formal lessons, or indirectly by a seasonable word of advice, as will make a deep and lasting impression. The incidental instruction of a teacher of wide culture and earnest convictions is an important factor in education, and will go far to establish correct habits of life in the pupil.

FOOD.—The most fundamental agency in the promotion of physical well-being is food. From food is obtained the material necessary for the growth of the body, and for the supply of the waste occasioned by muscular and mental action. In considering the subject, attention should be given to the kinds, the quality, the quantity, and the variety of food, and to the manner and times of taking it.

*Kinds of Food.*—In deciding upon the kinds of food best adapted to children, it would be well to follow the example of Pestalozzi and Froebel in regard to study, and learn of the children themselves. What food do they crave? or, What do they relish? are questions of more importance than, What food do I think they need? The practice of denying to children the food which they most crave is a remnant of the old asceticism which regarded the gratification of natural desires as a sin, and which finds its logical exponents in the self-immolated devotees on the banks of the Ganges.

The custom of forbidding sweets and vegetable acids are examples in point. Modern physiologists show that the almost universal desire of children for these things is but the expression of a universal need, and that to withhold them will be to the injury of the child.

It may be stated, as a general principle, that the kind of food craved by children is the very one that is most needed at the time; and that we should regard with grave suspicion any sanitary system or theory which ignores it.

*Limitation.* — While the general principle holds good, it does not follow that the ill-regulated desires of every child are to be taken as a guide in supplying him with food. These desires may have no basis in real needs. They may be vicious, from an inherited tendency, from the results of abnormal excesses, or from suppression in his previous experience. These aberrations, however, are exceptional, and should not be taken as an index of normal conditions, nor as a guide to proper control. To distinguish between the expression of natural needs and abnormal desires will require a large experience; and, in the meantime, it is safer to err on the side of liberty than on that of restriction.

*Quality of Food.* — The food of children should be specially nutritious. With adults, the special function of foods is to repair waste; with children, it has the additional function of promoting growth, and hence it needs be more nutritious for the latter than for the former. The practice of supplying children with coarse, innutritious food, is in every way mischievous. It diminishes the size of the body, or the quality of its tissues, so that there is less of strength and vigor. It necessitates an unnecessary amount of nervous expenditure in the way of digestion. It retards vital action in other directions, and renders both body and mind sluggish. It lays so poor a bodily foundation, as to seriously limit future physical and mental possibility.

Examples illustrating this principle may be found in every community. The families that are supplied with the most nutritious diet are the most active, physically and mentally. The ill-fed classes of city or country form the lower or inferior stratum of society. The ill-fed races are the lower races, and high civilization is possible only with a generous diet.

It is a great mistake to suppose that children, while attending school, or while engaged in study, should be put upon a low diet. The waste of tissue is much greater in mental than in muscular action, and calls for food of a correspondingly more nutritious quality. The student accustomed to exhausting physical labor, and to the food which is specially adapted to muscular waste, may need to change his diet when beginning study. His changed habits call for a change of food which shall be richer in the elements of nerve-tissue, but in no case should he choose a diet lower in all the elements of nutrition than the one to which he has been accustomed.

*Quantity of Food.*—The quantity of food should be ample as well as the quality excellent. The appetite of a healthful child is proverbially keen. To promote his growth, and supply the waste from his restless activity, a large amount of food is demanded.

In the case of quantity as well as quality, the appetite of the child should largely govern the supply, and all arbitrary restrictions should be avoided. Herbert Spencer says: "Not only is it that the *à priori* reasons for trusting the appetites of children are so strong, and that the reasons for distrusting them are invalid, but it is that no other guidance is worthy of any confidence. What is the value of this parental judgment, set up as an alternative regulator? When to 'Oliver asking for more' the mamma or governess replies in the negative, on what data does she proceed? She *thinks* he has had enough. But where are her grounds for so thinking? Has she some secret understanding with the boy's stomach—some *clairvoyant* power enabling her to discern the needs of his body? If not, how can she safely decide? Does she not know that the demand of the system for food is determined by numerous and involved causes—varies with the temperature, with the hygrometric and with the electric state of the air, varies according to the exercise taken, according to the kind and quality of the food eaten at the last meal, and according to the rapidity with which the last meal was digested? How can she calculate the result of such a combination of causes? In truth, this confidence with which most parents take upon themselves to legislate for the stomachs of their children proves their unacquaintance with the principles of physiology. If they knew more, they would be more modest. 'The pride of science is humble when compared with the pride of ignorance.'"

*Variety of Food.*—Natural or unvitiated relish is a fair indication of the food most needed at the time. A single kind of food exclusively used soon loses its relish, which shows that something is lacking in providing for the needs of the system. Usually good relish is a necessity to good digestion. The appetite of children is keener and more sensitive than that of adults, and while it is easily gratified, it more quickly palls upon a monotonous diet. The remark of the countryman that "he could eat liver for fifty or sixty meals, but would not like it for a steady diet," is but the application of the general law to a particular case.

An analysis of food shows that there is a great difference in the nutritive qualities of the different kinds. Some foods are entirely lacking in some of the elements necessary to repair the waste of the tissues of the body, and if exclusively used, the person starves to death as certainly, if not as quickly, as though he had been entirely deprived of food. In the use of such foods, variety is essential to the continuance of life.

Food should also be adapted to the changes of climate. In cold weather an excess of heat-producing food is demanded, and in summer this kind of food should be reduced to its minimum. To continue the same diet in summer that is best adapted to winter is to risk the raising of the temperature of the body to the fever-point. Persons engaged in manual labor need the foods that are rich in muscle-producing properties; while those engaged in study demand foods that best supply the waste of nerve tissue.

The best foods are those which are best relished by a normal appetite, and which contain the greatest number of nutritious elements in the proper proportion. The three kinds of food which are nearest perfect in their constituents are milk, the lean flesh of beef, and the entire grain of the wheat. Either of these will sustain life without resort to other foods.

*Caution to be Observed.*—The conditions of families greatly vary, and the habits of pupils depending upon these conditions also vary. Some have nutritious food plentiful in supply and agreeable in variety, and their entire system has a vigorous tone, and they are in a condition to respond to any reasonable demands made upon them. Others, on the contrary, are poorly supplied with food, and in consequence their nerves lack vigor and their muscles strength. To lay the same burden upon the latter as upon the former would be an injustice, and to bestow praise and censure for attainments and for good conduct equally in the two cases would also be unjust. Teachers who would deal justly with all, and who would reach the highest success, should make themselves familiar with the conditions and habits of each individual pupil, so that they can make the necessary allowances and discrimination.

*Time for Taking Food.*—Regularity in eating is an important element in the preservation of health. The stomach, like the other organs of the body, requires time to allow its forces to recuperate, and periods of rest should follow periods of activity. If stimulated to constant activity by the continual presence of food, its action becomes languid, and it performs its functions imperfectly, deranging the whole economy of the system.

It is impossible to establish a fixed rule that will decide for all persons the exact times for eating. The following principles, however, seem to be well established, and should serve as a guide in fixing the periods for each one: Food should be taken often enough to satisfy hunger; it should be taken regularly and at such intervals as will allow ample time for digestion, and the full recuperation of the stomach from the effects of its activity. Children need food more frequently than adults, but with the same regularity. The intervals between meals will vary with the varying conditions of climate, occupation, and health. While the practice of eating a hearty meal just before going to bed is a pernicious one, it is better to take a little food into the stomach at that time than to go to bed hungry. Children at school, and especially the younger ones, may need to eat before the noon intermission, and a time should be assigned them for that purpose; but the practice of eating at any time and at all times should not be permitted.

*Manner of Taking Food.*—The process of eating should proceed deliberately. Perfect digestion requires perfect mastication. The muscular action necessary to perfect mastication stimulates the salivary glands, and induces a flow of saliva, which not only lubricates the food so that it can be easily swallowed, but which performs an important office in digestion. Rapid eating and insufficient chewing do not induce a sufficient flow of saliva, and hence an extra amount of labor is imposed upon the stomach, producing exhaustion and derangements.

*Miscellaneous Suggestions.*—Food should not be taken when the body is exhausted by labor, physical or mental. A short interval of rest should precede the eating, to allow the vital forces to recover their tone, otherwise the food lies in the stomach a long time undigested, or is rejected altogether. Time should be given for digestion before work is resumed. Complete digestion demands vital force; and if this force is diverted to muscular or mental action, digestion is retarded or altogether ceases. It is better to have a short period of complete repose after meals, and especially after dinner.

These principles are well understood in regard to horses. A man would be considered as lacking in common sense who would feed his horse immediately after an exhausting drive, or who would put him to hard work or drive him rapidly immediately after eating. The same law should be heeded in regard to men. Teachers should recognize it, and never demand of their pupils exhaustive mental labor immediately after eating.

*Use of Drinks.*—Water taken in moderate quantities and at proper times is a necessity of existence. It moistens dry food so as to render it digestible, and it supplies the waste caused by perspiration. The quantity of drink necessary depends upon the quality of the food taken, the general temperature, and the amount of the work done. Most writers upon physiology condemn the habit of drinking largely at meal-time. If the drink is freely mingled with the eating, swallowing is performed with insufficient mastication, and without the flow of saliva necessary to perfect digestion. If a large quantity of fluid is taken into the stomach at the close of the meal, the gastric juice is diluted, and digestion is retarded, until the extra fluid is absorbed. The rule would seem to be moderate drinking at the close of meals.

Frequent drinking at irregular intervals is a habit almost as pernicious as that of irregular eating. It answers to no real need, and should not be permitted. Drinking large quantities of ice-water or very cold water is pernicious, as it absorbs the heat from the stomach, and arrests digestion until the proper temperature is recovered. Teachers can easily regulate the drinking of pupils when in school. In warm weather and after violent exercises which have caused perspiration, drink is a necessity. In general the pupils may be permitted to drink at stated intervals, depending upon the above conditions. Drinking at other times should be discouraged, as interfering with the order of the school, and as generally injurious to the pupil in the formation of habits. This regulation should not be made an inflexible rule, for needs must decide in each case, and the pupil must be permitted to interpret his own needs.

*Pernicious Drinks.*—In this age, when appetite in regard to drink is largely indulged, without consideration of consequences either to the person or to society, it becomes a matter of great moment to know what to avoid as well as what to use. It is now well established that, in our climate, the habitual use of alcoholic liquor as a beverage is hurtful in many ways. It injures the person using it by lowering the general tone of the system; by creating unnatural desires, which increasingly demand gratification; by turning vital forces to almost exclusively sensuous ends; by inducing neglect of the culture of the higher powers, and blindness to thrift and to domestic and social duties. So great is the train of evils which flow from habits of drink, and of so doubtful a character and of so little moment are the benefits which are claimed for it, that we may regard the formation of such habits as the negation of physical and spiritual well-being. The question is one in which educators are directly interested. Any system of education would be justly regarded as imperfect that either ignored this subject, or left a doubt in the minds of the pupils in regard to the degrading tendency of the habitual use of intoxicating liquors.

The teacher can do much indirectly and incidentally toward creating a healthful public sentiment among his pupils in regard to this subject. Very few of the pupils who attend our public schools have acquired a taste for liquor or a habit of drinking. There seems to be among them a natural and well-founded repugnance to drunkenness. By a seasonable word of advice, and by indirect allusions to the subject, this repugnance may be heightened, and the feeling rendered so strong as to become a safeguard in that critical period of life when temptations are strongest. With advanced pupils, more direct measures may be pursued. In connection with physiology, the effect of alcohol upon the nerves and bodily tissues should be fully set forth. In general exercises discussing moral questions and the laws of conduct, it should be shown that the formation of evil personal habits indirectly affects morals by the bad example set, by diminishing the power of the individual to perform his duties, and by the stimulus given to his lower propensities. The same habit becomes directly immoral by imposing upon the community the burdens of support which belong to the individual. The use of alcoholic drinks to any extent produces no good, and there is imminent danger that it may produce evil; hence it is better to shun it altogether.

*Tobacco.*—Although tobacco is not a food, its use may be considered in this connection. Like alcoholic liquors, it is an artificial stimulant or narcotic, which, to a man in health, is never a benefit, but always an injury. Although its use is so common, it answers to no universal human need, as is shown by the fact that with women, who constitute one-half of the race, its use is very limited, and is decreasing with each generation. The habitual use of tobacco so deranges the functions of the body that it creates a passionate desire, which tobacco alone can gratify. It turns certain of the excretions of the body away from their proper organs to the salivary glands, and ejects them from the mouth. It induces habits of filthiness and vitiates the breath, and so becomes an offense to others. It is an expense which, in many instances, entails essential privations upon the person or family, and in every case diminishes the ability to expend for good purposes. Whether considered in its relations to the individual, to society, or to posterity, it is a foul offense, and in every legitimate way it should be discouraged.

*Habits of the Teacher.*—Of course, no person addicted to the use of strong drink or tobacco should ever presume to take upon himself the office of teacher. His example, so powerful for evil, will go far to render nugatory any teaching of his that bears upon moral conduct. It is doubtful, on the whole, whether ignorance of the ordinary branches taught in school would not be preferable to intelligence accompanied by habits which go so far to derange the whole physical economy, and diminish the possibilities of life.

The prevalence of this habit in the community, and the approval given to it by the example of politicians, doctors, lawyers, and even by ministers of the Gospel, make it more imperative upon the teacher to use all the means which "Nature and Providence have put in his hands" to diminish this evil. He may be sure that his teachings and influence in this direction will be the true evangels of purity and beneficence.

WARMTH.—The next agency to be considered as promoting physical well-being is warmth. The temperature of the body must be maintained within certain narrow limits, or serious injuries result. As internal heat is the result of the action of the vital forces upon food, it has already been sufficiently noticed; but external heat, its sources, its degree, and its conditions, need further discussion. In climates where the temperature of the atmosphere is nearly uniform, and closely coincides with the temperature of the body, this subject needs but little attention; but in a climate like ours, subject to great extremes of heat and cold, health, and even the continuance of life, depends upon our ability to maintain a nearly equal temperature in spite of the changes of the atmosphere. We secure this uniformity by means of clothing, houses, and artificial processes of heating.

*Clothing.*—In summer, clothing is needed to keep out external heat, and in winter to prevent the too rapid radiation of the heat of the body; and to perform these various uses, it needs to vary in material, quantity, and color. Summer clothing should permit the free circulation of air, and reflect, rather than absorb, heat; and for these purposes it needs be thin and of a light color. Winter clothing should protect the entire body, and especially the extremities, against the cold; and for this purpose it needs be sufficient in quantity, and of a material that is a poor conductor of heat.

*Materials for Clothing.*—Experience has shown that light cotton and linen fabrics best answer the purposes of summer clothing, while thick, dark, woolen fabrics are best adapted to winter. When the fibre of cotton or linen is twisted and woven, the fabric becomes a good conductor of heat; and when the outside temperature is less than that of the body, it always feels cool. In the direct rays of the sun, however, it affords poor protection; and with cotton or linen clothing, there should always be an accompanying shade. When the fibre of these materials is loosely held together between thin sheets of fabric, as in quilts, the amount of air contained makes it a poor conductor of heat, and protects against the cold by preventing the escape of the heat of the body. Wool is a poor conductor of heat, and hence forms the best material out of which clothing can be made to protect from the cold. Woolen clothing is also needed as a protection from such sudden changes of temperature as are experienced in certain occupations.

*Relations of Clothing to Food.*—Food is the source of internal heat, while clothing is one of the principal means by which this heat is conserved and regulated. By insufficient clothing heat is wasted, and there follows a demand for a greater supply, which in turn demands more food. Intelligent farmers understand this principle, and save food by giving their stock proper shelter. Persons exposed to the weather in winter will require more food than those who are within doors. Children thinly clad require most food; and it so happens that often where food is most scanty, most food is demanded. To diminish the amount of food, and of clothing at the same time, must result in diminished vitality.

*Changes of Temperature.*—Sudden changes in temperature are experienced both by the change of weather and by going from a warm room into the cold without. When the temperature is suddenly lowered, a chill is produced, which closes the pores of the skin, arrests the insensible perspiration, and throws the excretions of the skin upon some of the vital organs. This produces the derangements which are called colds, and which are so often the precursors of more serious and even fatal diseases. To the end of protecting against chill, great care must be taken to make change of clothing conform to change of temperature. Adequate outer garments should be put on when going from a warm room into the cold air, and these should be taken off when coming into the room again. During the season of shifting conditions of climate, it is better to wear flannel underclothing, which may be a little uncomfortable for the warmest days, or parts of the day, but which is almost complete protection against sudden chill.

*Sanitary Suggestions.*—In winter great care should be taken to protect the extremities from the cold. For this purpose, adequate under-clothing and thick warm boots or shoes are indispensable. Girls usually are clothed less warmly than boys, and in consequence suffer more from exposure. This is an evil which should be remedied. When pupils are heated from exercise, they should not be permitted to sit down in a draft or in a cold place. At the close of an exercise in a cold day, it is safer to rest in a warm room, or at once to put on extra clothing.

The room in which pupils sit at recitation or study should have a uniform temperature of about 70°. During the periods when all the pupils engage in physical exercise, the temperature may be much lower than this. Dampness should be avoided. When the clothing is wet by exposure to the rain, the pupils should be permitted to dry it at once, even if the order of the school has to be changed for that purpose.

*Houses.*—Houses are built for shelter and warmth, and their form, structure, and materials, need intelligent attention. In the construction of schoolhouses economy is often carried to the extreme of parsimony. The objects which should be considered in their building are the health, comfort, and convenience of their occupants, and the perfect adaptation of the structure to its uses. But these objects are often lost sight of in the effort to save expense, and buildings are erected unsightly in appearance, flimsy in structure, coarse and rough in finish, and affording inadequate protection against the cold. Matters of comfort, convenience, and even of health, are entirely left out of account, and rooms are erected so small as to force pupils into uncomfortable proximity to each other, allowing no freedom of movement, and providing a very inadequate supply of air.

*Necessary Considerations.*—First of all, the schoolhouse should be well built, both for the direct benefit to the pupils, and for purposes of economy in the long run. A building well constructed will cost a little more at first, but it will not need repairs so soon nor so often, and it will last much longer than one that has been scrimped in quality of materials and workmanship. True economy is never conserved by bad work. Walls of stone or brick are better than of wood, as they last longer, and are cooler in summer and warmer in winter. When the walls are constructed of wood, they need a coating of sheathing-paper beneath the weather-boards, or an internal coat of plastering, as a protection in extreme cold weather. The foundation-walls should also be built entire and tight, that the floor may be kept warm.

The building should be large enough to allow a separate seat for each pupil, and perfect freedom of movement of pupils and classes, so that there need be no interference with each other. Room should also be ample for the use of apparatus, for the study of specimens in natural history, and for the allowance of separate space for the plays of the younger pupils. The room needed for air, and the means of heating, are considered under the head of Ventilation.

LIGHT.—In the construction of a schoolhouse, the disposition of light is a matter of prime moment. Windows should be large or grouped together, so as to afford opportunity for broad masses of light and a uniformity in all parts of the room. Small windows, placed at regular intervals with considerable space between, cause alternate bands of light and shade which are distinctly visible, and a shifting condition of light painful to the eyes. The light from large windows should be brought under control by the means of inside blinds which move in sections, admitting more or less light, according to the brightness of the day, and from any part of the window as may be desired.

*Direction of Light.*—It is much better to admit light upon but one side of the room. If windows are placed upon more than one side, they should always be provided with blinds which will effectually exclude the light upon one side when necessary. Cross-lights, or windows at right angles with each other, should always be avoided. The light coming to the eye in different directions, and at different degrees of intensity, the eye is continually engaged in endeavoring to adjust itself to incompatible conditions, and in consequence, its muscles become wearied and its functions deranged.

Windows should never be placed in front of the pupils. The continual glare of light coming directly into the eye, without any chance of mitigation, is both disagreeable and injurious. The light shines into the eyes while the shade is cast upon the book, reversing the conditions that are most desirable.

The seats of the room should be so arranged that the light comes in on the left side, in large masses, so modified and diffused as not to make deep shadows. This arrangement will allow the book to be illuminated, will keep the eyes in partial shade, and will allow the hand to write without an interrupting shadow.

*Defective Sight.*—Want of attention to the proper arrangement of light frequently results in defective sight on the part of pupils. In a late report from a commission appointed to examine the upper schools in Germany, it was stated that thirty-six per cent. of the students were found to have defective vision, directly traceable to the bad management of the lights in the schoolroom. This result may come from want of sufficient light, from too much light, from cross-lights, from front lights, and from changing lights. Windows are as easily arranged properly as improperly, and the only additional expense necessary to secure the proper adjustment of lights is that of the interior blinds. Direct sunlight in the room is very desirable on account of health, if the rays can be controlled and softened by the use of blinds.

AIR AND VENTILATION.—The ventilation of a room includes all the considerations relative to the circulation of the air, and to the artificial means of heating. In most of the schoolrooms throughout the country little attention is given to ventilation, and, in consequence, there is not only a loss in diminished work, but a positive injury in the form of various diseases. This evil is so formidable, and so nearly universal, that it should receive particular attention from teachers and all those who have the care of schools.

*Sources of Impure Air.*—The great mass of the atmosphere where the winds have free circulation is considered pure. The out-door impurities come principally from combustion, stagnant water, and from decaying vegetable and animal matter; and often considerable sections of country are rendered malarious from some of these causes. The winds, however, are the great purifiers, and injurious gases are usually dissipated nearly as soon as generated. Even swampy regions would soon be rendered wholesome, were it not for the continual supply of malarious matter which they furnish; and as it is, the air is contaminated only for a short distance upward.

*In-door Air.*—In the room, the conditions of the air are very different from without. The walls and ceiling necessary for protection arrest circulation, and impurities accumulate. These impurities, derived from combustion, and from the breathing and insensible perspiration of its inmates, consist of carbonic-acid gas and animal excretions, both of which are deleterious to health even in very small quantities. If breathing in a confined atmosphere is continued long enough, carbonic acid is generated in sufficient quantities to cause death; and when excretions from insensible perspiration are allowed to accumulate to any considerable extent, the air becomes so foul and offensive as to be almost unbearable.

*Conditions to be Observed.*—The problem to solve in ventilation is to secure and preserve a uniform temperature in all parts of the room, and at the same time to secure an amount of circulation of the air that will preserve its purity. To accomplish these results, advantage must be taken of forces incident to the heating; and the heating and ventilating apparatus must be so combined that the objects may be attained in the most effective and economical manner.

*Distribution of Heat.*—The heat of a room is distributed by the direct radiation from the heated surface, and by the circulation of heated air. With radiation alone the supply of heat in the different parts of the room is very unequal, and pupils near the stove are uncomfortably warm, while those at the greatest distance are uncomfortably cold. Heated air rises, and, in a room heated by a stove, there is always a current of warm air rising by the stove, and corresponding descending currents in the cooler parts of the room. By surrounding a common stove with a jacket of sheet-iron, open at the bottom and top, the ascending current of hot air becomes more pronounced, the intensity of radiation is diminished, and the heat is more evenly distributed in the room.

*Distribution of Impurities.*—Air breathed from the lungs, in consequence of its high temperature, usually rises slightly, but, soon parting with its heat, it falls, because laden with carbonic-acid gas, which is heavier than air. Afterward, by the operation of the law of diffusion of gases, it gradually mixes with the rest of the air.

*Egress of Air.*—When openings are made at the top of the room, the heat and comparatively pure air escapes, and no good arises except in case the room is overheated. Openings at the bottom, on the contrary, have a tendency to draw off the colder and impure air, and will do so, if so arranged that air does not come in instead of go out. As the room is always full of air, it follows that if air escapes, an equal amount must come in. Usually, this supply from without finds its way through the crevices of the windows and doors, producing draughts injurious to those exposed to them.

*Ventilating Arrangement.*—To make a successful system of ventilation that will give an ample supply of air without an unnecessary expenditure of heat, it is only needful to observe the foregoing conditions. Let the means of heating be a common stove of sufficient size. Surround this stove with a jacket of sheet-iron, reaching the floor and open at the top. Under the stove admit a current of air from without, and at the bottom of the room have openings which connect by means of boxes or ducts with the chimney. The size of the ducts will depend upon the size and number of the occupants of the room, and they should be so adjusted as to allow the passage of more or less air according to circumstances. With space in the room that gives each pupil 500 cubic feet of air, at least 600 cubic feet for each pupil should be admitted every hour.

*Method of Operation.*—The fire kindled in the stove

disturbs the equilibrium and produces an upward current. This occasions a flow of pure air through the cold-air duct at the bottom of the stove, which becomes heated in ascending between the stove and its jacket, and ascends and spreads out at the top of the room. At the same time the smoke and heat from the stove produce an upward current in the chimney-flue, and this occasions a draught through the ducts and ventilating registers at the bottom of the room, thus securing the escape of all foul air. Two forces are thus brought to bear to empty the room of its cold air—a pressure from the top and a draught from the bottom. If this simple apparatus is properly adjusted, the connections perfectly made, and the flues of proper size, the ventilation will be ample, the heat will be evenly distributed, and there will be the minimum waste of fuel.

*Cost of Construction.*—The three items of expense, in the construction of this apparatus, above that of a common stove, are the cold-air duct, the ventilating-duct connecting with the chimney, and the jacket to inclose the stove. Stoves are now constructed with reference to this system of ventilation which contain within themselves the two features of exterior covering and ventilating-duct, and these cost no more than equally good stoves of the common kind. This reduces the extra expense to the cost of the cold-air duct. Whatever may be the expense of a successful system of ventilation, it will be returned a hundredfold each year in the improved health of the pupils.

*Practical Suggestions.*—In schools where no provision has been made for ventilation, the teacher must exercise continual vigilance in regard to the air in the room. The attention given to this matter should be regular and systematic, as the air becomes foul by such imperceptible degrees that the teacher is unconscious of it as far as his own senses are concerned. Coming in from without, the impurities are perceived at once by the teacher. The practice of opening the windows at the top, except in case the room gets too warm, is a vicious one. The cold air coming in falls at once to the floor, exposing the unprotected heads of the pupils to the draughts, and producing chills and colds. A better plan is to open the window nearest the stove, at the bottom, the cold air falling immediately to the floor, and making its way to the stove. At the end of each hour the windows and doors should be opened a few minutes to allow a complete change of air, so that the air in the room shall never become very much vitiated. During this process the pupils should not be allowed to remain upon their seats. By making arrangements for calisthenic exercises to take place at these times, two important advantages will be gained—increased muscular vigor and a room filled with pure air.

DIRECT MUSCULAR TRAINING.—The course of physical culture recommended so far has had for its objects intelligence in regard to physical laws, the arrangements of conditions most favorable to their observance, and the formation of habits conforming to them. There remains the question of how much may be done for direct muscular training. That there should be an amount of muscular activity, each day alternating with the periods of intellectual activity, is obvious from the relations which are seen to exist between bodily health and vigor and correct thinking. Study determines the blood to the brain; exercise draws it to the extremities. In intellectual exercises nervous energy is concentrated at the nervous centres; in physical exercises it is diffused throughout the body. Thought and emotion, when carried to excess, tend to disturb the functions of the vital organs through the action of the sympathetic nerves; muscular activity, when carried to excess, equally disturbs the vital functions by depriving them of their proper amount of nervous stimulus. Exclusive devotion to intellectual pursuits, with a corresponding neglect of the physical, will reduce the physical powers to their minimum, and, reacting, will diminish the intellectual powers also. Exclusive devotion to muscular exercise will reduce intelligence to its minimum, and, reacting, will diminish the physical powers. To a complete development, both are needed; the one is complementary to the other, and each affords a relief from the weariness of the other. In schools, which from their very nature give prominence to intellectual pursuits, there should be sufficient attention given to physical exercise to preserve the proper balance of vital powers. The direct means at command to accomplish this purpose are calisthenic exercises, and the training for work.

*Calisthenics.*—Within the past few years calisthenics have been introduced into schools, and among the good results may be enumerated the following: The weariness of long-continued sitting is dispelled; the nervous restlessness which so often disturbs the order of the school is allayed; headaches and other forms of nervous ailments are diminished; the tendency to distortion incident to sitting in one position is overcome;

a strong, free, and vigorous movement is substituted for the listless shambling or the nervous jerking which are characteristics of schools where intellectual work is pushed to the utmost and exercise neglected; a greater amount of intellectual work is secured, and grace of attitude and gesture is developed.

*Kinds of Exercise.*—The kinds of exercise best fitted for public schools are the free calisthenics, as given in any of the manuals upon this subject. They include movements of nearly all the muscles of the body arranged in regular rhythmic exercises for class drill. Particular attention is given to the exercise of the muscles of the arms and chest, so as to give the fullest play to the lungs. When possible, the calisthenics should be accompanied by music, either vocal or instrumental, so that the rhythm may be fully preserved. In default of music, the simultaneous movement may be obtained by counting.

*Calisthenic Apparatus.*—For the purposes enumerated, little apparatus is needed, and in public schools generally the arrangement of the room is such that apparatus cannot be used. Even with ample room, simple apparatus is best for school purposes. Wooden dumb-bells, light clubs, wands, rings, and bags of grain not exceeding four pounds each, afford all the exercise that is demanded, and the variety necessary for keeping up the interest. By means of these, physical culture is obtained through a series of light and rapid movements, rather than by the heavy gymnastics which require a great expenditure of muscular force; and the ends attained are health, activity, and grace, rather than the greatest possible physical strength.

*Time Given to Exercise.*—Exercise should be frequent and not of long duration. In primary rooms it may with propriety be made to alternate with each of the recitations. In the higher departments and in ungraded schools, twice each session, about five minutes should be given to exercise, the time varying with the conditions of the school. In no case should it be continued to the point where it exhausts instead of invigorates.

*Caution to be Observed.*—The teacher should exercise a careful supervision over the calisthenics, and no pupil should be compelled or permitted to take part in them when ill, or when there is a liability that the exercise will produce illness. The whole subject of physical exercise has often fallen into disrepute from want of care in this direction.

REST.—Observation and experience show that, after an expenditure of vital force, time is needed to replace the elements used, and to restore the organs exercised to their full vigor. This interval for the recuperation, which we term rest, is as important an element of human well-being as exercise. The law seems to be that every period of activity, whether physical or intellectual, should be followed by a period of rest. When activity has continued to a point where rest is clearly demanded, we are said to be tired, and rest easily restores vigor. When activity continues beyond this point, vital force is derived from elements which enter into the composition of the organs themselves, and we become weary—a state which ordinary rest will not redress. Expenditure continued to the point of excessive weariness so destroys the vigor of the system, that there frequently happens a sudden failure of the nervous functions throughout the body, which we call paralysis.

*Rest of Change.*—When one set of muscles or faculties has become tired from use, a sense of rest is experienced by bringing another set into action, provided the aggregate vitality at command has not been exhausted. This is the rest of change or variety of employment. It is the method of relief from the dreariness of monotony, and one of which the teacher should take advantage in the arrangement of courses of study and daily programmes. Upon this principle the study of natural history is a rest from the study of mathematics, and calisthenics is a rest from all intellectual activity.

*Rest of the Attention.*—When the attention is fixed upon one subject for some time it becomes weary in one direction; and if given to a series of subjects, though each may afford a relief to the other, in time the whole stock of vital energy which is at the service of attention is exhausted, and the attention itself needs rest. The power of sustained attention varies with age and development. Children soon weary of the effort to fix their attention, and for this reason their lessons should continue but a few minutes at a time upon one subject, nor for any considerable time upon a variety of subjects. Calisthenics do not constitute a means of rest for the attention when tired, as they themselves require attention. The proper rest for wearied attention in children is spontaneous plays, and in students or business-men is the entire change which comes in the summer vacation by hunting, fishing, camping out, and visits to the sea or mountains.

*Complete Rest.*—Every human being has a certain

amount of vital force which he can spend in activities physical or intellectual, beneficent or vicious, in work or in play. If spent in one direction it cannot be spent in another. All kinds of activity are exhaustive, though not in equal degree. Exhaustive physical labor prevents any considerable mental activity, and exhaustive mental labor prevents any considerable physical activity. Dissipation, whatever form it may assume, is not only the waste of vital forces, so that no good purpose is possible, but it is usually the derangement of the vital functions diminishing the supply of force. When the stock of vitality at command is exhausted, no matter by what means, complete rest is demanded in the form of perfect quiet.

*Daily Rest or Sleep.*—By the constitution of human beings there seems to be an amount of extra vital force at command each day; and when the day ends, the force has been expended in some form—wisely in conserving and promoting human interests, or unwisely in dissipation by which forces are wasted, or in indolence by which they are expended in the morbid action of the organs themselves. This daily expenditure calls for the most perfect form of rest—sleep. During sleep all the powers are recuperated, and vital force is laid up for the next day's use. Regular daily undisturbed sleep is a necessity to well-being; and study, work, business, and play, should be arranged so as not to diminish its hours, or in any way to interfere with it.

*Amount of Sleep.*—The amount of sleep necessary to the full recuperation of the vital powers depends upon several conditions, among which are the constitution of the person, the nature of the employment, and the degree of the exhaustion. To prescribe the same number of hours of sleep for all would be as absurd as to prescribe the same amount of food for all. When tired but not weary, the proper amount of sleep refreshes the person, and restores his powers to full vigor. Intellectual activities in an especial manner call for plenty of sleep, and pupils in school should be instructed never to let any supposed necessity of study interfere with their natural amount of sleep. Nothing is more detrimental to the well-being of a student than attempted study when sleep is needed. Excessively late and excessively early hours are alike injurious. Besides the injury resulting from the loss of sleep, study at late hours bears but little fruit in the way of mental improvement. One hour of study in full vigor is worth six hours when the mind is half asleep.

*Rest from Weariness.*—When activity is long continued, without adequate intervals of rest, there results a general exhaustion, shown by a weariness which sleep does not overcome. The only remedy for this is perfect rest—an entire cessation from activities that demand attention. In the complicated arrangement of business affairs there often comes a continued strain upon the attention, and an abnormal expenditure of vital force, which exhausts not only the surplus stock, but all that the organs can yield. The redress of the weariness that ensues is only found in perfect rest, which must be taken to the full extent of restoration of vigor, or the vital functions will be permanently impaired or altogether cease.

A knowledge of rest in its several degrees and in its relations to activities is of vital importance to teachers. Ignorance of the laws which govern the recuperation of vitality often leads to absurd practices. In the olden time, students in the higher institutions of learning were obliged to get up at five o'clock in the morning, at all seasons of the year, to attend chapel exercises, observing divine worship by the disobedience of divine law. Teachers often stimulate pupils to an undue amount of study, by assigning too long lessons, and by censure expressed or implied when the lesson is not learned. In schools where the high-pressure principle in regard to study prevails, the most ambitious and delicately organized students are not uncommonly driven so hard that their powers of mind fail, and they either sink into premature graves, or pass the remainder of their lives the mere wrecks of what they might have been. In assigning too long lessons, the mistake of the teacher arises from judging of the capacity of the pupil by his own, and of expecting from children an amount of work which would tax the capacity of adults. When pupils have attained an age that gives them the power of independent study, the direction which should be given them is: "Give such time to your lessons as you can without encroaching upon your sleep, or hours of necessary recreation, and the amount of study required shall be arranged accordingly."

## CHAPTER XII.

### ÆSTHETIC CULTURE.

NATURE OF ÆSTHETICS.—In intellectual training the end is to ascertain the true—the true in the facts, relations, and laws of both the physical and mental worlds. In morals, the end sought is the good, which upon one side expresses the true in human relations, and upon the other converts it into action. In æsthetics, the end sought is the beautiful, which is the true in the relations of objects and their qualities as they affect the emotions through the senses. The true includes all phenomena; the good relates to human conduct; and the beautiful refers to objective relations which afford pleasure. The three are so united that the course which most certainly secures either is essential to the highest success in all, and that substantial attainment in each is necessary to the highest attainment in the others.

Æsthetic culture includes both a perception of the beautiful as it exists, and also the ability to arrange elements in such a manner as to produce the beautiful. It is not only an appreciative, but a creative power. Its highest ends are attained through the imagination, and it furnishes one of the principal means by which the imagination is cultivated. The æsthetic sense which we call taste, while greatly differing in individuals, can always be improved by systematic training.

*Standard of Beauty.*—In regard to the origin and nature of beauty, and the standard by which it is to be judged, there are two general theories. One, known as the intuitional, claims that in the spiritual world there is an absolute standard of beauty; that Nature is a realization of this standard to a greater or less degree; and that the human mind has an intuitive perception of the correspondence between the material and the spiritual whenever it occurs, and responds to the ideal standard. As natural forms approximate to the ideal standard, they are said to be beautiful; as they fall short in this respect, they are regarded as ugly.

*Ruskin's Views.*—Ruskin takes this view of the origin and nature of beauty, as is seen in the following extract: "Now I may state, that beauty has been appointed by the Deity to be one of the elements by which the human soul is continually sustained; it is, therefore, to be found in all natural objects; but in order that we may not satiate ourselves with it, and weary of it, it is rarely granted to us in its utmost degrees. When we see it in those utmost degrees, we are attracted to it strongly, and remember it long, as in the case of singularly beautiful scenery or a beautiful countenance. On the other hand, absolute ugliness is admitted as rarely as perfect beauty; but degrees of it, more or less distinct, are associated with whatever has the nature of death and sin, just as beauty is associated with what has the nature of virtue and of life.

"What Nature does generally is sure to be more or

less beautiful; what she does rarely will either be very beautiful or absolutely ugly; and we may again easily determine, if we are not willing in such a case to trust our feelings, which of these is indeed the case, by the simple rule that, if the occurrence is the result of the complete fulfillment of a natural law, it will be beautiful; if of the violation of a natural law, it will be ugly."

*Experience Theory.*—The other theory makes beauty the result of experience. In infancy, the beneficent gives pleasure, the harmful gives pain; the accustomed yields all needed ideas and gives pleasure; the unaccustomed inspires vague terrors and gives pain. A little higher in development, variety furnishes the mind with food and gives pleasure, while monotony starves it and gives pain.

In some combinations of qualities or of objects, the impressions harmonize with the human organism, and give pleasure; in others, they do not so harmonize, and give pain. For example: intense light is not in harmony with the structure of the eye, and pain is caused either by its admission or by the effort to keep it out. In like manner, cross-lights in a room produce continually varying degrees of light, so that the muscles of the iris become weary in endeavoring to adjust the internal structure to the outward conditions. So in color, certain combinations respond to the structure of the eye and are restful, while others are at variance with this structure and are painful. In all these cases, that which gives pleasure we call beautiful, and that which gives pain, ugly; the internal emotion passing judgment upon the external object.

In a still higher state of development, intelligence

reacts upon the senses and corrects the first vague notions. The harmful has been subjugated. Qualities are considered apart from objects. The harmonies between the external and internal are more clearly seen. The ideas which Nature represents are more fully comprehended. The imagination is busy in constructing new ideals. In consequence, notions concerning beauty continually broaden, become more discriminative, and exercise a more potent influence upon the emotions.

*Training in Art.*—Efforts to represent the beautiful are of great assistance to its full appreciation. The steps of representation are first imitation, and then an analysis and a rearrangement of the elements into new combinations. By this process we become more thoroughly acquainted with Nature; see more clearly the typical forms to which the real forms more or less imperfectly approximate; and are able to improve upon Nature by representing the typical rather than the real forms. This is the realization of the beautiful in human production, and is pure art.

Before considering the steps necessary to be taken in æsthetic culture, it is necessary to examine the elements which constitute beauty somewhat in detail.

Form.—One of the most fundamental elements of beauty is form. Observations of Nature give us forms in almost infinite variety and combination. We see daily the blue dome of the heavens and the green mantle of the earth, and nightly the stars in their procession, and each of these gives pleasure: not because of their known utility, but because they form a part of the established order of things, to which we have become accustomed. Mystery was one source of pleasure afforded by the contemplation of the starry heavens, but the pleasure becomes even greater, as the mystery is resolved into majestic law, which

> "Extends through all extent,
> Spreads undivided, operates unspent."

*Analysis of Form.*—Descending from the general to the particular, the features of a landscape and the special forms of vegetation give pleasure, and are said to be beautiful. At the same time a discrimination is made. A rugged landscape, unfit for human occupancy, would, at first, scarcely appear beautiful, because it is associated with no pleasurable emotions. The beauty of such scenery is appreciated only by those who have passed from the perceptive into the reflective state. So a tree gnarled and twisted by the wind is seen to poorly represent the typical tree which would grow up under the most favorable circumstances. To a higher culture, however, the very twisted appearance becomes an additional element of beauty, as it gives evidence of the operation of majestic forces, the contemplation of which is a stimulus and a pleasure to the mind.

*Geometric Divisions.*—Still further analysis separates form into its geometric elements, the main divisions of which are straight and curved lines. In Nature, straight lines are seldom presented, while curved lines are found in almost infinite variety, and it is equally true that curved lines usually give greater pleasure than straight ones, and are considered essential elements of beauty. A reason for the greater pleasure afforded by the curved line may be found in the fact that it is more restful to the eye. In forms made up of straight lines there is a monotony of vision along the single line to the end, where there is an abrupt transition, causing a sudden change in the muscular movements of the eye; while in curved lines and surfaces there is a continual change which avoids monotony, and makes a complete transition, as far as direction is concerned, by imperceptible degrees; the gradual change producing a more pleasurable feeling than the abrupt one.

*Forms used in Art.*—In the representation of beautiful forms, the first necessary step is the exact reproduction of natural forms as they appear. Next above this is the representation of natural forms so modified as to adapt them to industrial pursuits, when they are said to be conventionalized. The next step is the realization in art of the ideals which Nature suggests, or the separation of natural forms into their geometric elements, and the recombining of these new elements into essentially new designs, known as geometric designs or arabesques. In all these cases the forms of art give pleasure, as they faithfully represent Nature; as they idealize Nature by more fully realizing the idea which Nature suggests; or as they make complex designs which are hints of a perfection not fully embodied.

*Nature the Basis of Art.*—In most of the works of man the ideas of form seem to be directly derived from Nature. In one style of building, ascending through a series of changes, from the rude wigwam of the North American Indians to the stately groined arches of the Gothic cathedrals, the general idea of form is evidently suggested by the embowering branches of forest-trees. In another style of building, ascending from the underground abodes of the Borean races, through the rock-hewn cities of Arabia and India, and through the massive temples of Egypt, to the light and graceful structures of the classic Greeks, the leading idea of form seems derived from that of natural caverns; and all the changes which art has made in this long series are but modifications of this idea.

Almost any department of human art or industry furnishes additional examples of artificial forms growing directly out of natural ones. Norman castles, with their thick buttresses and stout turrets, were very faithful representations of mountains, crags, and rocks; and, as they are seen to crown the lofty summits along the Rhine, they constitute so harmonious a part of the landscape that they seem a part of the rocks upon which they stand, rather than the work of man. The Saracenic minarets and the Oriental pagodas, with their slender shafts and overhanging roofs, were developed in regions where the palm-tree is the typical form of vegetable life, and very faithfully the natural form is represented in the art structures. The lotus, a common product along the Nile, appears conventionalized upon all the monuments and ornamentations of the Egyptians; and the acanthus, a plant of Southern Europe, furnishes the idea for the exquisite capital of the Corinthian columns of the Greeks and the Romans.

PROPORTION.—The next element which enters into our ideas of beauty is that of proportion. In the full knowledge of an object, which results from examination, there are included ideas of use and adaptation to use. One of the elements of adaptation is size—and, from the correspondence of size to use, of the size of parts to their respective uses and to each other, and from the relative size of objects when compared with other objects, we get ideas of proportion. In natural forms these ideas are derived from the most perfect specimens in each department. For example, in the typical form of each species of trees there are certain fixed relations in size between trunk and branches which we call good proportion. When this relation is disturbed, we feel that the tree is imperfect and distorted, or, in other words, the parts are out of proportion.

*Proportion in Architecture.*—In architecture there are certain relations in the length, breadth, and height of a building which we call good proportion; and, while there is room for variation within proper limits, to transcend these limits is to occasion a sense of incongruity in those who see it. A theory has been advanced that true proportion in building, in its effects, is analagous to that of the natural scale in music; that correspondences in waves of light, as well as in waves of sound, produce harmony. In the construction of rooms there is the same necessity for the proper adjustments of the different dimensions, so that the greatest satisfaction may be produced. A square room gives a sense of incompleteness; when the room is too low, the ceiling seems to restrain us from full freedom of action, and when the room is too high the same feeling of restraint seems to come from the walls.

*Element of Safety.*—Ideas of proportion are often closely associated with a sense of safety. From experience, we get certain notions of the strength of materials, and of the effect of forces; and where we see an apparently inadequate support of a visible weight, or of a known strain, we have a sense of insecurity which determines our ideas of proportion in this particular case. A good example of this feeling is illustrated in the construction of bridges. The old massive stone structures are known to be perfectly safe, and are everywhere considered in good proportion and beautiful. Iron bridges, on the contrary, though we may know that they are just as safe, appear out of proportion and ugly. For this reason Ruskin says that true architecture demands that there shall be visible supports to all parts of the building; that while real supports, as iron rods, may be concealed, there must be entirely adequate apparent supports in the form of columns and buttresses.

*General Ideas of Proportion.*—This idea of proportion seems also to pervade the whole world of thought, and everywhere the mind is satisfied only by a proper adjustment of means to ends, and of cause to effect. When there is a great disparity in these regards the effect is grotesque, and is a legitimate source of mirth. Hood's comic illustrations were often of this character, deriving their fun from patent incongruities. One of these represents a small pony drawing a wagon crowded with people up a steep hill, and is designated "Drawing Lots;" and another represents an immense dray-horse apparently straining himself to the utmost in drawing a small baby-cart, under the title of "Anti-Climax." The caricatures of the comic papers, preserving the likeness of a person but exaggerating some peculiarity of feature, and the familiar Latin quotation, "*parturiunt montes et nascitur ridiculus mus,*" afford additional illustrations of the same principle.

*Ideas of Proportion applied.*—So universal is this idea of proportion, and so necessary to the proper adjustments of thought and action, that it should be considered in every department of school-work. Upon it are founded successful courses of study and daily programmes. It can be specifically cultivated in methods of study, and in the manner in which work is performed. Physically, ideas of proportion are developed by the proper spacing of letters and words, by adapting the size of letters and figures to the place where they are written, as upon the slate or blackboard, and by the methodical arrangement of all written work. In abstract matters, the same ideas may be developed by the proper division of time into periods of work and rest, and by giving to each study its proper amount of attention.

UNITY.—Another important element of beauty is unity. The most fundamental idea connected with every object is its use, not merely as contributing to the material welfare of man, but as occupying its appropriate place in relation to other objects. When an object is specially adapted to its uses, and all its parts, while adapted to their special uses, directly contribute to the general use of the whole, or when several objects are so related that they all contribute to one general use or design, in this adaptation to use we have the idea of unity.

*Example in Nature.*—A tree is beautiful from its graceful form, the proportion of its parts, and the undulating movement of its branches; but we are led to a closer observation and a higher appreciation of this beauty, when we see that the stalk is made strong that it may resist the wind; that the branches divide and subdivide so as to give support to almost innumerable leaves; that the leaves are broad, thin plates, hung upon slender stems, so that there may be the freest possible contact with the air; and that the leaves furnish the tree with the greater part of its sustenance by absorbing from the atmosphere the impurities detrimental to animal life. In this arrangement of the several parts we see adaptation to use, or unity.

*Unity in Art.*—In examining almost any of the works of man, our satisfaction, to a considerable extent, depends upon the idea that they are designed for use, and that in their construction this design is carried out. This is especially true of a machine. If it has no use, it is cast aside as a mere toy; if it is not well adapted to its use, then improvements are sought. Full satisfaction only comes when the proper work is performed in the proper manner.

In the structure of a building we look for the same unity of design. Whatever elements of beauty it may possess, if it does not serve its uses it is an offence. Then the several parts essential to the building must be arranged with express reference to this use, and all others omitted. The test of architectural ability is to make the best possible arrangement of necessary parts all strictly subordinated to the use. Within the limits of unity thus preserved there is opportunity for the exercise of a great variety in taste.

In the arrangement of a room, its furniture and utensils, the greatest satisfaction is taken when the principle of unity is fully preserved. Use determines the general character of the whole, and within its limits all ornamentation should come. In sitting-rooms and parlors, where considerable time is spent, pictures and beautiful objects of art are in place, as conforming objects of sight to the physiological conditions of the eye and to the needs of the mind. A fit variety in this direction is entirely consonant with ideas of unity.

*Disregard of Unity.*—In architecture the principle of unity is often entirely disregarded. Churches and lecture-rooms, for example, are built in accordance with some dogmatic canon in regard to proportion, and no attention is paid to acoustic effects, and they become an offence, alike to the speaker and the audience. Public edifices and dwellings are frequently erected in which use is entirely subordinated to external appearance.

The principle of unity is also violated in attaching features to a building expressly for ornament, or ornament for ornament's sake. In the structure of roofs, windows, doors, and other necessary parts of a building, beautiful forms and arrangements may be chosen; but the fundamental idea of unity forbids the addition of special features not necessary to the structure, simply for ornamentation.

*Aggregation not Unity.*—The absence of this idea of unity is felt in visiting a museum or public gallery of art. In the whole collection there can be no general idea except that of aggregation. An ordinary visit to such places leaves but confused and unsatisfactory images in the mind, and neither pleasure nor profit is gained. It is only when the attention is concentrated upon a single object that good can arise, and here the idea of unity is preserved by excluding all objects except the one studied.

SYMMETRY.—Observation in regard to almost any specimen of organic life shows a certain orderly arrangement of parts by which a balance is maintained on the two sides, and this arrangement is the same in all individuals belonging to the same species, and is analogous in the several species that constitute the more general groups. For example, the leaves of plants are arranged on the stalk sometimes opposite, sometimes alternate, and sometimes in other orders; but there is always a substantial equality maintained between the two sides. In like manner the anterior and posterior limbs of an animal balance each other, and the limbs and organs of sense are double, and placed on opposite sides. This arrangement of parts so that they balance each other is symmetry, and a perception of it gives a satisfaction to the mind and constitutes one of the elements of beauty.

*Symmetry in Nature.*—Our pleasure at the sight of a fine tree, to a considerable extent, depends upon the idea of symmetry which it suggests. While there may not be an exact reproduction of parts on each side, there is a general balance maintained. To see how much symmetry enters into our ideas of the beauty of a tree, we have only to observe one that has been riven by lightning, and we find that in the loss of one side all beauty is gone.

In the animal kingdom, so thoroughly is this idea of the symmetrical arrangement of parts impressed upon us that any deviation from it appears grotesque, and gives us an uneasy or painful feeling. This is illustrated by the sight of a flounder, where the relative position of the mouth and eyes, so different from that of most fish, suggests that some mistake has been made, which the imagination vainly attempts to rectify. A similar feeling of pain is experienced from the same cause when we see a person who has lost a limb or an eye.

*Symmetry in Art.*—The idea of symmetry is carried out in almost every department of construction. It is an especial element in architecture, where it demands a central idea, and a balance in the grouping of subordinate parts. When either of these conditions is absent, there is a disquieting feeling, a sense of incompleteness, and one element of beauty is wanting.

An analogous effect is produced by objects out of their true position. When a door, or window, or any other part of a building that should be vertical, is out of plumb, a painful sensation is produced; and this feeling is strongest in those whose observing powers have been best trained. This probably arises, in part, from the feeling of insecurity which is associated with leaning structures.

HARMONY. — Closely associated with unity, which considers the adaptation of parts to use, is harmony, which takes into account the dependence of parts and their relations as to style. In regard to dependence, harmony demands that the principal parts be made the most prominent, and that the minor parts shall not obtrude themselves upon notice. In this sense harmony is closely allied to proportion, but proportion in a general sense of considering all the parts which go to make up the structure or unity.

Examples of this want of harmony may be seen in doors much too large or too small for the walls in which they are placed; roofs so scanty as scarcely to be visible; in the kind of dwelling which is very justly described as a portico with a house behind it; in a small building surmounted by a large dome, looking like a child with his father's hat on; and in that general arrangement of farm buildings where the stable is made more conspicuous than the dwelling.

*Harmony in Style.*—In its second sense, harmony demands that, in the details of the arrangements of parts and in the finish, certain likenesses in style shall be preserved, and marked contrasts shall be avoided. When the laws of harmony are violated, a feeling is produced that the mistake has been made of putting together parts that belong to different objects, and that, though they may serve their uses, a different arrangement would serve them better.

*Harmony in Nature.*—We see this idea of harmony carried out in organic structure. Each species of trees has its own law of growth, and its typical form, and each individual in the species conforms to the law, and more or less closely approximates to the form. Coniferous trees are usually spire-shaped, and have branches and leaves peculiar to themselves; maples, in form and leaf, are of a quite different type, and there is no mixing of the characteristics of the two species.

In the animal world we find the same laws of harmony prevail in regard to general form, the arrangement of parts, and special characteristics. So much reliance can be placed upon this uniformity of structure in species that comparative anatomists are able to reconstruct an animal from a single bone, and even to reconstruct an extinct species from the impress of a single part left in the rocks. So strong is this idea of harmony in the structure of animal forms impressed upon the mind that the discovery of the remains of a species in Australia, with some of the characteristics of a bird and some of a mammal, was for a long time considered a fable; and, when the evidence was too strong to be doubted, the animal was regarded with feelings akin to those experienced toward monstrosities.

*Harmony in Art.*—In architecture, the element of harmony is of special importance. Many styles have grown out of different conditions and circumstances, each of the features expressing a definite idea, and all necessary to the completed whole. Between these different styles there may be but few features in common; and the effect of mixing parts is as incongruous as would be the growth of pine and maple branches and leaves on the same tree.

For example, Greek architecture was developed in the structure of large temples, and in a climate warm enough for out-door living during the greater part of the year. The temple consisted of four walls in the form of a rectangle, and of an exterior and interior portico supported by columns, and connected by open door-ways through the walls. The interior was an open court. All the decorative skill of the Greeks was expended upon the portico, which was a place of public assemblage, and the principal part of the building. When the Greek temple is built for modern purposes in a climate where protection from the weather is a prime necessity, the portico is found to be practically of little use in itself, and of decided disadvantage to the interior by shutting out the light. The chief part of such a building is out of harmony with its uses. When the forms which were developed in connection with the Greek temple are used to ornament buildings which have grown out of other circumstances and necessities, the effect is seen to be unpleasant from the violation of the laws of harmony.

*Want of Harmony.*—The same want of harmony is shown in mixing special and characteristic features of other styles of building. The Norman battlements and turrets were raised for defense in an age of perpetual warfare, and the Gothic groined arches grew out of religious fervor. To unite the forms of these two styles, and adapt them to the necessities of a modern dwelling, is to commit a double incongruity.

The violation of the laws of harmony is well illustrated by Lowell in his description of the house of Mr. Knott:

> "Whatever anybody had
> Out of the common, good or bad,
> Knott had it all worked well in;
> A donjon keep, where clothes might dry;
> A porter's lodge, that was a sty:
> A campanile slim and high,
> Too small to hang a bell in.
> It was a house to make one stare,
> All corners and all gables;
> And all the oddities to spare
> Were set upon the stables."

VARIETY.—The careful and minute study of Nature shows that, while there is a conformity to the laws of proportion, unity, and symmetry, there are no two things ever just alike. The leaves of a tree, although conforming to a common type, are all different; no two branches are alike in form, and no two trees are ever so near alike that they may not be readily distinguished from each other. In the animal world the same truth holds; no two animals are ever just alike, and, when the likeness is so perfect as in the structure of the two sides of the same animal, there are differences in detail which can be easily detected by nice observation. By these unlikenesses monotony is avoided, a perpetual pleasure is afforded by new impressions, and variety is seen to constitute one of the essential elements of beauty.

*Variety in Nature.*—Upon this point of variety in Nature, Ruskin says: " Gather a branch from any of the trees and flowers to which the earth owes its principal beauty. I will take, for instance, a spray of the common ash. Now Nature abhors equality and similitude, just as much as foolish men love them. You will find that the ends of the shoots are composed of four green stalks bearing leaves, springing in the form of a cross if seen from above, and at first you will suppose the four arms of the cross are equal. But look closer, and you will find that two opposite arms or stalks have only five leaves each, and the other two have seven; or else, two have seven and the other two nine, but always one pair of stalks has two more leaves than the other two. Sometimes the tree gets a little puzzled, and forgets which is to be the longest stalk, and begins with a stem for seven leaves where it should have nine, and then recollects itself at the last minute and puts on another leaf in a great hurry, and so produces a stalk with eight leaves; and all this care it takes merely to keep itself out of equalities, and all its grace and power of pleasing are owing to its doing so, together with the lovely curves in which its stalks, thus arranged, spring from the main bough."

Again he says: "You do not feel interested in hearing the same thing over and over again. Why do you suppose you can feel interested in seeing the same thing over and over again, were that thing even the best and most beautiful in the world? 'Nay,' but you will answer me, 'we see sunrises and sunsets, and violets and roses, over and over again, and we do not tire of them.' What! did you ever see one sunrise like another? Does not God vary his clouds for you every morning and every night? though, indeed, there is enough in the disappearing and appearing of the great orb above the rolling of the world to interest all of us, one would think, for as many times as we shall see it, and yet the aspect of it is changed for us daily. You see violets and roses often, and are not tired of them. True! but you did not often see two roses alike, or, if you did, you took care not to put them in the same nosegay, for fear the nosegay should be uninteresting."

*Variety in Art.*—The variety which is seen to constitute so important an element of beauty in Nature occupies an equally important place in art. This is especially noticeable in the architecture of our homes. A room is made more pleasant by windows varying in size and groupings on the different sides, and by panelings so that the walls do not appear as exact counterparts of each other. A building becomes a much more beautiful object, where exact symmetry is relieved by a judicious variety in the arrangement of parts. The plain monotonous front of a great factory, with its windows all exact duplicates of one form, placed at exactly regular intervals, is a synonym for ugliness, and any building is ugly as it approaches the factory type.

*Monotony in Cities.*—The same principle holds true in the aggregation of houses in a city. However fine the model of a building may be in its general proportions, its endless duplication through long streets becomes oppressive, and the mind derives a positive pleasure from the sight of even an old tumble-down rookery which relieves it from the wearisome monotony. When art is generally taught, and the principles of architecture are well understood, the house a man builds will be the expression of his individual taste, and the aggregation of such houses will have all the variety of individual character. Then the streets of a city will be a source of perpetual delight in their continual surprises, each change being but a variation of beautiful forms, and the whole will become an important educational influence.

*Contrasted Examples.*—In one of the principal cities in this country, two costly and solid public buildings stand near each other. The one is exactly symmetrical, with a central doorway and the same number of windows on each side. The door and the windows are ornamented by elaborate carved stone-work, and along the frieze there is also a great amount of costly carvings. The windows are, however, exactly alike, and the carved ornaments are such exact duplications of a single form that they appear as cast in the same mould. A single glance at this structure comprehends it all, and the observer turns away from all this exhibition of labor and expense, if not in disgust, at least in utter indifference.

In the other building, while there is a general balance of parts so as to satisfy the mind in regard to symmetry, the windows and other parts differ in regard to form, size, and ornamental carvings. Each window has its own separate design, and no two carvings are alike. The differences are not so great as to violate the laws of harmony, and the whole effect is that of unity in variety. The eye casually falling upon this structure is arrested by the beauty of its general form and color, and is thereby led to make more minute observations. The arrangement of the parts, each contributing to the beauty of the whole, next receives notice; and, lastly, the attention is attracted to the ornamental finish, where each successive form becomes a new revelation and excites a new interest. The pleasurable emotions aroused by the first glance are heightened by observation and study, and the sense of beauty is fully gratified.

Color.—Another fundamental element of beauty is color. The light by means of which the eye is enabled to see is principally derived from the sun; and we assume that there is such a substantial accord between the eye and the sun's rays that the ordinary light of day gives the greatest satisfaction, while light of an essentially different character would cause uneasiness. The direct rays of the sun, however, are usually subdued, and so distributed over objects that they come to the eye in differing degrees of intensity; and this variety is not only restful to the eye, but it is the only means by which we distinguish form through vision. Were it possible for all the light which enters the eye to be of uniform intensity, then form in objects would vanish, and all beauty would disappear.

*Standard of Beauty in Color.*—The analysis of the sun's ray gives the prismatic colors; and we think it safe to assume that the proportion of color most pleasing to the eye, and therefore the most beautiful, is that of the solar spectrum, and that, when separated, the colors that most largely enter into the composition of the sun's ray will be the ones upon which the eye will dwell longest without requiring a change.

For example, of the primary colors, blue constitutes nearly or quite one-half of the ray of light, and yellow something more than one-fourth. The combination of blue and yellow constitutes green. Experience shows that the eye will rest longer upon blue without uneasiness than upon either of the other primary colors, and upon green longer than upon any of the other secondary colors. In the blue of the sky and the green of the earth, we have the largest masses of color which Nature affords, and upon these the eye rests with a greater satisfaction than upon anything else, a fact confirming the idea of beauty of proportion existing in the sun's ray, and showing the conformity of internal conditions to objective realities.

*Complementary Colors.*—As the sun's ray furnishes just the proportion of color that the eye demands, it follows that the eye, sooner or later, will tire of observing any single color; and, when it is so tired, rest comes from the observation of complementary colors. The sun's ray being made up of the three primary colors, blue, yellow, and red, each one is complementary to the other two, either separately or in combination. The eye is pleased with green for a longer time than with any other of the bright colors; but, tiring at last, it demands the complementary color, red. In the same manner, the eye, tiring of violet, demands yellow, and, tiring of orange, demands blue. When the eye has become tired of a single color, as blue, if it be directed to another color partially composed of blue, as green, the blue element is not seen, and the green appears yellow.

When complementary colors are brought into proximity, the effect is to intensify both, and produce one kind of pleasing combination, as is seen in the violet and yellow of pansies, and in the appearance of bright red flowers, in contrast with the green of the grass. When two colors non-complementary, both of which contain a common element, as blue and green, are brought together, the effect is to modify or subdue the intensity of both, and to produce another kind of pleasing combination. We see this kind of effect in the natural mingling of flowers and colored lichens in rocky places, and in the mellowness of an extended landscape, where the intensity of the green is subdued by the faint and transparent blue of the atmosphere.

*Variety in Color.*—In the hues produced by uniting two primary colors in different proportions, in the tints and shades of the different hues, and in the more complex combinations of the several primary colors, we have variety in color limited only by the power of the eye to discriminate in regard to differences. With primitive people the brighter colors alone appear to be attractive; but, as æsthetic culture advances, greater beauty is seen in the delicate tints and shades of subdued and neutral colors.

*Attention to Color.*—As color so much enters into ideas of beauty, and is so largely employed in dress, in the furnishing of houses, and in the industrial arts, it should receive particular attention in school, both upon its theoretical and practical side. The late discoveries in regard to the nature of light have given to this subject a scientific character, and made it possible for teachers to approach it by scientific methods, and thus combine æsthetic and scientific culture.

SOUND. — Besides the beauty which is found in objects of sight, certain sounds and combinations of sounds produce analogous emotions of pleasure, and are called beautiful, and of this form of beauty the æsthetic sense takes cognizance. The sounds to which the term beautiful can be applied are found only in human speech and in music; the latter term including the natural song of birds, as well as the music of the voice in singing, and the music of instruments.

*Origin of Musical Perception.*—In music, as in form, two theories are advanced as to the standard of beauty, the one making it an intuitive perception of that which approximates to spiritual perfection, and the other deriving it from the complex experiences of the human race. Herbert Spencer, in sustaining the latter view, sums up his argument as follows: "We have seen that there is a physiological relation common to men and all animals, between feeling and muscular action; that, as vocal sounds are produced by muscular action, there is a consequent physiological relation between feeling and vocal sounds; that all the modifications of voice, expressive of feeling, are the direct results of this physiological relation; that music, adopting all these modifications, intensifies them more and more, as it ascends to its higher forms and becomes music in virtue of thus intensifying them; that from the ancient epic poet, chanting his verses, down to the modern musical composer, men of unusually strong feelings, prone to express them in extreme forms, have been naturally the agents of these intensifications; and that there has little by little arisen a wide divergence between this idealized language of emotion and its natural language; to which direct evidence we have added the indirect—that on no other tenable hypothesis can either the expressiveness or the genesis of music be explained."

Whether we adopt the one or the other of these theories in regard to the nature and origin of music, we are all agreed that the musical faculty can be cultivated; that musical culture is a part of a complete education, giving to the individual additional power and means of enjoyment, and that this culture is a legitimate part of school work.

*Æsthetic and Moral Value of Music.*—The importance of musical culture to full development and the exact place it should occupy are so well stated by Mr. Spencer that we again quote: "The tendency of civilization is more and more to repress the antagonistic elements of our characters, and to develop the social ones; to curb our purely selfish desires and exercise our unselfish ones; to replace private gratification by gratification resulting from or involving the happiness of others. And while, by this adaptation to the social state, the sympathetic side of our nature is being unfolded, there is simultaneously growing up a language of sympathetic intercourse—a language through which we communicate to others the happiness we feel, and are made to share in their happiness."

*Music in Schools.*—The controversies that have arisen concerning the introduction of music into schools have furnished incontrovertible arguments in its favor; and experience has more than justified the logic, so that we are safe in assuming that music should constitute a part of every regular course of instruction in school. Singing should be practised daily in every department for the immediate pleasure it gives, for the æsthetic culture which it affords, and for its beneficial results in school discipline. In the higher departments the art of music should be supplemented by its science, the attention being mainly given to singing, as being of much greater importance than any form of instrumental music.

*Character of School Music.*—As the function of music is to express emotion, which, reacting upon character, tends to stimulate emotion, and progressively give it more fit expression, the character of the music introduced into our schools becomes a matter of prime concern. Music, like literature, has its low and sensational forms which tend to degrade both taste and feeling. Dime novels have their counterpart in musical composition. This low kind of music includes the purely meaningless; the sentimental, which ends in mere sentiment, but never excites to generosity or action; the mocking, which parodies and vulgarizes that which is lofty and pure; the ignoble, which clothes puerility in the garb of piety; and the satanic, which appeals directly to the lower and baser passions. All this kind of music should be shunned, and that alone chosen which has a tendency to arouse the higher nature, to repress selfishness, and to restrain the lower propensities. Music of this kind, while directly aiding in æsthetic development, becomes an important element in moral culture.

*Tones in Speech.*—Speech has the double function of expressing thought and emotion, the former by words and their combinations, and the latter principally by the quality and variations of tone. In moral culture, the end is to subordinate the passions, the appetites, and the selfish propensities; to develop sympathy and the desire for the good of others; and to place all the activities under the control of reason. Æsthetic culture demands that the expression of these ruder emotions shall be correspondingly subordinated, and that the expression of the gentler emotions be cultivated until they become fixed habits.

*Unpleasant Tones.*—Loud tones in common conversation express a domineering spirit, coarse emotion, or a selfish determination to be heard in any event; shrill tones denote ill-temper; sneering tones indicate a disposition to hurt; and harsh dissonant tones show a want of thought or a lack of human sympathy. Should these tones be used simply from imitation, they would have the effect to arouse the emotions of which they are the natural expression in the person using them and in others. In consequence, the teacher cannot be too careful in regard to his own manner of speech, nor too attentive to that of his pupils. By proper training in regard to speech, the æsthetic sense is cultivated, and this, reacting, produces greater beauty of speech; and, in the end, the tones used by both teacher and pupil will be those which express kindliness and tender emotion, and none other.

GENERAL SUMMARY.—From the foregoing analysis, we get an idea of the nature of beauty and of the universality of its elements, and we see how æsthetic culture reaches out toward science upon the one side, and toward morals upon the other. We also see how erroneous is the notion which so extensively prevails that the æsthetic sense is confined to an appreciation or production of pictures or other works which come under the general designation of the fine arts. It is true that the fine arts constitute the proper field for æsthetic activity; but the limits of these arts must be extended so as to embrace all possible arrangements of objects and materials that give to the mind the satisfaction which is afforded by beauty. The processes to secure this end are two—a mental conception of what constitutes beauty, and a practical ability to arrange available materials in such a manner as to approximately satisfy this conception. These processes may be separated in thought, but scarcely in practice, each step in the one being accompanied by a corresponding step in the other. An endeavor to do, results in a better knowledge of what should be done, and increased knowledge gives greater power to do.

*Æsthetic Teaching.*—The processes of teaching in our schools leading to æsthetic culture need be both direct and indirect—direct in developing ideas in regard to beauty, and in giving to them practical expression, and indirect, in so arranging all matters pertaining to the school that the same ideas may be insensibly imbibed.

*The Schoolroom.* — In the construction of the

schoolroom, due regard should be paid to proportion, unity, and harmony, so that the room itself may be a satisfaction rather than an offense to the æsthetic sense. The shape of the room, the finish of the walls, and the character of the furniture are all matters of importance. A room one-fourth longer than wide, with windows grouped to admit broad lights, finished with the natural grain of wood instead of paint, and with walls delicately tinted, costs but little more in the outset than the caricatures of buildings which are so often erected for schoolhouses. It will be seen also that the arrangement for the admission of light and the apparatus for heating and ventilation have their æsthetic as well as sanitary bearing.

The business of building belongs to the school directors, and the teacher's office in this connection is only advisory. In the care of the room, however, where the teacher has control, equal regard should be paid to æsthetic effects. The room must always be kept scrupulously clean. There is no ugliness or deformity so fatal to æsthetic culture as filth. The furniture should be preserved unmarred, and every piece of apparatus should have its appropriate place and be kept there when not in use.

The untinted and often dingy walls of the ordinary schoolroom may be so decorated in some cheap way, that ugliness will be converted into beauty. A few hardy vines may be trained to run over them; or, failing in this, evergreen branches may be used with excellent effect. In summer, bouquets of flowers may be made available, the perfume as well as the beauty producing agreeable impressions.

*School Surroundings.*—In the choice of a site, regard should be had to its beauty as well as to its healthfulness. A fine slope near a grove of trees, an outlook upon a body of water or over a valley, or a sheltered nook among the hills, will furnish beautiful images, which will insensibly take possession of the minds of the pupils. As the influence which the site affords will affect favorably or unfavorably many generations of children, it seems that much more than the usual amount of attention should be given to this matter. In regard to the condition and care of the school-yard, grass and trees are indispensable, and flowers are very desirable. On the negative side, rank weeds should be exterminated, and no foul places should be tolerated.

*Dress.*—Attention to personal appearance is one of the fundamental requirements of æsthetic culture, and this includes dress. Perfect neatness in dress is an indispensable requisite demanded alike by health, morality, and beauty. In addition, the latter requires proper attention to form, color, and adaptation to special use. Neither costly material nor fashion necessarily has any connection with the intrinsically beautiful, but there is a demand that the best disposition shall be made of the material at command.

*Habits and Manners.*—Personal habits and manners have a direct bearing upon this subject. The sharp, abrupt words of command, so frequently used by teachers, not only tend to excite antagonism, but they become sources of unamiable expression on the part of pupils, leading directly to boorishness of behavior. Courtesy upon the part of both teacher and pupils is demanded alike by æsthetics and morality. Obedience is much more quickly and willingly yielded to a pleasant request than to a stern command; and, when yielded in the one case, it is a spontaneous and cheerful act, and in the other it is the sullen compliance, offspring of fear. Culture in this direction also demands that attention should be given to cleaning shoes upon entering the room, to the manner of walking in the room, and to proper position in study and recitation.

In the detail of work performed by the pupil, there is an opportunity for direct æsthetic culture. Books should be kept neat and in their places. The desks should be without blot or mar. The writing on paper and slates should always be neatly done. All blackboard work should be neatly arranged, and in such order that the successive steps can be easily followed. While pupils are sometimes impatient of criticism of slovenly work, they are always pleased when the process of instruction has resulted in their ability to do neat work.

DRAWING.—While the manner of performing work in all the branches may be made to contribute to æsthetic culture, the special work to that end is drawing, and for this reason drawing should be made a part of the daily work in every grade of school. Drawing is not, as is quite generally supposed, a study merely for artists, but it is of the highest use to all, physically in training the muscles of the hand, intellectually in inciting to correct observation, and æsthetically in the appreciation and production of beauty in form. It is also the handmaid of other branches, and no study in school can be pursued in which drawing in some form may not be made an important aid. It is so important in its bearing upon æsthetic culture, as well as in its other relations, that a somewhat detailed statement of its successive steps seems to be demanded.

*Muscular Drill.*—Experience shows that when drawing is introduced into schools, the lessons alternating with penmanship, the latter is more quickly learned than though the whole time had been spent upon it alone. The training derived from drawing gives to the muscles of the hand flexibility and accuracy of movement, of the greatest value in all departments of industry where delicacy of touch is demanded. The exercises that give this training comprise both free-hand drawing and the invention of new designs from given elements.

*Cultivating Observation.*—The end next to be attained in drawing is the habit of correct observation. Success in this is of great importance in the study of the physical sciences, as the study gives the matter for drawing, and the drawing leads to nicer observation in the science. This power to represent real objects is also of great value in almost every kind of mechanical pursuit, and it lies at the very foundation of all successful art.

*Perspective and Shading.*—Real objects must be drawn as they appear, and the efforts to accomplish this develop the facts from which the laws of perspective are derived. These laws are then applied to the representation of objects, either single or in combination, greatly facilitating the operation. In a similar way the manner of representing light and shade is practised as an art, and the laws are developed and applied in practice.

*Use of Colors.*—The fondness of children for color may be turned to good account in this direction. The regular color-lessons in the primary grades are mainly for the purpose of giving the pupils the names and qualities of the primary colors, and their more simple combinations. In the more advanced grades, the pupils may be led to gradually substitute color for the black lines in shading, and by easy stages to the use of color in painting. By such practical exercises, ideas of beauty in color may be developed and practically applied.

*Industrial Art.*—In the higher grades the principles of drawing should be turned in the direction of the industries. As in the advanced courses of every branch of science, the methods change from induction to deduction, from discovery to application. The laws which have been inferred from practice and verified, and the skill obtained in the lower grades, need now be applied to specific fields of industry, and the æsthetic sense employed in engrafting the beautiful upon the useful, or rather in so constructing the useful that it becomes the beautiful. At this point, the courses of instruction, which before have been general, may now diverge, and conform to individual tastes or to prospective vocations.

*Art Proper.*—The greatest advantage to be derived from drawing in school is the aid which it gives to the development of the æsthetic sense in all. A feeling of respect and admiration is engendered for all beautiful things, and with it a corresponding feeling of disgust at the essentially ugly and vulgar. The æsthetic sense lends its sanction to morality by its recognition of the "beauty of holiness." It sees harmony of relation in human conduct when it conforms to the Golden Rule, and selfishness, vice, and crime are as repulsive to good taste as to good morals. But these lessons have another value. They afford the best means for the discovery of those who have a peculiar aptitude for artistic work, and they furnish the best opportunity for the cultivation of the artistic faculty. When drawing in our schools becomes general, we may expect not only a more universal appreciation of beauty in Nature and art, but a large accession to the ranks of true artists.

*National Art.*—As the æsthetic sense becomes developed, and æsthetic ideas are disseminated, the question of the formation of a distinctive school of American art is frequently discussed, and speculations are indulged in as to what will be its character. We believe that in the future such a school will appear, but only its more general features can now be outlined. It will evidently not be a copy of the art of antiquity, nor of any of the schools of modern Europe, for the life out of which these schools grew was provincial compared with the cosmopolitan character of American society. It cannot be a mere school of foreign growth grafted upon American life. It must be an outgrowth of our own conditions and necessities. If it is to have more than a mere ephemeral existence, its roots must be deeply and firmly set in Nature, and it must find its first expression in personal appearance and manners, and in the best possible ordering of homes. The care and arrangement of the common material necessary for daily comfort must be made a matter of consideration, so that children may imbibe ideas of beauty from the first moment of conscious existence. This implies artistic setting for our lives, of which pictures, statuary, and noble architecture are only elements. National art will come from individual culture, as national morality comes from individual character.

The common schools furnish the opportunity for the dissemination of æsthetic ideas, and the teachers of the country are the custodians of the future of national art, as well as of national intelligence. If true to their trusts they will strive as earnestly for æsthetic as for intellectual culture, both as an element of personal character and as a means of instruction. The pupils under their care will be trained to the production of beautiful forms, and to the appreciation of the beautiful in Nature and art. The taste acquired in school will influence all the homes of the land; and from these homes, transfigured by the spirit of beauty, an American art will arise, as varied, as comprehensive, and as original as the intelligence and character of the American people.

# CHAPTER XIII.

## *MORAL CULTURE.*

MORAL AIMS.—To attain a high moral character, a modern writer says: "We must consider the demands of the present time; become enlightened concerning our practical duties; learn to make the best of all human conditions; seek, amid all obstructions, confusions, and corruptions, the way of a true life; bear testimony against all iniquity, and in favor of all righteousness; and dedicate our lives to the reasonable service of God and man, as children of the Highest, and as brothers of the lowest."

This exalted aim may be considered the fruitage of education and of life, and it becomes a question of great moment as to how far it may be attained through the instrumentality of the schools.

*Neglect of Moral Instruction.*—It has been charged, with some show of reason, that in our modern system of schools intelligence is more directly sought than morality, that the discriminative and executive powers are cultivated to the neglect of the regulative. Making due allowance for exaggeration and prejudice, there remains enough of truth in this charge to demand that its causes should be investigated and a remedy devised.

*Reasons for the Neglect.*—The most obvious reasons for the neglect of moral instruction in schools are that the sciences and the branches that treat of purely intellectual matters are better known and systematized than those that treat of morals, and hence are more easily taught; and that little effort has been made to examine morals upon the scientific side, and to formulate its principles in accordance with the general ideas of human development.

Another reason bearing upon the same subject has been the prevalence of two, crude philosophic notions, antagonistic to each other, but equally opposed to sound moral training. The first of these claims that moral conduct is incident to intellectual culture, and hence that the ordinary exercises of the schools are sufficient for moral purposes; the second, that morality belongs exclusively to theology, and hence has no place in the secular scheme of State education, or, indeed, in any but strictly sectarian schools.

At the present time, however, the fact that morality does not receive proper attention is regarded by the most thoughtful teachers and friends of education as a grave if not fatal defect in any system of education; and the reasons for such neglect in the past are not considered so formidable or fundamental as necessarily to apply to the schools of the future. The old philosophic notions are seriously called in question, and there is an evident desire for a new departure. The first steps looking toward reform require an examination of fundamental principles.

WHAT IS MORALITY?—The field of morality is humanity, and it includes all the possible relations which exist between human beings. A man has duties religious toward his Maker; duties personal to himself; duties moral toward his neighbor; and duties humane toward the lower animals. All these duties are imperative, but the domain of each may be considered separately. It is only when relations are established between man and man that morality arises or is possible.

It is a question of relations between creatures of the same order. The instinctive feeling we call sympathy acts only in so far as we attribute to others a likeness to ourselves. It is instinctive inasmuch as it is instant in action, so soon as the intellect has supplied the information necessary to establish the relation of likeness between us and another creature. The hard, unsympathetic nature is, in the main, the result of narrow experience and limited knowledge. The imagination also has its part to play in vividly representing the situation; but imagination is dependent for its material upon the intellect and upon the feelings for its stimulus. Hence the value of fairy tales, of fables, of story-telling, of biographies, and of literature generally, in the strict sense of the word, as a powerful agent in moral culture through its nurture of the imagination.

When the time has come in the development of the pupil's mind that he naturally demands a scientific analysis of the subject of duty, and of its sanctions, it can readily be shown that duties to self are imperative, if duties to others are acknowledged, for only by a strict observance of duties regarding self can we attain the best conditions for the performance of our duty to others. So of our duties to animals, their likeness to human beings is a question of degree. They are sensitive to pain and pleasure, and to this extent our sympathies go out to them and bind us to treat them humanely.

Our morality is also much influenced by our knowledge of science. Without a scientific comprehension of our relations to others we have no guide in emergencies and in new situations.

In a loose and vague way, morality is made to define all of human duty, and in discussing the subject much confusion arises from the different definitions which different parties give to it. While one is urging the importance of duty toward God, the other is thinking about duty toward men, the trouble arising from confounding religious and moral duties. We are thus careful to give the exact limits to the subject, as we regard it, so that vexed questions not germane to it may be excluded, and so that the attention may be confined to the precise subject under consideration. Should an objection be made that our definition is not sufficiently comprehensive, we reply that we will in this chapter confine our discussion to that branch of morals which considers human relations.

Morals thus defined, while restricted to that which is human, in its applications includes the whole field of social activities; and upon its principles only can any rational system of civil government or political economy be established.

*Basis of Morals.*—Every human being has needs inherent in his being, and directly depending upon the fact of his existence. These needs create demands that must be satisfied, or his existence soon terminates. For example, he needs to eat, to breathe, and to preserve a given temperature; and food, air, and warmth must be at his command, or life, which is his by the divine right of being, ceases.

*Extent of Needs.*—These needs are coextensive with the whole nature of man, physical, mental, and moral. He needs physical agencies, that his body may grow, attain strength, and be kept in health; he needs materials of study and guidance, that his mind may be nurtured; and he needs good example, social intercourse, and instruction in regard to conduct, that his moral sensibilities may be made acute and excited to action.

*Equality of Needs.*—Differences in environment, in civilization, in national characteristics, and in individual character, would seem to indicate a difference in needs. Indeed, many needs are brought into existence only by the development of the individual or the race. But the general needs of all are the same, and the special needs are the same under the same conditions. Potentially, then, the needs of one human being are exactly equal to those of any other human being.

*Basis of Rights.*—The demands flowing from these needs give rise to individual rights; and to every need there is a corresponding right. We have physical needs, and a right to all the physical agencies which the needs demand; mental and moral needs, and a right to all the mental and moral agencies which these needs demand. The right of every human being to these agencies inheres in his very constitution, and is a part of his being; and to deprive him of these rights would be to rob him of a portion of his life.

*Basis of Duty.*—But man is a social being, and, as a member of community, his existence is bound up with other existences. Relations are established which, while they restrict individual freedom on one side, vastly multiply individual power and possibility on the other. His activities are supplemented by the activities of others. From his position as a member of society he receives help from others, and there devolves upon him an obligation to help others in turn. High-minded, sensitive persons are scrupulous in paying debts due to individuals, but few in all the world's records have realized their debt to society, in the past as well as in the present, and have honestly labored through life, sensible of the fact that at best they were paying the merest fraction of their obligations. The world's heroes and martyrs have, whether consciously or not, felt this sense of obligation, and the self-forgetful in all times have worked in the same spirit, though the majority of these have lived and died in obscurity. This obligation, which we call moral duty, is simply another name for his debt to society, and is the exact reciprocal of his individual rights, and there can be no possible right without a corresponding duty.

*Examples.*—We all have a need of air, and, in consequence, a right to air. But, as air is supplied to us naturally in abundance, the only duty of others in regard to our supply is that they shall not interfere with it, either restricting its quantity or vitiating its quality. The duty in this case is negative.

We all have a need of food, and consequently a right to food. This need is imperative at all times, and the right is just as inherent when we are infants or disabled as when we are able to procure our own food. It follows that somebody must administer to our necessities while we are helpless; and it equally follows that we should minister to others' necessities under like circumstances. The duty of others to supply us with food, when able to do so ourselves, does not inhere, for the performance of such an act would be a sacrifice of their rights, and a consequent diminution of their ability to perform their real duty. This duty to serve others is positive.

*Negative and Positive Duties.*—Moral duties are thus seen to be twofold—negative, leading to a respect for the rights of others, and positive, demanding service. Respect for rights implies that our every act, in which others are interested, or which in any way affects others, shall be based upon the principle that every human being has potentially the same rights as ourselves; while service demands that we shall actively supply needs when by so doing we shall promote human welfare.

The demands of negative duty are imperative, that we shall refrain from injuring the quality or diminishing the quantity of our neighbor's food; from injuring his person; from converting his property to our own use; from restricting his liberty to think and to form opinions for himself; from imputing to him unworthy motives in differences of opinion; and from diminishing his opportunities to earn his own living by misinterpreting his acts and misrepresenting his motives.

The demands of positive duty are equally imperative. They require of us tender nurture for every child, wise and adequate provision for the sick and unfortunate, and affectionate care for the aged who have finished life's work. Duty, as thus defined, is the embodiment of that ethical law known as the "Golden Rule," and our constant endeavor should be to make this rule a practical reality.

*Standard of Moral Duty.*—In every act that comes within the domain of morals there are two parties, the actor and the receiver of the action. The actor may perform his duty or he may neglect it. If he acts in such a manner as he thinks will conduce to human welfare, then the act from his point of view is *right*. If his motive is malicious, then the act from his point of view is *wrong*. He may through ignorance do serious injury by the very act which he intended as a benefit, and which from his point of view was *right*. From the point of view of the receives the action is *good* if it promotes welfare, *bad* if harm is the result.

In every moral act there is then a double judgment, the one considering its results upon the person directly affected or upon the world at large, and the other dealing with the motive of the actor, and, in case of bad results, passing judgment upon his innocence or guilt. The highest morality, or the interests of society as a whole, demands that not only should an action be *right*, springing from good motives, but that it should also be *good*, producing beneficent results.

The fact is constantly forced upon us that, with the best of intentions, persons are constantly performing acts injurious to those affected by them, and we are led to inquire into the cause of the evil results, and to ascertain what element besides good motive should enter into moral action.

*Concrete Examples.*—A mother desires the welfare

of her child, and is unwearied in her care and devotion. By continual self-sacrifice, she gratifies its every desire and caprice, until she develops in it selfishness to such a degree as to entirely vitiate its character.

A father, in his desire to repress all evil tendencies in his child, threatens and cajoles by turns, is terribly severe or forgetful of his promises, and the child grows up, very acute as to parental moods, but with little control of temper and with little regard to truth.

A teacher, intent upon securing good conduct and intellectual progress upon the part of his pupils, visits each offense of omission or commission with severe penalties, thus stifling affection and developing in them ideas of brutality and revenge.

A physician desires to relieve the pain of his patient, and effect a speedy cure; yet, by a mistake in the nature of the case, or in the medicine used, he administers a poison which aggravates the disease or terminates the life.

The captain of a ship, in stress of weather, to prevent his vessel from foundering, battens down the hatchways, and, when the storm has passed, finds his passengers smothered, his measures to preserve their lives having caused their death.

A clergyman, impressed by the tremendous consequences of an impenitent life, visits a sick man, and by his endeavors to save, produces a nervous exhaustion which results in death.

*Factors of Morality.*—In all these cases the motives have been good while the results have been evil; and we see that by a wiser judgment, coming from a higher intelligence, the evils might have been avoided. The factors of morality are thus seen to be *good motive* and *intelligence*, the highest morality demanding both in the highest degree.

Good motive is a fixed factor. It is the disposition to do right, or to perform the acts demanded by duty, and is of the highest importance in determining conduct. It may exist in individuals mixed more or less with selfish desires and propensities, but in essential character it is always the same.

Intelligence, on the contrary, differs with the individual, the age, and the race. With advancing civilization, ideas of what conduces to human welfare change, and the morality of one age is considered very imperfect in the next. Absolute morality must be associated with infinite wisdom.

*Individual Morality.*—The demands of morality upon every individual are that he should perform every duty that devolves upon him, both negative and positive; that, in every act in which others are concerned, he should consider their welfare equally with his own; that in every case his acts should conform to his highest intelligence, and that he should neglect no opportunity to become more intelligent.

MORAL INSTRUCTION IN SCHOOLS.—The foregoing analysis shows the nature of the problem which we are to solve in education, and serves as a guide in regard to the methods to be pursued in making moral instruction a part of the school course. Without discussing the question whether the disposition to do right comes from the operation of a single faculty of the mind, or is the resultant of the combined action of several faculties, we assume this position as incontrovertible, that moral power, like physical and intellectual power, is developed by exercise, and can be greatly increased by systematic training.

*Force of Example.*—"As is the teacher so is the school," is an old adage. Children are imitative beings, and, consciously or unconsciously, they copy the manners of those with whom they are associated. If the teacher is domineering, discourteous, and unjust, through the operation of this imitative propensity the pupils will show the same traits; and, unless corrected by some strong counteracting influence, they will become life-habits. On the contrary, if the teacher is reasonable, kind, just, and courteous, the same imitative propensity will lead the pupils to copy these traits, and to form corresponding habits.

The manners and habits of the teacher are thus seen to be of fundamental importance in moral training. Trustees and directors of schools cannot be too careful in the selection of teachers; and teachers, knowing that example is one of the most powerful of all the agencies operating upon childhood, should carefully scrutinize their own conduct, and see that every act not only springs from the right motive, but that it be performed in such a manner as to carry the conviction of its motive to the minds of the pupils.

*Manners.*—In this connection, it may be observed that manners are intimately associated with morals; that the expression of the act, as well as the act itself, has its moral bearings. Kindliness will generate its like, even if uncouthly expressed; but it will make a much more favorable and lasting impression if it is shown in such an easy and appropriate way that no part of the attention is turned from the act itself to the manner in which the act is performed. There should be no occasion that the admiration for moral goodness should be accompanied by excuses for coarse language and improprieties of attitude and gesture.

*Example of Ill-Manners.*—Dr. Samuel Johnson was noted for his kindliness and for his sympathies with imperfect and suffering humanity. His writings are full of the most elevated sentiments, and in all his works there is nothing ignoble. So tender was his conscience that, in middle life and at the height of his renown, he made a pilgrimage to his native town of Uttoxeter, and stood all day, with head uncovered, in the open market place, to atone for refusing a request of his father in boyhood. All admired the greatness of his genius and the goodness of his heart; yet in his social intercourse he was loud, overbearing, and often insolent, and at the table his manner of eating was so gross as to excite universal disgust. To his intimate associates the coarseness of his manners in a great measure nullified the pleasure which the brilliancy of his conversation created, and the influence which his wisdom merited.

*Limit of Responsibility.*—As the influence of home and of general society is much greater than that of the school, the teacher can be held responsible for results only so far as his own influence extends. If that influence, both directly and indirectly, has always been in favor of the highest moral excellence, no blame can attach to him if other and adverse influences, over which he has no control, have proved stronger than his own.

*Moral Sensibility.*—The moral sensibilities of pupils should be awakened and made acute. To this end, in all social intercourse they should be taught to respect the rights of others to freedom of opinion, as well as to the control of their own persons and property. They should be made to see that the hoyden game, so common, where one pupil takes hold of another without his consent, is a violation of personal rights. The care of older pupils for the young, and of the strong for the weak, should be encouraged, as developing in them ideas antagonistic to mere selfish gratification. Bullying and outrage on the part of the strong should be repressed, gently but firmly, and an endeavor should be made to eradicate all tendencies in this direction. All selfishness should be made odious to the one exhibiting it, by contrasting the act with one of an opposite character, and all unselfish acts should receive from the teacher a quiet recognition that the pupil can well understand. By continual vigilance, stimulating right conduct and repressing wrong, a public sentiment will be developed in the school in the direction of justice and kindliness, and the discipline of the school will go on by the action of social forces without the direct interference of the teacher. The good conduct which this public sentiment demands will gradually become a settled habit, lasting through life.

INCIDENTAL MORAL LESSONS.—Pestalozzi's first experience as a teacher was at Stanz, where he had the entire care of a hundred destitute children living in an old convent. The accommodations were poor and the food coarse and scanty. While there a fire took place in the neighboring village of Altdorf, by which a large number of people were rendered homeless. The sudden calamity called for immediate relief. Pestalozzi gave an account of the fire to the pupils, and described the destitution which had followed. He told them how many little children like themselves were suffering from cold and hunger. When their sympathies were excited, he asked, "Can we do anything to relieve this suffering?" Several of the pupils at once proposed that the children be invited to Stanz as members of their own little community. "But," said Pestalozzi, "if they come they must share your accommodations and food, and, in consequence, your own comforts will be less, and probably many times you will not have food enough to satisfy your hunger."

The pupils, however, insisted, and the invitation was given and accepted. Not a single murmur was ever heard in consequence of the privations which this act entailed. On the contrary, the guests were eagerly welcomed, and treated with special marks of respect and honor. This lesson in practical benevolence sank deep into their hearts, enriching and ennobling their lives for all time; and the event goes into history and literature as a monument to the wisdom of the teacher and the acute moral sensibility of the school, and as an incentive to higher endeavor on the part of all teachers.

Incidents arise in every school which the skillful teacher may turn to good advantage in inculcating a moral lesson. A child has lost his dinner; who will share theirs with him? Who will contribute to the cleanliness, the comfort, and the adornment of the schoolhouse? Who will refrain from injuring or soiling the schoolhouse in any way? Not a day or an hour passes without affording an opportunity for repressing actions that will give pain to others, or for the performance of acts that will give pleasure to others. The attendance at school of a deformed child, or one so differing from the others as to attract attention, may be made the occasion for deep and lasting moral impressions, and the school-life of the unfortunate may be made so pleasant by the affectionate attitude of his schoolmates as to compensate, to a large extent, for the privations which his unfortunate condition entails. A case of destitution in the neighborhood may occasion the voluntary offer of service which requires sacrifice of pleasure, time, and comfort; and when this is accomplished a great step is gained in the triumph of duty over selfishness.

> "The Holy Supper is kept indeed,
> In whatso we share with another's need;
> Not that which we give but what we share,
> For the gift without the giver is bare!"

Care must be taken by the teacher, in all such cases, that the good deed has a distinct recognition; and care must also be taken that the feeling excited, and the consequent benevolent action, shall be directed to cases of real distress; for misapplied benevolence and sacrifice always lead to evil results.

*Negative Results.*—The moral sensibilities of pupils may be blunted or destroyed by unwise action on the part of teachers. An unmerited punishment may inflict an injury for life. Dr. Carpenter says: "Nothing tends so much to prevent the healthful development of the moral sense as the infliction of punishment which the child feels to be unjust; and nothing retards the acquirement of the power of directing the intellectual processes so much as the emotional disturbance which the feeling of injustice provokes." A pupil accustomed to see others treated brutally becomes hardened, and loses that acute sympathy with suffering which is the impelling force to service when such duty is demanded. In cases where brutality is frequent, children may learn even to take delight in suffering, thus nullifying moral culture, reversing the moral law, and developing a demoniac rather than a moral character. Denunciations, sarcastic remarks calculated to wound the sensibilities, scoldings, uncharitableness, exhibitions of favoritism, unnecessary rules and commands, and all forms of caprice upon the part of the teacher, have a tendency to produce these negative moral results in the minds of the pupils. By a careless discipline and a slip-shod administration of justice in school, children grow up with little idea of self-control, with their regulative faculties entirely undeveloped, and they often pass through life intent upon the gratification of personal desires, but entirely insensible to the welfare of others.

*Labor and Service.*—To arouse moral sensibility is one thing, to direct it in the channels of proper expenditure is quite another. The feeling of sympathy which has been developed may be wasted in mere sentiment, as when a tale of suffering causes tears, and tears only; or it may be expended upon unworthy objects as when alms are given to professional beggars, directly encouraging idleness and vice; or it may be expended in cases where it relieves distress or encourages worthy and noble effort. In the latter case only does the act make its proper impression, and the feeling become an element of character. It is incumbent on the teacher, then, not only to arouse sensibilities but to direct them to legitimate ends, to encourage the conversion of sympathetic feeling into acts of service. The importance of securing the manifestation of kindly intentions in muscular action can scarcely be overestimated.

One of the first lessons in unselfishness which a child learns is when it performs an act of real service for its parents, and the glow of pleasure which results from a knowledge that it is a service, and is recognized as such, leads to a repetition of similar acts. The teacher may make use of this principle of action, and stimulate the moral powers, by asking little acts of service; though the requests of this character should not be too frequent, nor should they convey the idea that they are made through the indolence of the teacher.

*Caution.*—Every emotion has its natural and proper channel of expenditure. Pity for suffering finds its proper expenditure in acts of relief. To witness distress that we cannot in any way alleviate is to excite sensibilities which cannot be properly expended, and the effect is an intellectual and moral derangement. The aroused emotion may react, producing physical and mental prostration, or it may be expended in channels quite different from the legitimate one. For example, the sight of squalor, sordidness, and misery, which cannot be relieved, may excite an emotion of pity, which may assume the form of frenzy, and expend itself in rage; or the emotion may expend itself in sensual indulgence, and the person seek relief in the forgetfulness of intoxication.

In his endeavors to excite moral action, the teacher should take care to avoid cases of this character, when the emotion excited cannot be expended in legitimate acts of relief. To this end details of stories of horrible destitution and suffering, of fire and shipwreck, of railroad accidents, and of war and pestilence, should be avoided altogether.

*Recognition of Well-Doing.*—In the matter of recognition of well-doing, two extremes are to be avoided. By praise, the pupil loses the glow of satisfaction that comes from an unselfish performance of service which has afforded relief or assistance to others, and there is substituted for it a self-satisfaction, in which the virtue of the act and the praise are mingled; but, by repeating the process, the pleasure derived from the praise becomes more pronounced, until the quality of the act is lost sight of in the desire to secure the praise.

On the other hand, if service is received with entire indifference, the pupil has little guide as to the nature of the acts which he performs, and little encouragement to persevere in well-doing. With an adult, whose judgment has been matured by experience, the matter of recognition may be of little or no importance in the performance of duty; but with children it is one of the most potent forces which urges them to action, and which leads them to discriminate between desirable and undesirable acts.

This recognition may be made by a glance of the eye, a modulation of tone, or a word of approbation, which, adjusted to time and circumstance, will make deep impressions, and become powerful incentives to a repetition of similar acts in the future. In this recognition motives should be considered, and the praise should not be withheld even if the service has not been productive of good. In case of evil results, the faults of judgment may be pointed out, with no censure either expressed or implied. In the bestowal of approbation a strict impartiality should be observed toward all. The sensibilities of children are often wounded, and the moral tone of the whole school lowered, by praise and censure bestowed through caprice or favoritism.

SCHOOL GOVERNMENT.—All the agencies used to secure good order and good conduct in school should be considered only as means for moral instruction and training. The objective point in all school government is to so develop the regulative powers of each pupil that unruly desires and passions are kept within their legitimate sphere; that the lower propensities are brought under the control of the higher sentiments; and that good conduct be the result of a growth from within, rather than of an enforcement from without. The end is entirely a moral one, and all considerations outside of the strict letter of moral relations should be discarded as obstructive to this end and as demoralizing to the school.

*Obstructive Considerations.*—In times past there has been great effort wasted in the supposed necessity of "sustaining the dignity of the teacher," of "vindicating the majesty of the law," and of "maintaining order for order's sake." All these considerations disappear when we see the character of the relations which exist between teacher and pupil, and fully understand that all policies in regard to government are to be settled solely upon moral grounds. The question which the teacher should ask, when he performs an act toward an individual pupil, or devises a measure that affects the school, is the same that morality demands should be asked upon all occasions when an act is contemplated in which others are interested: "Will this act conduce to the welfare of those affected by it, or to general welfare?" If this question is answered in the affirmative, then the act is right, and the result will be beneficial, provided the relations in all particulars have been fully comprehended. If the question is answered in the negative, then the act is wrong, and no considerations of dignity, law, or order can make it right, or justify the purpose in performing it.

We may say, in passing, that if the attention of the teacher is solely directed to moral aims; if he sincerely wishes to promote the welfare of his pupils, and has the intelligence requisite to understand the moral questions involved in his relations and acts; and if, acting upon these principles, he adjudicates each case as it arises in the spirit of justice and kindness: incidentally he will better maintain his own dignity, vindicate the law, and sustain order, than though he should consciously devote himself to these ends.

*Changes desirable.*—With the moral idea dominant, that inflexibly demands good motive as prompting to every act, and is content with nothing less than good results, and with the old crude ideas of the nature of school government and of the exceptional position of the teacher eliminated, all the old brutal notions in regard to methods of maintaining order, will disappear, and the reign of justice will supersede the reign of force.

The highest morality demands, upon the part of the teacher, a genuine desire to make every act tell for the benefit of his pupils; a knowledge of relations which will enable him to wisely adapt means to ends; a forgetfulness and subordination of self in the work in which he is engaged; and an original force of character which will assert itself, and exact that deference which is due worth and worth only. He must not only feel kindly but he must make kindliness felt; he must not only deal justly but he must enthrone justice, and make it so altogether lovely as to exact a willing homage of all. Courteous in his intercourse with his pupils, he receives courtesy in return; kindly in his feelings, he begets kindness in them; just in his acts, he creates a sentiment of justice as a fundamental motive; patient and gentle in his manners, he elevates and refines; zealous in his work, he kindles enthusiasm and awakens aspiration; devoted to the welfare of others, he checks selfishness and induces a noble emulation for the attainment of the higher life.

*Restraint.*—Evil conduct must not be permitted, but the teacher must discriminate in regard to its character, and give to each case its appropriate treatment. Habits of self-indulgence must be broken up by inciting to active services; selfishness must be counteracted by exciting sympathy for others; and thoughtlessness must be cured by the inflexible demand that atonement must be made for the fault. Teachers must also keep in mind that bad conduct is more frequently the result of moral ignorance, or of physical disability, than of moral depravity, and calls for instruction rather than censure or punishment. Turbulence, violence, and open disregard of common decorum must be restrained by physical means, if others fail, until opportunity is given for the operation of moral influences and the awakening of moral powers.

*Indirect Moral Influences.*—So far the practical course of moral instruction recommended has been mainly *incidental*. The teacher's work has been to surround the pupil with influences and agencies calculated to awaken and strengthen moral impressions, and to check selfish propensities. The pupils insensibly imbibe and assimilate moral sentiments. Their moral nature is developed through *affection* which is awakened by parental and friendly care; through *imitation* when they witness unselfish acts on the part of others; through *sympathy* with suffering and distress whenever cases of the kind come to their notice; and through *experience* which progressively enables them to put themselves in another's place, and so fully realize the results of their own action. Moral actions practised during the school-days crystallize into principles and become fixed habits, which not only regulate moral conduct in specific cases, but which finally so take possession of the whole being as to make moral action instinctive and unconscious.

*Dangers of Neglect.*—A neglect of this indirect moral teaching is fatal to the formation of the highest character. Habits of self-indulgence formed in childhood are seldom or never fully eradicated. While it is comparatively easy to give direction to the unfolding thought and to the unformed habits, the bent once established, and the vital currents flowing in a given way, a change can be effected only by violent effort, and by a great loss of power. In point of time the *incidental* instruction should *precede* formal moral instruction, so that when the time has come for the demonstration of moral principles, an appeal may be made directly to consciousness and experience. As in all other branches of thought and activity, the art precedes the science; and the philosophic principles which the science unfolds are derived directly from the art which has insensibly grown and been put in practice during all the years of conscious existence.

DIRECT MORAL TEACHING.—The moral impressions made by the indirect method of teaching need be supplemented by direct lessons bearing upon the same subject. The emotions arising from sympathy should be supplemented by an intelligence in regard to the circumstances which excited them, and to the methods in which they may be properly expended. Moral art should finally terminate in moral science.

In teaching moral science, the same laws prevail as in teaching other branches. The mind must first be trained to observe, compare, and classify facts, and then to draw inferences from them. These inferences will successively become more abstract, until they arrive at the most comprehensive moral law; and the law derived from observation and experience can be taken as a guide in new experiences.

*Precept and Practice.*—Precept has but little influence upon the mind in awakening the moral nature. Homilies, the repetition of moral rules and sentiments, and what pupils call "preaching," disgust the child and deaden the moral sensibilities. The truth embodied in the precept is usually so general in its character that it weighs little against concrete wants and personal desires. The lesson sought to be enforced, having no root in experience, takes but feeble hold of the mind. Repetition only intensifies the difficulty. The words, which at first had little meaning, soon become a mere formula with no more sense than a succession of inarticulate sounds. Finding that the formula is considered important, independent of his ability to comprehend it, the pupil falls into the habit of regarding the words and of neglecting the thoughts which the words were designed to convey, a habit fatal to both intellectual and moral improvement. Before a moral precept can be fully comprehended, the moral sensibilities must be aroused in the direction of that particular truth, and the sensibility exhibited by some beneficent deed.

*Use of Common Incidents.*—Besides their indirect use, as has already been indicated, common incidents may be made the texts of direct moral lessons. Some event has happened in the neighborhood, or is related in the newspapers, in which the pupils take a lively interest. The matter is taken up and discussed before the class or the school. All the facts bearing upon the case are given. Conflicting statements are harmonized as far as possible. The whole is made into a continuous narrative, so that the relations of the facts may be seen. The pupils assist in the process. Their sympathy is excited, and they are called upon to pass judgment upon the different acts, the probable motive of the actor, and the effect of the acts upon all the parties interested. Such a process accustoms the pupil to look at the moral side of every act; and by it three things are accomplished—moral feeling is aroused, intellectual approval of the right course is secured, and a stimulus is given to practical good conduct.

Sometimes controversies arising in the school itself may be made the occasion for deriving important moral inferences. The school may be organized into a court, in which testimony is taken and decisions rendered. In exercises employing common incidents connected with the school or neighborhood, great care must be taken to avoid subjects which will arouse prejudice and ill-feeling, or will array the school in opposing factions.

*Use of Literature.*—For the purpose of illustrating a moral truth, suitable literary selections may be substituted for the formal reading lessons of the text-book. With study and care selections may be made, that are adapted to any grade of school, and to almost any special occasion. The value of the lessons derived from these exercises is in direct ratio to the interest which may be excited in discussing them. A mere reading of the most exalted sentiments without note or comment is productive of little good. Such a practice is equivalent to the teaching of morals by precept, the ideas failing to reach the mind, and the words producing only reflex nervous action. It is in its power to awaken interest and stimulate the imagination that literature excels as a moral force.

Besides the immediate moral lesson to be derived from these literary selections, a great good arises from making the pupil familiar with the best productions of the world, increasing his intellectual grasp and filling his mind with noble thoughts and images. The taste is also cultivated, and both feeling and judgment unite in giving preference to that which is pure and elevating.

*Abuse of Literature.*—Nothing is more fatal to intellectual and moral growth than a familiarity with low and sensational literary works. The mind is kept in a state of dreamy indolence, or of a feverish unrest. Interest is excited in unreal and impossible events, and abnormal desires are awakened which cannot be gratified in the ordinary process of human affairs. Like the growth of a poisonous fungus, the taste for this literature absorbs the vital forces and destroys all that is noble in life. It awakens no moral sentiment and renders the mind impatient of all kinds of moral restraint. It ends by the complete destruction of the regulative powers, and the surrender of the whole being to impulse and caprice. To prevent this disastrous result, ceaseless effort should be made to cultivate a taste for the works of the great masters of human thought. Experience shows that the mind is best protected from the degradation of gross and impure thoughts by furnishing it ample material for activity in unselfish and impersonal directions.

*Use of Biographies.*—There can be no more effective stimulus to patriotism than the story of the trials, the sufferings, and the sacrifices of our fathers in grappling with Nature, in converting a savage wilderness into fruitful fields, and in engaging in a long and desperate war rather than submit to a policy which deprived them of their just rights. The struggles of heroes for their country's freedom, the more obscure struggles of brave men for individual liberty, the sufferings of martyrs for conscience' sake, and the battles and triumphs of truth everywhere all tend to excite deep emotion, and a warm admiration for an unselfish devotion to truth. These records may be made the inspiration of childhood in very tender years. The picture of Sir Philip Sydney, mortally wounded, motioning away the cup of water from his parched lips, to relieve the thirst of a dying soldier " because his needs are greater than mine," is one of such moral grandeur that it ennobles every heart where the lesson finds lodgment.

*Use of History.* — The study of history may be made to bear directly upon morals. The acts of different personages in history may be carefully examined in connection with surrounding conditions and relations; and from all the circumstances, inference may be drawn in regard to the motives which prompted the acts, and to the effect of the acts upon the community. Comparisons may be instituted between the careers of different persons, both in regard to motive and influence. The effect of personal character, whether selfish or unselfish, upon the nation or the age should receive particular attention. From individuals the examination may be carried to policies as affecting national welfare, and to the general character and career of nations as affecting civilization and the world.

History should also be presented in such a way as to show how national greatness and national decay have largely depended upon moral causes. It should deal with principles and show the inevitable result of conduct, whether of individuals or nations; and, finally, it should show the gradual change of the existing nations of the earth, from a state of barbarism where brute strength was the only element of control, to that of civilization where moral and intellectual forces are progressively becoming more powerful.

*Defects in Historical Study.*—Much of that which passes as historical study is of little value from the moral point of view. The process of committing texts to memory in historical study is directly antagonistic to moral as well as to intellectual progress. So great a stress is laid upon words that the meaning becomes of secondary importance, or is altogether neglected; the mind fails to notice relations in which morals have their root, and there results a mental habit which overlooks relations everywhere. The mere chronologies of nations, the details of battles, and the succession of dynasties, by themselves, are of little importance for mental development or practical guidance, or as a stimulant to good conduct. The study which contents itself with the mere facts of history, without considering their relations and significance, lacks all those elements which give to history its greatest value, and is unworthy of practice in any intelligent system of teaching.

*Moral Science.*—With the more advanced classes the inductions and inferences which have been made from the practice and the objective study of morals may be brought together, and presented in a subjective form, constituting the science of morals. The principles of morals, as given in the beginning of this chapter, should be thoroughly treated and illustrated. The limits of moral action and the field of moral duty should be strictly defined. The sequence and dependence of needs, rights, and duties should be brought to the comprehension of all. The standard of moral judgment should be made so familiar that its use would become an ordinary habit of the mind, and an analysis of the moral character of an act would antedate the act itself, with the certainty and celerity of automatic action. The pupil should be made to see and feel that beneficent motive is a necessary element in every life worth living; that consideration for the welfare of others is just as much a necessity as attention to personal welfare; and that one of the great purposes of life is to adjust our acts so that the desire to promote human welfare shall always be attained to its fullest extent.

This view of human duty makes personal and public welfare identical, and shows that their apparent antagonism has grown out of unintelligent and imperfect knowledge of human relations, and of practices in accordance with such imperfect knowledge. It gives broader and higher ideas of life and its possibilities. Finding the basis of morals in the constitution of the universe, and hence in the constitution of the mind, the moral law has added weight and significance. It is not a rule from without, but is a law of our being, dependent as to its degree of perfection upon the development of the individual, and acting directly and involuntarily in the control of conduct. The education given in the school should, in a large measure, determine the elements that enter into and constitute that something we call character. So long as conduct requires outward restraint the end of education has not been attained, and only when conduct spontaneously conforms to the true, the good, and the beautiful is character established.

As will be readily understood, absolute perfection, entire adaptation to environment is not attainable. The facts of heredity alone, to say nothing of circumstance and condition in life, must always modify results. Viewed in this light, the maxims of the sages, and the Golden Rule itself, have new meaning. They are no longer commands to be obeyed, but conditions to be observed. They no longer come as arbitrary mandates, thwarting our desires and abridging our freedom, but as the expression and revelation of those beneficent relations by means of which alone can we attain fullness of life.

SOCIAL RELATIONS.—The intelligence specially demanded as a guide to moral action is in regard to social relations. We need to know what will conduce to human welfare, before we can decide what course to pursue as far as others are concerned. Knowing that with the purest of motives we are liable to make serious mistakes unless we possess this antecedent knowledge, the study of sociology becomes a matter of necessity. Teachers who have made themselves familiar with the subject will have no difficulty in interesting the pupils upon the questions involved. Perhaps at first short general exercises, once or twice a week, would be sufficient. In these exercises the various social problems should be clearly presented, leading the pupils to bestow as much thought upon them as possible; then they should be familiarly discussed, the pupils deciding them according to moral principles.

The advantages gained by such a course are many.

A new field of thought is opened to the pupil outside the ordinary routine of the schoolroom; the reasoning powers are taxed to see all the relations involved, and to place all the facts in definite order; the judgment is trained in making decisions in accordance with well-settled principles; and the moral powers are awakened by the necessity of measuring all actions by the standard of duty, and of considering all questions from the moral point of view.

*The Family.*—At the basis of the whole social superstructure are the family relations. How shall duties, conjugal, parental, filial, and fraternal, be adjusted, so that in all family concerns there shall be the least waste of effort, an equable division af labor and cares, the least restriction of individual liberty, the most scrupulous care for individual rights, the greatest desire to be of service one to another, the most careful and generous nurture for children, and the highest and best opportunity for the development of a strong and noble character? The general moral law affords the key for the perfect solution of these questions; but the law needs be analyzed and specifically applied, to the end that the spirit of the law shall permeate the whole being, and moral habits be made deep and lasting. We would say in passing that a careful study in this direction will doubtless reveal the fact that hitherto in the world too much relative stress has been laid upon the duties of children to their parents, while too little attention has been given to the duties of parents to their children; and this for the reason that books upon duty have been written by parents, and the children's side of the question has not been properly represented.

*General Society.*—Next above the family come the interests of neighborhoods and general society. What are the relations that exist between us and our fellows in the same community, and what obligations rest upon us in consequence of these relations? Why should we tell the truth, be honest in our dealings, keep our engagements, and fulfill our contracts? The examination of this subject brings in all the questions relating to buyer and seller, employer and employé, and laborer and capitalist. With the development of the moral nature and intelligence in these directions, grinding oppression on the one hand, and brutal revolt on the other, would alike be impossible. It would be seen that the welfare of each is bound up in the welfare of all, and that to seek personal ends regardless of public good is to array against us the moral forces of the world. This subject covers the same field as law; and so far as law is synonymous with justice, it is but another expression for morality. Indeed, the whole warrant of law is found in moral relations, and the law is of benefit to man just so far as it embodies moral principles.

*Civil Government.*—The social organization that takes the form of government represents one phase of human relations, and hence lies strictly within the field of morality. It has sometimes been said that legislation has no right to touch moral subjects, but from the definition of morals we see that it can deal with no other. The just powers of government being derived from the consent of the governed, it follows that in kind the functions of government, its powers and duties, must coincide with the powers or rights and duties of the individual, and hence must have for its object, not only the protection of rights, but the performance of service. In degree the extent of these functions depends upon expediency. By expediency we mean that the people draw no hard and fast line when they, consciously or unconsciously, willingly or unwillingly, delegate certain of their powers and duties to an official class. The functions of government are therefore dependent upon the condition of society as existing at the time. A knowledge of the relations of government to community, of the powers and duties of civil rulers, of the limits of governmental action, and of the tests to be applied to statutes to decide upon their validity, must be antecedent to intelligent moral action in regard to these questions. It will be seen that a nullification of just laws, and a revolt from necessary restraint, produce anarchy, which is the negation of morality; while submission to unjust statutes subverts liberty and prevents moral development. All governmental work must be judged by moral standards.

*Practical Morality.*—The mind having become enlightened in regard to social relations, the moral law, which was objectively developed, may now be subjectively applied, and taken as a guide to future conduct and in new experiences. Actions in particular cases need no longer be tentative, but they may be deliberately taken in the full assurance of beneficent result. Dependence upon the moral law may be made with the same assurance as upon gravitation.

*Applications in School.*—In school the teacher should give to the moral law a wide and varied application to as many of the occurrences of daily life as possible, to accustom the pupils to examine the moral bearing of all their acts. What moral principles are involved in cleanliness of person and clothing, and attention to neatness and order in the room? Is there anything immoral in bringing dirt on the feet into the schoolroom or into the sitting-room at home? or in neglecting to put things in their proper places? or in carelessly breaking and destroying things? What has morality to say in regard to interruptions of school order? to play in study hours? to inattention? to neglect of study? to waste of time?

The scope of the discussion may be widened by the introduction of questions like the following: Are amusements necessary, and in accordance with the moral law? What of dancing, ball-playing, card-playing, and other games? How much of our likings or dislikings of these amusements is the result of educational bias, and how much do they depend upon moral considerations?

What has morality to say in regard to lotteries, gambling, and horse-racing? to drinking intoxicating liquor, and to making and selling the same? To the use of tobacco, to overreaching in trade, to adulterations, to concealing defects in articles sold?

What obligations rest upon every one to earn his own living? Why should he not live upon the earnings of another? Why should he be economical in expenditure? What incentives are there to thrift, and forethought for the future? What duty rests upon youth and maturity in regard to old age?

The solution of these questions cannot be obtained from a book, nor can they be dogmatically stated by the teacher. The value of these exercises depends upon their full and free discussion in class, the collection of facts made by the pupils bearing upon each case, the inferences derived from such facts, and the detection of fallacies of statement and inference. The teacher's work is principally directive, and he should avoid giving decisions with the air of authority, for the good to the pupils comes from the thought elicited, rather than from the conclusions stated.

*Results of Moral Training.*—The outcome of this moral training in homes and in schools will be individual lives enriched, ennobled, and exalted; selfishness duly controlled, and motive based upon considerations of human welfare; intelligence informing in regard to relations and obligations, and guiding to beneficent results; homes in which the gratification of personal desires is always subordinated to the general good; communities where human rights are sacred, and the patent of nobility is " service to humanity; " States founded, upon individual purity, throwing their mantle of protection around the humblest and weakest, furnishing opportunity for the most complete development of all, and establishing public justice upon the sure foundation of private character; and the final realization of the prediction upon the advent of the great Teacher: " Peace on earth and good-will to men."

## CHAPTER XIV.

*GENERAL COURSE OF STUDY.*

IN 1878, when this book was issued, the principles it advocates, although not in any sense new, and although accepted theoretically by many teachers, had not as a whole been embodied in any course of instruction, nor applied systematically, except in the State Normal School at Warrensburg, Missouri. In 1872 the author organized this school, selected the teachers, and for three years conducted it under circumstances peculiarly favorable to educational experiment. The State Superintendent and Board of Trustees gave him sympathetic support and entire freedom in devising his course of study, and also in choosing his teachers. A brief sketch of the school may be found by referring to The Popular Science Monthly of February, 1889.

The ends sought in this school, the aims set forth by the writer of this book and the methods suggested, have since then been widely accepted, here and there adopted, and in some instances developed along the lines indicated much further than was possible, for various reasons, in 1872 or 1878.

At that time very few teachers could be found possessing the broad culture, the professional training, and the sympathetic knowledge of children necessary in creating a harmonious school environment. Besides this, public opinion would permit only the most guarded and unobtrusive departures from the beaten track; and much the largest share of the author's work was expended in enlightening public opinion through lectures. While the author based his treatise on biological and psychological science and on such a *consensus* of opinion as could then be ascertained, it is plain that a detailed course of study arranged at that time must now need a considerable revision in the light of further investigation by specialists in these fields.

It is further to be considered that at present the various schools illustrating the principles herein advocated afford in their published reports valuable material for comparative study, and teachers are earnestly advised to profit by them.

*Principles to be taken as a Basis.*—In preparing a " Course of Study " the following principles exemplified in the preceding chapters should, however, be kept in mind, and will serve as a guide in the selection and orderly presentation of the materials needed by the child for its nurture and discipline. The *subject-matter* will comprise the whole domain of Nature, including, as of course, man and his thoughts and works. The *elements* of these subjects are found in the experience of every child, and furnish the foundation for instruction. The principles are:

*First:* That the object of education is the harmonious development of all the powers and faculties of the child.

*Second:* That the powers and faculties of the child

should be cultivated in the exact order of their growth and relative activity.

*Third:* That the perceptive faculties are the most active in childhood, and that the facts obtained through the senses are an essential foundation for instruction.

*Fourth:* That the "object-lessons" used for the development of the perceptive faculties should be so arranged that by progressive steps they will lead directly into the sciences and arts.

*Fifth:* That "the mental circuit is not complete" until impression has passed on into expression.

*Sixth:* That the order and the mode of expression should be governed by the natural activities of the child and by the order of their development.

*Seventh:* That reason and judgment, the reflective faculties, are best developed by inferences derived from a wide basis of facts obtained through the senses, and assimilated by the aid of appropriate expression.

*Eighth:* That the subjects of study should be so coördinated that each shall be complementary to every other, thus promoting harmony of development and intensity of impression.

*Ninth:* That the studies and conditions which best unfold the capacities of the child are the studies and conditions which best fit him for his environment.

*Tenth:* That the course of study for general development is substantially the same for all, irrespective of their future fields of activity.

*General Arrangement.*—In the general arrangement six lines of instruction are carried forward throughout the course, two principal and four subordinate. The former are, first, Natural Science, treating of the outward world; second, the Humanities, a study of man in all his relations. These two are classed as principal because their value is intrinsic and independent; they furnish the *subject-matter* for the exercise of the other four.

The four subordinate lines may be classified under one general head. They are modes of expression when considered as arts, and are then to be acquired by doing. Interest in the subject-matter and imitation are the chief factors of success in the mastery of the arts of expression. The four divisions may be considered, for purposes of instruction, under the following heads: Music, Language, Manual Arts, and Mathematics. Instruction in each has its time, place, and method, systematically correlated with its appropriate subject-matter in the two main lines provided by the course of study. By means of the four subordinate lines of instruction the child uses the impressions and ideas he has derived from the two great realms of knowledge above indicated. In using and expressing them he assimilates them, and is thus enabled, through the reenforcement of his interests, to enter into possession of an ever-widening " circle of thought " and feeling, and thereby to re-create himself.

*The Natural Sciences.*—These, systematically studied, make the child intelligent in regard to his physical nature and environment. They furnish him with a knowledge of the conditions which he must observe for the preservation of life and health; and also with the kind of knowledge which lies at the foundation of all productive industry.

The materials for the study of these sciences are

found ready at hand, and every child before he enters the schoolroom has begun the study of Nature, prompted by his inherent activities. These natural activities, the collecting of objects, the handling and use of them in his plays, the observation of their qualities, and the expression of his feeling and thought in connection with them, are to be guided and encouraged by the teacher in conformity with the requirements of child nature, and will be found to correspond to the order of dependence in the sciences themselves.

*Course in Science.*—In arranging the topics for the scientific course two things are to be considered: first, the order of dependence of the sciences themselves; and, second, the order of dependence of the topics in each science.

In the succession of the sciences it is obvious that mineralogy, botany, and zoölogy, treating of objects in the inorganic and organic world, should receive first attention. The order of precedence of the three is to be determined by the interest on the part of the child, and this will be found to attach itself first to objects having life, motion, brilliant color, and obvious use.

Next after these sciences, which deal with objects, come physics and chemistry, treating of the forces which control matter in the mass and in atoms; and, lastly, geology and astronomy, which grow out of and are based upon the preceding sciences. Geology, without chemistry to show the composition of the rocks, and without botany and zoölogy to interpret the meaning of the embalmed remains of organic life which they contain, is of little scientific value; and astronomy, without the laws and principles derived from physics, is an incomprehensible maze.

Practically, however, as the sciences are so interwoven that the elements of each are needed for advance in every other, and, as in the primary classes, only the most obvious facts are presented, all branches of science are in some degree brought into the course of instruction from the beginning.

In the more advanced classes each science is treated again upon successively higher planes, leading to more minute investigations and to broader scientific generalizations.

*Philosophy, or the Humanities.*—In this one of the two main lines of instruction man is considered as a spiritual being. The Humanities treat of his activities as manifestations of thought and feeling. This line of instruction begins by a careful estimate, on the part of the teacher, of the habits and dispositions of the children. The material for instruction is found existing in actions and situations arising in their daily lives; and these experiences are extended and multiplied by means of stories, songs, ballads, myths, and fairy tales, appropriate to the existing instincts and interests of the children.

For this reason the songs, the ballads, the tales, that have passed from mouth to mouth for centuries, and are heard to-day in almost the same words to which our ancestors listened on the slopes of the Hindoo-Koosh, are the best introduction into the Humanities. With the child, as with primitive peoples, the imagination has no definite limits; reason and judgment, which in the mature mind curb and direct this faculty, are not well developed. The nations of antiquity were in many respects like children, especially in their lack of accurate knowledge in the field of natural science. Their tales are full of life and movement, which appeal vividly to children, and the improbabilities in no way offend the childish sense. Myths, fairy tales, fables, stories from the Bible, and from the Greek and Roman classics, will lead gradually into a systematic course in literature.

The lessons in place will gradually lead into Geography, which treats of Nature on the one hand and of man upon the other. It treats of man as an inhabitant of the earth, of the races of men, and of their divisions and distributions. It considers man as a being acted upon by material forces and as an agent active in changing material conditions; and, besides, it furnishes a general description of the works of man in his various fields of activity.

The same conditions, circumstances, and events which on the imaginative side lead out into Literature, will on the narrative side lead into History, and must be kept closely correlated with Geography. Geography and Literature re-enforce each other. A fact or event in history, which through some chain of association has become of interest to the pupil, sets up in him a new interest, but he cannot thoroughly assimilate the historical narrative till he has located and visualized it.

As to the extent to which the correlated studies, Literature, Geography, and History, should be carried, there is no hard and fast line to be drawn. Always, the possession of knowledge leads to further inquiry and an insatiable desire to find related facts, and to this activity there is no limit, except the limits of practical life, which demand that *use* must wait on attainment. The same consideration must control the course in the objective sciences.

Civil Government, which treats of the organization of men into communities and states; of the laws which control such organizations; and of the different forms of government which have grown up out of varying conditions, is next in order. It should also be studied objectively in the local institutions, before attention is called to the more remote departments of government. Later in the light of mental and moral philosophy, the subject should be resumed under the head of Political Economy, and from the history and conditions of society will be derived those general laws which best promote the welfare of communities.

Mental Philosophy is the next general topic, turning the attention from the objects of thought to thought itself, and the conditions of its vigorous and healthful exercise. It seeks to collect and observe the facts of mental development, to note their order of succession, and to consider the sequences in the activity of faculty, as related to educational methods, and to the ordering of the affairs of life. Higher in the course, this subject is again considered, in its relation to the sciences, and its place as the indispensable keystone in the arch is shown.

The subject of Moral Philosophy having received its objective treatment in every grade of the school, *incidentally* it is true, but the more effectually, is now to be considered logically and by analytic methods. In its essence it is shown to be a question as between beings of a like kind. True moral relations must have their origin in sympathy, and this in turn must have its origin in the feeling of likeness, the instinctive feeling with another, inherent in our spiritual constitution. A strong sense of needs on our part has its correlative in a strong sense of the needs of others. Obtuseness, dullness, inertness, insensibility to pain or pleasure is, on our own part, certain to be accompanied by indifference regarding others. A vigorous tenacity in maintaining our own rights has its correlative in a sensitive respect for the rights of others. This course of instruction in moral philosophy will show the growth of rights out of needs, of duties out of rights, and will thus furnish a basis for moral law.

Next in order, as completing the mental circuit by giving play to the creative instincts of the mind, we find the *four subordinate lines of instruction.* The term subordinate must not be misconceived. It does not imply inferiority of importance, since expression or creation is a natural activity, without which little progress can be made. Merely to acquire knowledge, to *know*, does not bring into exercise the whole mind, and hence the need for the Manual and Fine Arts, for Language and Mathematics. These are subordinate because they are dependent upon Science and the Humanities for their material.

For the purposes of a Course of Study we must consider Music by itself, as a representative fine art. It is expressive of the emotional nature, and should receive special attention' throughout the whole school life. In the primary department the exercises should consist of melodies that will give pleasure to the pupils; that will progressively cultivate the musical taste; and that will promote the general harmony of the schoolroom. Elementary exercises in the science of music also begin in the primary department. In the higher departments the art and science of music should be continued by means of a series of thoroughly objective lessons. The choice of Music as first in a course of study is not wholly arbitrary. All normally constituted children are early susceptible to harmonies of sound, although in a varying degree, and the mother instinctively cultivates this sensibility while seeking to soothe and charm the infant with song. The teacher in the primary school takes advantage of this already developed capacity, to establish harmonious relations between the members of the school dwelling together for the time being as one family. This would seem a good reason for giving music precedence in the programme.

Language furnishes one means by which the facts and thoughts of science and philosophy are expressed. Although subordinate to thought, it is an inseparable accompaniment to it; and, in the study of every branch of knowledge, language demands and receives a very large share of the time and attention. In the past it has monopolized in an undue degree the consideration of teachers, but in the reaction against this mistake we must not rush into the opposite extreme and neglect the most *comprehensive* of all the modes of expression.

The objective points in the study of language are accuracy and facility in the expression of thought, both orally and in writing. This mastery over language so that thought may be expressed in the best words, arranged in the most effective order, is at once one of the most important elements of human power, and one of the most accurate tests of the possession of knowledge itself. The language lessons should be arranged so that expression shall have a solid basis in thought. The *primary* attention should in every case be fixed on the thought instead of on the expression.

Skill in the use of language comes from a clear understanding of the thought, and from a continuous effort to express it in the most effective manner. Appropriate language must be as strictly required in oral as in written exercises. Every lesson and every school exercise should contribute to the pupil's power over language.

Language as a means of expressing thought is best taught *incidentally* through its use. Language in its scientific relations and history is a branch of philosophy and belongs to the advanced course of instruction.

*Course in Language.*—The course in language should be arranged to include daily exercises both in speaking and writing, such as will insure a most thorough drill in the technical details of reading, spelling, and penmanship; in the etymology of words; and, finally, in the laws of construction as embodied in the rules of syntax.

*Use in Speaking.*—The correct use of language in speaking is taught in the primary schools by means of questions which demand complete sentences for answer; of lessons which require verbal description; of stories told by teachers and reproduced by pupils; and of original incidents related by pupils. The vocabulary is enlarged by giving a new word to express every new idea acquired, so that thought and expression go hand in hand. These oral exercises are continued for several years, and gradually give place to topical recitations, and in that form are continued throughout the entire school course.

*Use in Writing.*—The correct use of language in writing is taught by exercises directly from objects, in which but a single fact is stated, forming a complete sentence, then two or more facts, until the whole description is given in connected discourse. These descriptions are followed later by written narrations of incidents from daily life; by reproduction of preceding lessons; and by writing out the substance of at least one of the daily school lessons.

In the more advanced classes these written exercises consist of the results of original investigations in natural history; of historical and philosophical sketches derived from the study of books; and, finally, of essays embodying the results of research and reflection.

In these special language lessons pupils should be taught first to collect the facts bearing upon a subject; second, to arrange them in a logical order; and, third, to express them in well-considered discourse.

The topics selected as themes for the formal written lessons in language should be closely connected with some subject studied at the time, or something that rounds out and complements the studies already pursued. Each of these themes is then thoroughly discussed in the class as a preliminary to writing, so that the principle is practically enforced that well-arranged thought should precede all attempts at systematic expression.

The written exercises upon these elementary topics serve as a guide to all subsequent logical arrangement of thought; show the relations that exist between thoughts that are usually presented in a disconnected and fragmentary way; and fix them in the mind more permanently by the processes of philosophic association.

The events and questions of the day, as they are recorded in newspapers and magazines, furnish matter for written exercises. This kind of study should begin with the neighborhood, extend to the State and nation, and finally be made to embrace all questions of national importance in the principal countries of the world. Through several grades of the intermediate department the leading occupations of men may be made the basis of written exercises.

This method of study leads to a knowledge of the various branches of industry, and to their classification on the basis of their relative usefulness. In the philosophic summary it will be shown how each has grown out of some human need or desire, and how the peculiar development of each has been determined by the special circumstances of the case.

In the advanced course, after the student has acquired an elementary knowledge of natural science, history and literature, and is somewhat conversant with the operations of the mind, he may take for the subject of his essays the historical development of art, including architecture, painting, sculpture, music, and poetry. Lastly, his attention should be called to philosophy, its history, and the characteristics of the various systems both ancient and modern.

Reading exercises are not to be confined to the school text-books. A wide variety of supplementary reading leading directly into the great fields of thought should be used to break up the monotony of drill in school readers and induce a habit of mind which spontaneously rejects puerile or demoralizing writings.

The technical details of language, including reading, spelling, the use of capitals and punctuation, are *progressively* taught in all the previously described exercises of the language course, and should be thoroughly mastered and automatically observed in practice before the pupil enters on the study of grammar.

Language as a science deals with abstract logical relations and principles, and hence properly belongs to a more advanced stage of culture than that required by the Nature studies. In most schools grammar is introduced much too early, but at the present time many teachers gradually call attention to the parts of speech, and step by step, objectively, lead the pupil into a consideration of the logical relations which constitute the foundation of formal grammar. Rhetoric should follow grammar, and later systematic exercises in the analysis of words should receive attention. In the latter exercise the pupil is made familiar with the results of philological research in regard to the formation of words and the growth of language. By the careful study of his own vernacular, he obtains a knowledge of the roots derived from all the languages which enter into the English; he gets the nice and discriminating use of words which is usually sought in the study of a foreign language; and he acquires a power of etymological analysis which will be of great use should he continue his linguistic studies. While study of this kind cannot take the place of thorough culture in the classic languages it will be found an excellent preparation for such culture, and of much greater practical value than superficial classical study.

*Manual Arts.*—Under this head, as suited to the use of schools, will be found all the occupations of the kindergarten—drawing, painting, modeling in clay, writing, tool-work, cooking, gardening, sewing, and all the manipulations of objects incident to the study of science. We must not assume that manual training has been wholly lacking in the schools. The manual arts in all times have had some share in the process of obtaining ideas, and have been still more generally employed in expressing them. The advocates of manual training, however, urge upon the teacher a much more extended and systematic training of the hand. The next step in the improvement of school-work lies in this direction, and cannot much longer be delayed without danger of discredit to the whole school system.

Instruction in the manual arts is in the experimental stage as regards many of its phases. So far as these arts are subordinate, and are used incidentally, in gaining and expressing ideas, the methods have been determined by the practice of the best teachers, and a general uniformity prevails. Such manual arts as cooking, gardening, and sewing, which require instruction independent of the other branches of study, will need further time to develop the methods of training best suited to educational needs.

Drawing and modeling in clay have long been matters of experiment in many of the best schools, and teachers will find a plan of work, based on sound educational principles, in actual operation which they will do well to study before arranging a course of instruction.

*Mathematics.*—By means of the various branches of mathematics, quantitative relations become known and are expressed. Directly derived from the concrete sciences, they are indispensable to the complete mastery of them; and throughout the entire school course, their pursuit should exactly keep pace with that of the sciences.

The practice of allowing the mathematical studies to monopolize so much time, or to be pursued greatly in advance of the sciences in which they have their origin and to the investigations of which their chief value is owing, is not encouraged.

*Course in Mathematics.*—In the primary grades the elements of numbers should be taught by means of objects, and the pupil should be drilled upon simple combinations until the fundamental operations of arithmetic are thoroughly mastered. The best exercises for practice are derived from the work in science, and the natural interest awakened by this method will be of great advantage in securing attention. Throughout the entire course this principle should be observed.

The drill derived from the mastery of the ordinary practical arithmetic is considered sufficient in this direction. The curiosities of numbers exhibited in the so-called higher arithmetic are wholly omitted.

In the academic course, algebra, geometry, and

trigonometry should be thoroughly mastered so far as their fundamental principles and processes are concerned, and each step should be illustrated by examples which will serve to connect scientific demonstration with daily experience. .The principles of geometry and trigonometry should be applied to surveying, to mensuration, and to mechanics and astronomy sufficiently to unfold the elements of these sciences.

In a complete, philosophic system of education the cultivation of the taste to an appreciation of the beautiful in all its forms is considered as important as the cultivation of the mental and moral faculties to an appreciation of the true and the good respectively. Taste, however, is rather the outcome of the whole course than of any special line of instruction; and the training suited to our public schools carries us but a little way on the road leading to production in the fine arts.

*Cultivation of Taste.*—Good taste is promoted by attention to the accepted rules of behavior, to neatness of person and clothing, to color in dress, in the decoration of the schoolroom, to color and form in the furniture, and to the harmony and fitness of all the surroundings, both in school and home. In this connection the cultivation of flowers and their use in decoration may be made effective.

In all the purely literary studies the development of a critical taste is kept constantly in view. The pupil is so directed as to recognize the beauty of the literary forms, created by the great poets and the masters of literature.

Drawing, too, throughout the course is valued not

merely as a means of expressing ideas of form, of educating the eye and hand, but as an aid to culture of the artistic sense. Pupils should be taught to draw directly from objects in Nature, and to make such combinations of form as will lay the foundation for creative art. We must not concern ourselves as teachers with the cultivation of taste in any one-sided direction, as, for example, in music, form, or color. The same spontaneous discrimination in moral relations should be recognized in its merely outward manifestation as essential to good taste.

# CHAPTER XV.

*COUNTRY SCHOOLS, AND THEIR ORGANIZATION.*

COMPARATIVE STANDING.—In city and country the objects of education are alike, but the conditions of the two are so dissimilar that the schools are necessarily unlike in organization and general methods. The aggregation of pupils in the city allows of a gradation and division of labor quite impossible in the country; and the concentrated wealth of the city gives superior advantages in the way of school-houses and all the appliances of education. Still there are compensations in the country; and in excellence of results country schools, intelligently conducted, approach nearer the ideal standard than is possible for city schools.

The low condition of schools in many parts of the country is owing in part to intrinsic defects, and in part to accidental causes. The former can be much ameliorated and the latter removed by making the most of all favoring conditions, and by a wise administration that fully comprehends their needs.

*Advantages.*—The advantages of situation possessed by country schools will be more and more appreciated as instruction progressively approximates to rational methods. In the country the study of natural history, the foundation of all primary instruction, can be carried on without cost for material; and as the children are daily brought into immediate contact with Nature, the study may be made doubly interesting and profitable. The growth of mind is a slow process, requiring periods of alternate activity and rest. The perpetual din and motion in the city stimulates mental activity, but there is no opportunity for the rest which the quiet of the country affords. If the proper means are taken to awaken the mental powers, the conditions of healthful mental growth greatly preponderate in the country schools. There devolves upon the teacher, however, the duty of arousing thought, to prevent the mental stagnation which comes from uncultivated perceptions, and the narrowness incident to limited experiences.

Another advantage in country life favorable to scholarship is the general mingling of work and study. Both boys and girls have something to do as well as something to learn; and when the work is limited to the proper amount, and not pushed to the point of exhaustion, it becomes a source of additional intellectual vigor. Teachers who have had experience in both city and country schools, with great unanimity, testify that the pupils in the latter take greater interest and make greater progress in a given time. This is doubtless owing in part to the work, which affords a natural outlet to their activities and gives them motive and vigor, and in part to the shorter terms of country schools.

Dr. Seguin, the eminent physiologist and physician, advocates out-door study as the most conducive to bodily health and mental vigor. He thinks pupils from a very early age should be brought in direct contact with Nature, and no lesson should be given in-doors that can be given without. To accomplish this end he proposes to make the public parks of the city great educational institutions, where Nature may be studied at first hand. While this plan may not be practical at present, it indicates the direction of the improvements which are demanded for education. In the country are found the conditions which this improved system of education calls for to a much greater extent than in the city, and it seems possible that country schools will soon take the lead in reducing these ideas to practice.

*Defects.*—The greatest intrinsic disadvantage of country schools is the limited number of pupils, and the consequent impossibility of a proper system of grading. Pupils of all ages and degrees of advancement meet in the same room, each grade diminishing the opportunities of the other: primary and advanced instruction go on together, mutually interfering with each other; and so wide a range of employment is given to the teacher that he cannot become an expert in any department, and he fails to do justice to any class. While these evils are incident to the situation of country schools, the ill effects may be diminished by greater flexibility in organization and administration.

*Boards of Control.*—That organization has proved the most successful which has brought several schools, as those of a township, under one board of control. The advantages which this system has over that of single districts are a more intelligent management, the employment of better qualified teachers, the erection of better school-houses, greater care in the preservation of school property, a wiser supervision, and a more equable distribution of taxes. When the board is invested with the power of grading and establishing central schools for the higher classes, and when they exercise this power judiciously, the greatest inherent defect of the country school system is largely overcome, and the schools in efficiency are made to approximate very closely to the city schools. The teacher may also do much to diminish the evils of mixed schools, by reducing the number of classes to the minimum, by more frequent general exercises, by the adoption of rational instead of mechanical methods, and by the more general introduction and practice of written work. The other evils connected with country schools are wholly remediable by the State, the district, and the teacher.

*School-houses.*—In many parts of the country the condition of the school-houses and the premises about them is a disgrace to the community. A building made ugly to the extreme of parsimony in its construction, affording no adequate protection from the elements, destitute of ordinary comforts within, and wanting in the conveniences demanded by decency without, is the place where all the children of the district are to pass their school-days, and receive the most durable impressions of their lives. The only satisfaction to be gained from a consideration of this matter is in the fact that improvements are being made, and that these conditions, so disreputable to the people who are responsible for them, are undergoing a change for the better.

The school-house should be conveniently and pleasantly located, and well built. It should afford ample protection from the weather, and it should be arranged for the comfort of the pupils. Attention should be specially given to the admission of light, and to the heating and ventilation, so that a uniform temperature may be preserved, and an ample supply of pure air secured. At the present time there can be no reasonable excuse for poisoning pupils with foul air. In other respects the schools should be supplied with those conveniences which are considered indispensable to respectable households. The country school has a high mission here. All the conditions should conform to the standards dictated by science, and thus afford a most valuable object-lesson in some important details of practical life.

*Apparatus and Books.*—Another defect in the country schools generally is the want of the apparatus and books necessary for successful instruction. No man would think of employing a farm-laborer without supplying him with the tools for farm-work; and it is no less absurd to expect a teacher to do the best work without apparatus than to expect a laborer to make the best crop without a plough and other farm-implements. The neglect in this direction is in part owing to a mistaken notion in regard to the importance of apparatus, and in part to the desire to reduce the expenses to the lowest possible amount. Economy, however, it is easy to show, is on the side of wise and proper expenditure, as by it the efficiency of the schools is so greatly increased.

Costly apparatus is not needed in the average country schools. Most of the things needed to illustrate instruction can be collected by teachers and pupils at very little expense. The things which are indispensable to the best results are a globe, a set of outline maps, local maps of the town and county, a large amount of excellent blackboard, and a cabinet containing specimens sufficient to illustrate the elements of the different departments of natural history, and the different manufactures. The books indispensable are an unabridged dictionary, a comprehensive history of the United States, a biographical dictionary, and some brief encyclopædia of science. An encyclopædia of general knowledge, freely used by pupils, would so multiply the general results of education as to pay for itself each year. After the books enumerated have been provided, the expenditure of a small sum each year will soon procure a valuable library of reference which will be a source of enlightenment not only to the school, but to the whole neighborhood.

*Short Terms.*—Another of the disabilities under which the majority of the country schools labor is the short terms of instruction. While the city schools usually continue in session ten months each year, the country schools average but little more than one-half of that time. The opportunity for education is thus less than it should be, and intelligence is correspondingly less. By irregularity of attendance also there is a failure to make the best of the opportunities offered, and the amount of possible good to be derived from the schools is still further diminished.

The sessions that would seem most suitable to the conditions of the country are a term of eight weeks beginning about the 1st of September, a session of twenty weeks beginning from the 1st to the 10th of November, and a session of eight weeks beginning about the 1st of May. This would give thirty-six weeks of school, which could be extended to forty weeks by making the intermediate vacations less. By this arrangement the long continuous term is in winter when there is the least demand for labor, and the long vacation is in midsummer, so as to avoid exposure of children to the great heat and to give teachers time for recreation in the form of rest and study. Since the experiment of Agassiz, at Penikese, summer schools for teachers are springing up all over the country, and the terms of the country schools should be so arranged that country as well as city teachers may be able to attend them.

*Change of Teachers.*—In most country districts the older pupils attend school only in winter, and the summer term is made up mostly of the younger ones, constituting in reality a primary department. This condition of affairs has given rise to the custom of changing teachers each term, employing a higher-priced teacher in winter than in summer. This custom works injury to the schools in numerous ways. No two teachers have exactly the same methods of instruction, and it always takes time for pupils to get accustomed to the new methods, and hence there is a waste of time at the advent of every new teacher. At the close of the short term the teacher has become thoroughly acquainted with the peculiarities of the pupils and of the district, so as to be able to perform the best service; but at the commencement of the next term another comes in, and the process of making the acquaintance of the pupils is repeated. Teachers employed for only a single term at one place take comparatively little interest in their work, and have but little incentive to improvement. The people, accustomed to migratory teachers, show them scant courtesy or ignore them altogether, and the school is altogether lacking in that mental vigor and high moral tone which would result from the interest and coöperation of teacher, pupil, and parent.

The true policy in regard to the employment of teachers would seem to be the payment of the highest wages that the district can afford, the standard of ability to pay being an enlightened appreciation of the value of education; the employment of the best teacher which the money will secure; and the retention of the teacher for the longest possible time. All proper encouragement and facilities should be given the teacher for attending Institutes and special summer schools, and a lively interest should be shown by the parents in the teacher's work. A new idea or a new method introduced should be judged by its results, and not denounced in the outset. By careful attention to the selection and moral support of the teacher, the value of the schools may be more than doubled.

QUALIFICATION OF TEACHERS.—The one thing indispensable to the success of a school is a good teacher. In comparison, the functions of all other officers are of little moment; and could we be sure of a supply of competent teachers, superintendents and examiners would at once become superfluous, and directors would be useful only in furnishing necessary supplies for the schools. Practically, however, it is found that all teachers are not properly qualified, and that the utmost vigilance must be exercised continually to keep aspiring incompetence out of the schools. All the machinery of superintendence and of examinations is devised to this end; but when the competent teacher is once secured, the work of the school goes on without the aid or interference of any other person.

*Scientific Knowledge.*—The first and lowest qualification demanded of teachers is that they shall have a knowledge of the branches which they are expected to teach. It is not enough to be able to read, and so ascertain from the text-book whether the pupils repeat the text accurately, but the knowledge should be so thorough that text-books would never be a necessity in recitation. The knowledge demanded for the successful conduct of even a primary school is varied and extensive.

Officers who have charge of the examination of teachers have curious experiences in the discharge of their duties. Persons are continually presenting themselves as candidates for certificates, who cannot spell; who make fearful blunders in reading the easiest narrative; who are not able to solve the simplest problems of arithmetic outside of the accustomed routine, and who continually blunder in expression both orally and in writing. Such persons are usually very persistent in their demands, and not unfrequently the refusal of a certificate is followed by the denunciation of the office. The literary qualifications now demanded for a first-grade certificate are the least that any teacher of any grade of school should possess.

*General Culture.*—Besides the technical knowledge of the branches to be taught, teachers should have a wide and varied culture in matters of general human interest. It has been well stated that no person can be in full possession of his own powers until he is acquainted with the history of the past; and certainly it is scarcely possible to exaggerate the importance of historical knowledge in promoting the interest and efficiency of the school. This knowledge in its widest sense includes every department of literature; and there is no form of literary attainment that may not be turned to advantage in school processes.

This general culture should include also a knowledge of the present state of affairs in the leading countries of the world. Our morning newspapers bring us intelligence fresh from every known part of the earth, but a wide knowledge of present history is necessary to profit by this intelligence ourselves and to turn it to good account in teaching. Teachers in possession of this knowledge can make profitable use of newspapers, magazines, and everything that relates to current events, and the value of the school will be vastly increased by such processes.

*The Mental Powers.*—A knowledge of the mental powers, their modes of activity, their limitations, and the order of their development, is indispensable to the highest success in teaching. Without this knowledge good instruction may be given, but the processes are necessarily empirical and the work that of mere routine. With it, teachers have a key to most of the educational problems that are continually coming up for solution; they have a principle to guide them in new experiences; they can adapt their work to the needs of the pupils, and adjust courses of study to produce the best results;

they are sufficient for any emergency that may arise in instruction, and they are not driven to make doubtful experiments which may increase the evils rather than diminish them.

*Professional Knowledge.*—The teacher should in every instance possess very thorough knowledge of the economics of instruction, such as organization, classification, tactics, and discipline. Organization includes the general scope of the instruction, the course of study, and the proper distribution of the studies as far as time is concerned; classification has reference to the division of the school on the bases of attainment for the purpose of recitation; tactics considers the movements of pupils, so that there shall be no interference, and no time wasted; and discipline has to do with the means to secure order and promote the best interests of the school. Experienced teachers have written upon all these topics, treating them from both the theoretical and practical points of view; and there are now so many valuable treatises readily accessible that no teacher can have an adequate excuse for neglecting them.

The means of professional culture are within the reach of every teacher. The cost of instruction at Normal Schools is usually less than at other schools where the same branches are taught, and these schools are now provided in nearly all the States. In some of the States, in addition to the Normal Schools, there are teachers' classes in academies and high schools, where tuition is free. Another agency for the instruction of teachers is the Teachers' Institute, now held annually in each county in those States where much attention is given to school matters. The lowest demand that should be made upon teachers in regard to these agencies for professional culture is that they should attend the professional course of a normal school or academy before commencing their work, and that they should be constant in their attendance upon Institutes after entering upon their duties, and should take an active part in the exercises.

*Self-Improvement.*—It is incumbent upon all teachers to continually study and improve themselves. This is especially true in regard to those who, for any cause, have been deprived of the opportunity for a thorough professional preparation. The new subjects investigated should be in the direction of natural history, mental philosophy, and general history and literature, as these are most neglected. Several of these subjects may be taken up in direct connection with school-work, and the improvement of the teacher made incidental to his class-duties. For example, a teacher has never studied botany, and he wishes to give some elementary instruction to a class of children upon plants. He would do well to procure some little work like Miss Youmans's "First Book in Botany," or Gray's "How Plants Grow," for the purpose of getting the method of study.

The summer schools for professional instruction afford teachers an admirable opportunity for studies in the direction pointed out, and it becomes a question of grave moment whether a teacher who neglects these opportunities, or who has not sufficient energy to overcome the ordinary difficulties in the way of attending these schools, has the desire for improvement, the energy, and the will, which are necessary to successful teaching.

*Details of Work.*—The course of study prepared for country schools should be founded upon the same general principle as that for graded schools, given at length in the chapter upon "Course of Study." It is necessary, however, to condense the longer course in regard to time, and the studies to be pursued, so as to adapt it to the needs and conditions of the country schools. The problem to solve is to prepare a course that shall broaden the present instruction, introduce more rational methods, provide for more practical work, and stimulate teachers to higher endeavor, and at the same time not to set the standard so high as to be unattainable by a majority of teachers now employed, and so to act as a discouragement rather than an incentive to effort. The changes in the present practices which are proposed are entirely practical, as has been proved by actual trial in many schools, and there is no good reason why the better results which will follow from the adoption of this improved course may not be realized in all parts of the country.

*The Alphabet.*—Pupils should be taught to read by the sentence methods: The unit of attention is the sentence. By this method the letters and words are learned incidentally, while the pupil is intent on the thought represented, and the least possible amount of time is directly spent for this purpose.

*Reading.*—Sentences should always be read as a unit, and the pupil should not be permitted to pronounce each word as though disconnected from the others. In all primary reading, pupils should fully understand the thought before trying to express it. They should never be allowed to read what they cannot understand, and they should always express the thought from the book, as they would the same thought in conversation. By observing these simple directions, the conventional school-drawl may be broken up, root and branch, and an onerous mechanical exercise may be changed into an interesting and intelligent one.

*Spelling.*—An almost complete revolution is recommended in teaching the art of spelling. As soon as the pupil learns a sentence, let him be taught to copy it on the blackboard. This copying of lessons from the chart and book should be continued as a daily exercise for at least three years, although it will not be necessary to copy all the lessons. Before the close of the first term, the pupil should also commence writing descriptions of objects, beginning by telling one thing and adding one detail after another until full descriptions are given. In this way spelling and penmanship are both taught incidentally while other lessons are studied, and the time for teaching them directly is saved. By this method the pupil never guesses at the spelling of a word; never spells orally except with the written or printed characters before him; never hears or sees a misspelled word; and he spells every word he knows correctly. The words that he does not know, he does not try to spell until he has looked them out, and this leads to good spelling all the time.

*Object-Lessons.*—The object-lessons are systematized, and from the very first are made to include the elements of the sciences. They are made so progressive that any teacher of ordinary intelligence can give them, and gradually become acquainted with the science of which they form a part in the way already pointed out. More or less time may be given to this part of the instruction, depending upon the condition of the school and the skill of the teachers. It may be made to constitute the best half of teaching, awakening mental activity and storing the mind with the most useful knowledge. These object-lessons may frequently be made general for the whole school, thus effecting another saving in time.

*Rural Affairs.*—It is a fact much to be deplored that in country schools there are no exercises which take into consideration country life. The occupation which absorbs the greater part of the life of the people, and all its varied and contingent interests, are scarcely recognized in school-work. Children fresh from the farm, with an extensive but unsystematized knowledge of the farm processes, and an active interest in them, are set to tasks which have no relations to these activities, and which usually are abstract and uninteresting. A rational system of instruction would seem to indicate that the first step in the school-work shall be to make the child conscious of what he already knows, to arrange the knowledge in proper order, and to stimulate observation and inquiry in the very direction in which the mind has already been developed.

These country children know a great deal about plants, their names, their forms, their uses, and their manner of growth. A little guidance only is necessary to awaken a great interest in the general subject of plant-life, leading on by short steps to systematic botany and vegetable physiology. They know also a great deal about domestic animals, their characteristics, their habits, and their products. Starting from this knowledge it is easy to lead them to make further investigations in the same direction, cultivating their perceptive powers in the most efficient manner, and storing their minds with knowledge that reaches out toward the material world on the one side, and toward the phenomena of life upon the other, and indispensable as a basis to a wide and general culture. The knowledge which the child has in regard to bees and other insects; to the succession of farm processes from seed-time to harvest; to the manipulations necessary to produce a crop and prepare it for the market; and to the processes and products of household labor and economy—all can be turned to good account in the process of education, doubling the interest in study and increasing the products many fold. As a result of such a system of instruction children would find rural life full of interest in all seasons of the year.

In following this method, the teacher is but obeying one of the most fundamental of all the laws of mental development, proceeding from the known to the unknown, and making the previous experience of the child the basis for its future growth. Besides the advantage to the child itself, this method aids education in other ways. It takes away from instruction the reproach of being unpractical, it excites an interest in all school affairs on the part of parents, and it leads to continually more intelligent action in home and farm affairs. We may hope it will also have the effect of leading to a higher appreciation of country life and of arresting the present tendency of migration toward the cities, and of the abandonment of the farms for trade or for the professions. "Abandoned farms" are in the last analysis but a result of discontent, either with the meager profits of farming or with the dullness of the farmer's life. More attention to Nature Studies and a better training in the Manual Arts should go far to remove the causes of this discontent. If the farmer is as well trained for his work as the mechanic he will succeed as surely, and he will find even his odd moments precious.

# APPENDIX.

## THE STORY OF A SCHOOL.\*

**BY JAMES JOHONNOT.**

IN this age of wholesale educational machinery the faithful record of any school, individual in its character, ought to be of interest to all who seek better results in practical ability than our present systems of instruction succeed in giving. But when the school departs widely from recognized standards, its record is of double value, as calling in question prevalent customs, and affording a new criterion for the judgment of current methods. The tendency of instruction is to become set in its ways. Teachers follow precedent and reach formalism.

But from time to time particular individuals are found who ask the reason of this or that practice, and call in question its value as a means of culture. Hence arose the "teachers' institutes" in this country. They were first organized in the State of New York, in 1846. They grew naturally out of the progress in liberty of thought. Time-worn methods of teaching were brought up for discussion, and judged by their results and in the light of reason.

Credit is surely due the founders and conductors of institutes, in that they brought about and persisted in this habit of questioning and discussing educational

---
\* Republished from the "Popular Science Monthly," February, 1889.

practices and principles. This was their special field of work. Their method was the true one, but the laws of life and of mental development were not then well enough understood, even by the best thinkers, to furnish safe guidance in this difficult work.

"The new education" means a revolt against all precise, ready-made forms, and an adoption of such methods as science may from time to time discover and point out. The "Story of a School" tells of the trials and triumphs of an experiment designed to test educational principles at which I had arrived through many years of "institute" instruction. In this constant comparing, discriminating, and sifting of methods I had obtained a special preparation for normal-school work. Herbert Spencer, in his treatise on education, had laid a solid foundation for scientific education, and Prof. E. L. Youmans had with voice and pen succeeded in arousing among thinking people a lively interest in the subject.

In the year 1872, through the agency of the Hon. John Monteith, Superintendent of the Schools of Missouri, I received a call to take charge of the newly established normal school at Warrensburg in that State. In the interview with Mr. Monteith I said suggestively to him, "You do not want me, and your board of regents will not want my services when they learn the conditions I shall exact." "What may these be?" said he, with some curiosity in his tone. "Entire control of the school, without interference from the superintendent or from the regents," was my reply. Laughing, said he, "You are the very man we want," and added, by way of caution: "You understand that liberty implies responsibility. Give us right results, and we will trust to you for methods." I accepted the situation, and took up my work under circumstances singularly propitious to the experiment I was about to make.

The first thing that engaged my attention was the preparation of a course of study. It was an easy matter to select the required document from the catalogue of some noted institution, or I might have made a mosaic, adopting parts from several. A brief inspection of various catalogues showed that little thought had been bestowed upon the order of subjects in the course. One study might be made to take the place of any other, without the slightest disturbance in their relations. Of the natural order of growth in mind, and of the corresponding sequences in the sciences, they had taken no account. To these laws I now turned for guidance, and tried to forget that a school curriculum had ever been constructed, so that custom should in no wise interfere with the free play of philosophic principles.

The subjects were arranged in their order of dependence as determined by comparative science. The course of study thus worked out differed quite materially from the ordinary, in spirit and in principles. It emerged as *an organic whole,* rather than as a loose array of disconnected subjects.

The physical sciences had first place, their treatment beginning with an observation of material objects and passing to a consideration of forces and of the laws of physical relations.

Another line of study treated of man and his environment. It began with a consideration of man as an inhabitant of the globe, dealing with geography, and it led up through history, literature, civil government, to mental and moral philosophy, and later on to rhetoric, logic, and political economy.

Besides these two main lines of thought there were two subordinate ones, dealing respectively with language as a science and with mathematics. In our treatment of language the widest departure from the customary was made. Latin and Greek were excluded, as the State University already offered a much more complete course in the classics than our school could hope to give. But a still weightier reason constrained me in this decision. The time at our disposal for linguistic study was needed chiefly for constructive work in the vernacular. I determined to make the study of English thorough. I realized the power gained by an accurate and easy mastery of our own tongue, and I fully appreciated the æsthetic value of English literature in the cultivation of a refined and discriminating taste.

The constructive work was so managed that familiarity with composition preceded analysis, and the principles and rules of language were developed out of the pupil's own work. Grammar came out of language, not language out of grammar. The critical work of grammar and rhetoric was placed in the advanced course along with logic.

In this spirit, and by the general method here indicated, the whole course of study was arranged. The place occupied by each subject was not a matter of accident, but of philosophic dependence. The success of my scheme demanded intelligent and harmonious co-operation on the part of the faculty. I needed a select corps of teachers, and the freedom of choice secured to me by Mr. Monteith now proved of great importance.

For my first assistant I chose Prof. L. H. Cheney, who some years later was accidentally killed while making an excavation in connection with the work of a geological expedition under direction of Prof. Shaler, of Harvard. In years long gone by Prof. Cheney had been a pupil of mine; later we had worked together, so that I knew well his peculiar worth and fitness for the place.

Next came Prof. and Mrs. Straight, representatives of the most advanced thought of the time in educational philosophy. They brought original and fruitful contribution to the work now in progress, and henceforth were to me as my right and left hand. At the close of his stay in Missouri, Prof. Straight was called to the charge of a department in the Oswego Normal School. Later he went with Colonel Parker to the Cook County Normal School, Illinois. He gave all the energy of an intense nature to his profession, but died in middle life, his mind a storehouse of educational material ripe for use. Mrs. Straight's refined intelligence and professional skill found equally ready appreciation, and she took a high position in each of these normal schools. Since her husband's death, she has been called to a responsible position in one of the state schools of Japan. The remaining members of the faculty were chosen for their fitness in special directions. The plans of each had their recognized place in a *co-ordinate work.* One of the chief defects in colleges and academies to-day is this lack of co-ordination. Without it the scientific method in its integrity is impossible, and instruction proceeds as though each science were independent. Time and strength are laboriously frittered away, with the result of chronic discouragement on the part of both professor and students.

"I declare," said one of our most observant pupils, as he came out from recitation one day, "the teaching in all the classes is somehow alike! It makes no difference whether we are in natural science, mathematics, or language, we are going the same road, and each lesson throws a new light upon all the others."

When the summer school at Penikese was organized, we made prompt application for a share in the rare opportunities offered. Only fifty students could be accommodated. Three of our teachers received the appointment, and accompanied me across Buzzard's Bay on that eventful summer morning in 1873. Agassiz "the master" was there, his face hopeful and inspiring. The last and noblest experiment of his life was about to be tried, and everything promised success. The promise was fulfilled. The many summer schools of science springing up all over the land are the direct offspring of Agassiz's realized dream; and the increasing recognition of the fundamental value of science by numerous prominent schools is also largely a result of his Penikese experiment. Our teachers again, the second summer, made haste to profit by the advantages of the Penikese school, and returned to their work in Missouri with added skill and devotion.

Our pupils represented every class of society. We opened with seventeen, and rapidly increased till the roll contained four hundred names.  Within the limits of this paper only the bare outlines of our methods can be given.  We began with the properties of things. The gardens and fields were open to us and furnished us the objects.  When familiar with these and their relations, books were brought in to extend our knowledge beyond the limits of personal experience.  The zoölogy and physiology classes, under Prof. Straight, were at once engaged in laboratory practice.  They obtained their knowledge of the animal world from direct observation and through actual dissections.  The neighborhood was laid under contribution for cats.  Any feeling of repugnance at first shown for the work soon passed away as interest in the study grew eager and absorbing. The absurdity of rote-teaching was shown by an incident in the professor's class-room.

One day he called the attention of the class to the description of a certain sea-animal, as given in a popular text-book.  This description he asked the pupils to commit to memory, which they proceeded to do, wondering why.  One morning, only a few days later, the table was furnished with a specimen of this same animal preserved in alcohol.  Not a member of the class recognized it.  The elaborate verbal definition had given them no correct idea of the animal, if, indeed, any image whatever had been present in their minds.

In botany, books were unopened, except to aid in analysis.  Materials for study the students found in their walks, and the keen delight awakened when examination revealed to them this new world of facts left no doubt that this was the very method of Nature. The study went deeper than systematic botany, and led to an extended investigation of life processes in the plant.

Physics was taught in the laboratory and illustrated by apparatus which teachers and pupils united in making. This proved of double value; for, while primarily it helped to solve the problem in physics, incidentally it constrained the pupil to test knowledge previously gained by its practical application. The inventive powers were also stimulated, and a long step was taken in the development of faculty.

The teacher of geometry followed the method of Prof. Krüsi, of Oswego. This, in essentials, is the same as that outlined by Herbert Spencer in his work on education. It was developed incidentally out of the needs of constructive art, and was carried forward slowly, as the gradual progress of the pupil called for further applications of its principles. It was specially gratifying to witness the cheerful activity of pupils in this line of work, so often dreaded and shirked, and to watch the stimulating effect of power gained in mastering a difficult problem.

Drawing came in everywhere, being a mode of expression as natural as language, and indispensable to the acquirement of clear ideas; pupils soon made constant use of it, though, from lack of early training, their efforts had no pretensions to artistic merit.

Our lessons took various forms, depending upon the object we had in view. In the development exercises, by a series of questions quite in the Socratic spirit, we brought together the wandering, disconnected ideas which the class possessed upon any subject, and directed attention to the more obvious relations. The pupils were then left to work over the lesson, and arrange and present it in due order. This process became a guide, and pointed out the way for the next step in investigation. Lessons of instruction were usually given in the form of lectures. We, however, varied this exercise by substituting for the formal lecture a more or less familiar conversation, in which, after a little, all pupils took part.

Topical recitations included all knowledge obtained from books or reported from investigation. Day by day pupils were called upon to tell what they knew of given subjects in clear and connected discourse. The words of the text-book were not accepted; so every lesson became a language-lesson of the most practical kind. As a matter of fact, we found that, whenever a new thought was clearly understood, the mind sought expression in some form, either through constructive work, drawing, or language, and was not content until it had clearly imparted its meaning to another mind. The mental circuit was then complete.

In this reaching out after words and forms individual character asserted itself, the imagination was awakened, the invention quickened, and the dead monotony of the old-school recitation disappeared completely. This training finally resulted in an unusual mastery of spoken language.

Written work held a large place in our school. Our plan made provision for at least one written exercise a day for each pupil. As these exercises were in connection with the studies pursued at the time, the pupils entered upon them without any consciousness that they had begun the dreaded composition. Lessons from text-books, and aided by books of reference, were treated topically, and were frequently written out. Investigations in science were reported in writing, and in due time the pupils came to think easily and naturally, pen in hand.

In another regard we made a serious innovation upon custom. The teachers were not required to correct the wearisome mass of papers prepared daily. For this we had good reasons. The free use of criticism is a dangerous practice. It paralyzes the imagination of the pupil, and so depresses and discourages him that original constructive work is next to impossible. And if, as so often happens through the training given, the critical faculty of the pupil is developed in advance of the constructive ability, and of the power to use language with ease and accuracy, the result is fatal to progress in composition. The first rude efforts fall so far short of the polish demanded by the critical spirit that the sense of discouragement is overmastering.

There is still another view of the case that makes for the same distrust of promiscuous criticism. The errors of the early compositions are soon naturally and spontaneously outgrown through the constant effort at clearness of expression, and through the rapidly increased power over language gained by this continuous practice. In this way the mastery of language came *incidentally*, and we avoided the stiff awkwardness of the conventional composition.

In the study of English we did what we could to awaken the literary sense to some degree in all our pupils. We knew that each one came into the world with definite mental limitations. The literary sense, like any other form of the artistic faculty, seems, with rare exceptions, to require several generations of culture in a scholarly atmosphere before it attains to a fine discrimination. But we could at least make a real beginning. We could find out the present state of their taste, and carry forward their development by guiding their course of reading. Advantage was taken of events to bring before them some special poem, or some impassioned prose composition, having relation to the event in question. We could thus awaken a susceptibility of the soul, that through repeated impressions would develop into an instinctive sense of the beauty of true literary art-forms.

This was our aim, and quite subsidiary to this was the acquisition of knowledge *about* literature. The history, bibliography, and philosophy of English literature must come later instead of usurping the first place, as is commonly the case in schools.

In language, Prof. Campbell prepared an exercise which proved of great value. He selected about three hundred of the most productive roots of English words, and gave them one by one to the class. They traced these roots back to the various languages entering into the English tongue, and thus acquired a broader view of the origin and relations of English words. The study thus bestowed upon the vernacular was further valuable as furnishing a basis for the study of other languages.

When the student in Latin, French, or German finds that a large number of the new words he is learning have the roots with which he is familiar in his mother-tongue, the difficulties of his work are greatly diminished.

Mental and moral philosophy were taken up objectively and without the aid of books. Prof. Straight first developed the relations which knowledge sustains to mind, and the action of mind under varying conditions. He then took up some familiar subject and called upon the class to apply the knowledge thus far gained. For example, a flower was brought in and analyzed according to the laws of systematic botany. Then came introspection: what powers of mind had been used, and in what order? A lesson in geometry came next, and this was followed by the other school studies, until the list was exhausted. Next came the industries: what mental powers are brought into play in raising a crop, in building a house, in boiling a potato, in the making of bread? By this plan mental philosophy was lifted out of the fog of dreary abstractions and set on its feet in the broad light of every-day life.

Moral philosophy fell to my share. No books were used. My methods were quite similar to those of Prof. Straight. In a series of discussions, extending over several weeks, the human being was taken where Prof. Straight left him, and the relations developed that existed between him and other human beings. Needs were shown to exist by virtue of the "constitution of things," and deeper than this we did not attempt to go.

Human beings were seen to be *potentially* equal in needs, hence the necessity for equality before the law, that all might have opportunity for their natural development. Out of needs grew rights, and out of rights duties. A study of experience soon showed that duty assumed two phases—positive and negative. Confucius is credited with a maxim covering the ground of negative duty—forbidding injury to your neighbor. Jesus enunciated a law that summarized both positive and negative duty.

Next, the principles derived from this preliminary study were applied to the conditions which exist in school, home, and neighborhood. Why should a person work? What time should be given to recreation? What shall we do with the tramp? what with worthy but destitute men and women? what with needy orphans?

The discussion was conducted almost solely by the pupils. When it took too wide a range, the teacher quietly led it back to the question at issue. The lesson on one occasion dealt with card-playing. One young woman charged that it led to gambling and bad company. To this another replied that she had often played but never for money, nor had she the least inclination to gamble. As for bad company, she played with her sister, who was no worse company at the card-table than at the dinner-table. When I found that the discussion had become a mere assertion of opinion, I interposed: "You seem to disagree. Why?" "Yes," said one, who recalled my method of treating such cases, "we have not facts enough to enable us to form an intelligent opinion." "But," said another, "what is your opinion?" "My opinion is not the question. What are you to do next?" Wait, observe, and continue to study, was the conclusion.

Our history grew out of our geography, and as we labored to build up in the mind of the pupil a connected and distinct picture of the skeleton—the mountain system of the globe—and then clothed these gaunt outlines with the trailing robes of continental divisions, showing also the necessary dependence of the water systems upon the great backbone of the continents, so in history we aimed at a unity of conception, we sought to develop an historic sense, which, once acquired, serves as a guide through the mass of unrelated facts filling so large a space in historical works even of the higher order. This kind of training is too complex for description here.

And so of our methods of discipline: they were all intricate and intimate parts of our whole work. We had no rules, no class-markings, no roll of honor. We rejected the whole military system, as tending to produce mechanical, routine work. The abrupt tone of command was not heard within our walls. Directions were given in the form of requests. Teachers and pupils observed toward each other the usual courtesies of social life. No premium was offered for study. We relied on the natural incentives. Exercise of faculty is the chief source of pleasure in the young, and we furnished abundant scope for it. The time being filled with pleasurable occupations, calling into activity the whole nature, there was less temptation to misdemeanors than in the ordinary conditions of home life.

Herbert Spencer's essay on moral education will best describe the work as it went on in our school, subject to the imperfections of human nature, it is true, but with a result in general most gratifying.

The school as a whole soon attained a character of its own, derived from the aggregate of its members, and, reacting upon them, it became a potent force in stimulating the moral growth of individuals. This aggregate moral power was exerted for the most part unconsciously, but it was effective, and in time reached proportions which rendered my interference unnecessary.

An incident will here illustrate the operation of this power. A youth entered our school who had formerly been employed as train-boy upon the railroad. His experiences had greatly sharpened wits naturally keen, and as he came among us he was plainly seen to be an alien element. His evil propensities soon showed themselves. He told foul stories, but could get no listeners. He tried to pick quarrels with the younger members of the class, but a quiet word from one of the older pupils soon put an end to that; and, finally, he became angry and disgusted, and took himself away permanently. I watched this affair with much interest as a psychological experiment, but with some anxiety lest the moral leprosy should spread; but the character of the school told, and I was superfluous.

Another instance discloses something of the spirit prevailing among our students. The use of tobacco was discouraged incidentally in a variety of ways. We had a beautiful new building, and great care was taken to preserve it free from filth of any kind. A tobacco-stain, when observed, was removed at once with scrubbing-brush and sand. The physiology class, too, came upon the question of the action of tobacco upon the tissues of the body, and, besides, there was felt to be a social discredit in its use. One evening, while waiting for the mail at the post-office, a number of students on the same errand gathered about, and our talk turned on school matters. Allusion was made to our freedom from the restraint of rules. A late comer remarked: "But you have one rule, I understand. No one must use tobacco on the school premises." I assured him that, though I was opposed to the use of tobacco, I did not prohibit it. "But," I said, "no gentleman will soil the floor of a room occupied by ladies; and this fact, being understood, prevents its use more effectually than a positive prohibition." So powerful was the social reprobation of this filthy habit, that forty young men, of their own will, gave up the practice. It will thus be seen that our moral training, too, was largely *incidental;* it was implicit in every detail of school-life.

As will already have been anticipated, we dispensed with all distinctive religious services. I had carefully observed the effect in school and college throughout a long period of years, and had been forced to conclude that the evil results vastly outweighed the good. I had noticed that stated Bible-reading often became a mere lifeless form, in which many took no interest. This was contrary to the whole spirit of my system. "Vain repetitions," leading to a habit of regarding words apart from thought, were to be carefully avoided. Then, again, the teachings were dogmatic, appealing to authority, while science regards authority as an impertinence. Besides, the Constitution of the United States places its whole machinery upon a strictly secular basis, and religious services in a State school are there upon sufferance. No matter how carefully guarded, the daily performance of any religious service degenerates into formalism, and excites in the community sectarian animosities.

But, above all, I wished to place morals upon a scientific basis, so as to furnish a safe guide to conduct, independent of the shifting standards of theological belief. We, who received our appointments from the State, could not, honestly, either promote or attack any form of religious belief. Happily, the scientific method equally forbids doing either of these things, and, if strictly adhered to, will prevent all possibility of such quarrels between religious sects as have recently agitated Boston, and have from time to time interrupted the work of many schools in this country.

Our position on this question occasioned widespread comment, and, among the clergy of the more ignorant and bigoted sects, there arose an opposition, instinctive rather than outspoken.

The Missionary Society voted us a Bible, and I received a formal note from the secretary announcing the fact, and requesting me to appoint a time for the presentation to take place. I had been informed privately that, as soon as I fixed the time, a public meeting was to be called, and an address made denouncing our neglect of religious observances. In answer to the secretary, I informed him that our library was richly supplied with Bibles, but that, as a token of confidence and good-will, their gift would be highly prized, and we would gratefully receive the promised Bible at the president's office in the normal-school building, at such time as was most convenient to the secretary. The Bible never came.

Prof. Campbell, of our faculty, gave testimony of

considerable significance concerning the moral atmosphere of our school. He had been educated in a sectarian college, and had been graduated at a theological seminary. All his prejudices were enlisted in favor of a daily religious service. He said: "I am at a loss to account for the uniform good feeling existing between teachers and pupils here. No student seems disposed to annoy or vex a teacher, and the moral tone of the school is much higher than I have before known." At first he had thought that the good-will prevailing was in spite of the omission of religious services, but a more careful study had convinced him that the system, in its integrity, had created the moral atmosphere that pervaded the school.

Examinations, as usually conducted, had proved fruitful of serious evils. They gave opportunity for cram, and were often an occasion for cheating. When formal and stated examinations are held, on which class promotion depends, there is a strong inducement to make spasmodic efforts of memory serve in place of sound learning. We avoided these evils by a simple device. Examinations were held at irregular intervals, and were of such a nature that no miraculous feat of memorizing could meet our requirements. Repetitions of text-book formulas were habitually in disfavor, and necessarily there grew up habits of genuine study. These reviews were found sufficient aids in testing progress, and we dispensed with all other examinations.

After some effort toward conformity to prevailing custom, we found ourselves constrained by the guiding principles we had adopted to devise some more genuine representation of our year's work than is possible in "closing exercises" of the regulation pattern. Essays upon the subjects usually chosen had no essential relation to the student's past researches, and, being prepared for the occasion, represented nothing in particular. Besides, they are not uncommonly doctored by the teacher of rhetoric till they are of doubtful originality. We finally dispensed with all special preparation, and discarded all the spectacular features of the ordinary commencement.

One day was given to the public. Every four weeks during the year our pupils had been accustomed to select some subject having close relation to their studies, and to give time and care to the preparation of an essay upon it. These papers were preserved, and from among them each member was required to choose and bring one. On the last day of the term the public came in, and those interested stayed and listened to the reading of these essays. The truthfulness of every step was plain to all concerned, and was thus in accord with the spirit of the school.

Our experiment came to an end. Of the various innovations made upon custom each had justified itself. The effort to make character the end of education had more than fulfilled expectation. During the last year not a single case of misconduct was reported to me, nor was the behavior of one of our students criticised by the citizens. We had a reign of influence. The forces that govern conduct came from a growth within of just and kindly impulses. A watchful supervision had always been maintained, but into this had entered no element of espionage. The peculiar character which the school attained, both on its mental and moral side, was due to the several factors of influence—scientific methods in study, philosophic succession of subjects, and a never-ceasing but an apparently *incidental* attention to moral training.

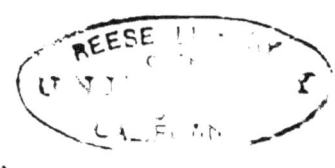

THE END.

D. APPLETON & CO.'S PUBLICATIONS.

## Recent Volumes of the International Scientific Series.

*ICE WORK, PRESENT AND PAST.* By T. G. BONNEY, D. Sc., F. R. S., F. S. A., etc., Professor of Geology at University College, London. No. 74, International Scientific Series. 12mo. Cloth, $1.50.

The student of ice and its work frequently finds that books upon the subject are written more with a view to advocating some particular interpretation of facts than of describing the facts themselves In his work Prof. Bonney has endeavored to give greater prominence to those facts of glacial geology on which all inferences must be founded. After setting forth the facts shown in various regions he has given the various interpretations which have been proposed, adding his comments and criticisms. He also explains a method by which he believes we can approximate to the temperature at various places during the Glacial epoch, and the different explanations of this general refrigeration are stated and briefly discussed.

*THE SUN.* By C. A. YOUNG, Ph. D., LL. D., Professor of Astronomy in Princeton University. New and revised edition, with numerous Illustrations. No. 34, International Scientific Series. 12mo. Cloth, $2.00.

Since the original publication of this book, in 1881, great advances have been made in our knowledge of the sun; and although, in subsequent editions, notes and appendices have kept the work fairly up to date, the author has deemed it best to thoroughly revise it, embodying the notes in the text, and rewriting certain portions. This edition is therefore representative of the solar science of to-day, including important spectroscopic discoveries which have been made during the revision.

*MOVEMENT.* By E. J. MAREY, Member of the Institute and of the Academy of Medicine; Professor at the College of France; author of "Animal Mechanism." Translated by Eric Pritchard, M. A. With 200 Illustrations. No. 73, International Scientific Series. 12mo. Cloth, $1.75.

The present work describes the methods employed in the extended development of photography of moving objects attained in the last few years, and shows the importance of such researches in mechanics and other departments of physics, the fine arts, physiology, and zoölogy, and in regulating the walking or marching of men and the gait of horses.

*RACE AND LANGUAGE.* By ANDRÉ LÉFÈVRE, Professor in the Anthropological School, Paris. 12mo. Cloth, $1.50.

"A most scholarly exposition of the evolution of language, and a comprehensive account of the Indo-European group of tongues."—*Boston Advertiser.*

"A welcome contribution to the study of the obscure and complicated subject with which it deals."—*San Francisco Chronicle.*

"One of the few scientific works which promise to become popular, both with those who read for instruction and those who read for recreation."—*Philadelphia Item.*

New York: D. APPLETON & CO., 72 Fifth Avenue.

# D. APPLETON & CO.'S PUBLICATIONS.

JOHN BACH MCMASTER.

*HISTORY OF THE PEOPLE OF THE UNITED STATES*, from the Revolution to the Civil War. By JOHN BACH MCMASTER. To be completed in six volumes. Vols. I, II, III, and IV now ready. 8vo. Cloth, gilt top, $2.50 each.

". . . Prof. McMaster has told us what no other historians have told. . . . The skill, the animation, the brightness, the force, and the charm with which he arrays the facts before us are such that we can hardly conceive of more interesting reading for an American citizen who cares to know the nature of those causes which have made not only him but his environment and the opportunities life has given him what they are."—*N. Y. Times.*

"Those who can read between the lines may discover in these pages constant evidences of care and skill and faithful labor, of which the old-time superficial essayists, compiling library notes on dates and striking events, had no conception; but to the general reader the fluent narrative gives no hint of the conscientious labors, far-reaching, world-wide, vast and yet microscopically minute, that give the strength and value which are felt rather than seen. This is due to the art of presentation. The author's position as a scientific workman we may accept on the abundant testimony of the experts who know the solid worth of his work; his skill as a literary artist we can all appreciate, the charm of his style being self-evident."—*Philadelphia Telegraph.*

"The third volume contains the brilliantly written and fascinating story of the progress and doings of the people of this country from the era of the Louisiana purchase to the opening scenes of the second war with Great Britain—say a period of ten years. In every page of the book the reader finds that fascinating flow of narrative, that clear and lucid style, and that penetrating power of thought and judgment which distinguished the previous volumes."—*Columbus State Journal.*

"Prof. McMaster has more than fulfilled the promises made in his first volumes, and his work is constantly growing better and more valuable as he brings it nearer to our own time. His style is clear, simple, and idiomatic, and there is just enough of the critical spirit in the narrative to guide the reader."—*Boston Herald.*

"Take it all in all, the History promises to be the ideal American history. Not so much given to dates and battles and great events as in the fact that it is like a great panorama of the people, revealing their inner life and action. It contains, with all its sober facts, the spice of personalities and incidents, which relieves every page from dullness."—*Chicago Inter-Ocean.*

"History written in this picturesque style will tempt the most heedless to read. Prof. McMaster is more than a stylist; he is a student, and his History abounds in evidences of research in quarters not before discovered by the historian."—*Chicago Tribune.*

"A History *sui generis* which has made and will keep its own place in our literature."—*New York Evening Post.*

"His style is vigorous and his treatment candid and impartial."—*New York Tribune.*

---

New York: D. APPLETON & CO., 72 Fifth Avenue.

# D. APPLETON & CO.'S PUBLICATIONS.

**WITH THE FATHERS.** Studies in the History of the United States. By JOHN BACH McMASTER, Professor of American History in the University of Pennsylvania, author of "The History of the People of the United States," etc. 8vo. Cloth, $1.50.

"The book is of great practical value, as many of the essays throw a broad light over living questions of the day. Prof. McMaster has a clear, simple style, that is delightful. His facts are gathered with great care, and admirably interwoven to impress the subject under discussion upon the mind of the reader."—*Chicago Inter-Ocean.*

"Prof. McMaster's essays possess in their diversity a breadth which covers most of the topics which are current as well as historical, and each is so scholarly in treatment and profound in judgment that the importance of their place in the library of political history can not be gainsaid."—*Washington Times.*

"Such works as this serve to elucidate history and make more attractive a study which an abstruse writer only makes perplexing. All through the studies there is a note of intense patriotism and a conviction of the sound sense of the American people which directs the government to a bright goal."—*Chicago Record.*

"A wide field is here covered, and it is covered in Prof. McMaster's own inimitable and fascinating style. . . . Can not but have a marked value as a work of reference upon several most important subjects."—*Boston Daily Advertiser.*

"There is much that is interesting in this little book, and it is full of solid chunks of political information."—*Buffalo Commercial.*

"Clear, penetrating, dispassionate, convincing. His language is what one should expect from the Professor of American History in the University of Pennsylvania. Prof. McMaster has proved before now that he can write history with the breath of life in it, and the present volume is new proof."—*Chicago Tribune.*

"Of great practical value. . . . Charming and instructive history."—*New Haven Leader.*

"An interesting and most instructive volume."—*Detroit Journal.*

"At once commends itself to the taste and judgment of all historical readers. His style charms the general reader with its open and frank ways, its courageous form of statement, its sparkling, crisp narrative and description, and its close and penetrating analysis of characters and events."—*Boston Courier.*

---

New York: D. APPLETON & CO., 72 Fifth Avenue.

## D. APPLETON & CO.'S PUBLICATIONS.

*GUSTAVE FLAUBERT, as seen in his Works and Correspondence.* By JOHN CHARLES TARVER. With Portrait. 8vo. Buckram, $4.00.

"It is surprising that this extremely interesting correspondence has not been Englished before."—*London Athenæum.*

"This handsome volume is welcome. . . . It merits a cordial reception if for no other reason than to make a large section of the English public more intimately acquainted with the foremost champion of art for art's sake. . . . The letters are admirably translated, and in the main the book is written with skill and *verve*."—*London Academy.*

*LIFE OF SIR RICHARD OWEN.* By Rev. RICHARD OWEN. With an Introduction by T. H. HUXLEY. 2 vols. 12mo. Cloth, $7.50.

"The value of these memoirs is that they disclose with great minuteness the daily labors and occupations of one of the foremost men of science of England."—*Boston Herald.*

"A noteworthy contribution to biographical literature."—*Philadelphia Press.*

*DEAN BUCKLAND.* The Life and Correspondence of WILLIAM BUCKLAND, D. D., F. R. S., sometime Dean of Westminster, twice President of the Theological Society, and first President of the British Association. By his Daughter, Mrs. GORDON. With Portraits and Illustrations. 8vo. Buckram, $3.50.

"Next to Charles Darwin, Dean Buckland is certainly the most interesting personality in the field of natural science that the present century has produced."—*London Daily News.*

"A very readable book, for it gives an excellent account, without any padding or unnecessary detail, of a most original man."—*Westminster Gazette.*

*PERSONAL RECOLLECTIONS OF WERNER VON SIEMENS.* Translated by W. C. COUPLAND. With Portrait. 8vo. Cloth, $5.00.

"This volume of straightforward reminiscence reflects new credit on its author, and deserves a high place among the records of great inventors who have made a name and a fortune in ways which have been of immense public benefit."—*Literary World.*

"The general reader need not be deterred from taking up the book by the fear that he will have to wade through chapters of long technical terms which he does not understand. Whether he is describing his simple home life or his scientific career and its manifold achievements, Von Siemens writes plainly, unaffectedly, and in a uniformly attractive fashion. The whole work is, as the publishers of the translation say with truth, 'rich in genial narrative, stirring adventure, and picturesque description,' and stamped throughout with the impress of an original mind and a sterling character."—*London Times.*

New York: D. APPLETON & CO., 72 Fifth Avenue.

## D. APPLETON & CO.'S PUBLICATIONS.

### THE ANTHROPOLOGICAL SERIES.

"Will be hailed with delight by scholars and scientific specialists, and it will be gladly received by others who aspire after the useful knowledge it will impart."—*New York Home Journal.*

#### NOW READY.

**WOMAN'S SHARE IN PRIMITIVE CULTURE.** By OTIS TUFTON MASON, A. M., Curator of the Department of Ethnology in the United States National Museum. With numerous Illustrations. 12mo. Cloth, $1.75.

"A most interesting *résumé* of the revelations which science has made concerning the habits of human beings in primitive times, and especially as to the place, the duties, and the customs of women."—*Philadelphia Inquirer.*

"A highly entertaining and instructive book.... Prof. Mason's bright, graceful style must do much to awaken a lively interest in a study that has heretofore received such scant attention."—*Baltimore American.*

"The special charm of Mr. Mason's book is that his studies are based mainly upon ctually existing types, rather than upon mere tradition."—*Philadelphia Times.*

**THE PYGMIES.** By A. DE QUATREFAGES, late Professor of Anthropology at the Museum of Natural History, Paris. With numerous Illustrations. 12mo. Cloth, $1.75.

"Probably no one was better equipped to illustrate the general subject than Quatrefages. While constantly occupied upon the anatomical and osseous phases of his subject, he was none the less well acquainted with what literature and history had to say concerning the pygmies.... This book ought to be in every divinity school in which man as well as God is studied, and from which missionaries go out to convert the human being of reality and not the man of rhetoric and text-books."—*Boston Literary World.*

"It is fortunate that American students of anthropology are able to enjoy as luminous a translation of this notable monograph as that which Prof. Starr now submits to the public."—*Philadelphia Press.*

"It is regarded by scholars entitled to offer an opinion as one of the half-dozen most important works of an anthropologist whose ethnographic publications numbered nearly one hundred."—*Chicago Evening Post.*

**THE BEGINNINGS OF WRITING.** By W. J. HOFFMAN, M. D. With numerous Illustrations. 12mo. Cloth, $1.75.

This interesting book gives a most attractive account of the rude methods employed by primitive man for recording his deeds. The earliest writing consists of pictographs which were traced on stone, wood, bone, skins, and various paperlike substances. Dr. Hoffman shows how the several classes of symbols used in these records are to be interpreted, and traces the growth of conventional signs up to syllabaries and alphabets—the two classes of signs employed by modern peoples.

#### IN PREPARATION.

*THE SOUTH SEA ISLANDERS.* By Dr. SCHMELTZ
*THE ZUÑI.* By FRANK HAMILTON CUSHING.
*THE AZTECS.* By Mrs. ZELIA NUTTALL.

New York: D. APPLETON & CO., 72 Fifth Avenue.

## D. APPLETON & CO.'S PUBLICATIONS.

### THE LIBRARY OF USEFUL STORIES.

*Each book complete in itself. By writers of authority in their various spheres. 16mo. Cloth, 40 cents per volume.*

**NOW READY.**

*THE STORY OF THE STARS.* By G. F. CHAMBERS, F. R. A. S., author of "Handbook of Descriptive and Practical Astronomy," etc. With 24 Illustrations.

"One can here get a clear conception of the relative condition of the stars and constellations, and of the existent universe so far as it is disclosed to view. The author presents his wonderful and at times bewildering facts in a bright and cheery spirit that makes the book doubly attractive."—*Boston Home Journal.*

*THE STORY OF "PRIMITIVE" MAN.* By EDWARD CLODD, author of "The Story of Creation," etc.

"No candid person will deny that Mr. Clodd has come as near as any one at this time is likely to come to an authentic exposition of all the information hitherto gained regarding the earlier stages in the evolution of mankind."—*New York Sun.*

*THE STORY OF THE PLANTS.* By GRANT ALLEN, author of "Flowers and their Pedigrees," etc.

"As fascinating in style as a first-class story of fiction, and is a simple and clear exposition of plant life."—*Boston Home Journal.*

*THE STORY OF THE EARTH.* By H. G. SEELEY, F. R. S., Professor of Geography in King's College, London. With Illustrations.

"Thoroughly interesting, and it is doubtful if the fascinating story of the planet on which we live has been previously told so clearly and at the same time so comprehensively."—*Boston Advertiser.*

*THE STORY OF THE SOLAR SYSTEM.* By G. F. CHAMBERS, F. R. A. S.

"Any intelligent reader can get clear ideas of the movements of the worlds about us.... Will impart a wise knowledge of astronomical wonders."—*Chicago Inter-Ocean.*

*THE STORY OF A PIECE OF COAL.* By E. A. MARTIN.

*THE STORY OF ELECTRICITY.* By JOHN MUNRO, C. E.

New York: D. APPLETON & CO., 72 Fifth Avenue.

# D. APPLETON & CO.'S PUBLICATIONS.

## THE WARFARE OF SCIENCE WITH THEOLOGY. A History of the Warfare of Science with Theology in Christendom. By ANDREW D. WHITE, LL. D., late President and Professor of History at Cornell University. In two volumes. 8vo. Cloth, $5.00.

"The story of the struggle of searchers after truth with the organized forces of ignorance, bigotry, and superstition is the most inspiring chapter in the whole history of mankind That story has never been better told than by the ex-President of Cornell University in these two volumes. . . . A wonderful story it is that he tells."—*London Daily Chronicle.*

" A literary event of prime importance is the appearance of 'A History of the Warfare of Science with Theology in Christendom.' "—*Philadelphia Press.*

"Such an honest and thorough treatment of the subject in all its bearings that it will carry weight and be accepted as an authority in tracing the process by which the scientific method has come to be supreme in modern thought and life."—*Boston Herald.*

"A great work of a great man upon great subjects, and will always be a religio-scientific classic."—*Chicago Evening Post.*

"It is graphic, lucid, even-tempered—never bitter nor vindictive. No student of human progress should fail to read these volumes. While they have about them the fascination of a well-told tale, they are also crowded with the facts of history that have had a tremendous bearing upon the development of the race."—*Brooklyn Eagle.*

"The same liberal spirit that marked his public life is seen in the pages of his book, giving it a zest and interest that can not fail to secure for it hearty commendation and honest praise."—*Philadelphia Public Ledger.*

" A conscientious summary of the body of learning to which it relates accumulated during long years of research. . . . A monument of industry."—*N. Y. Evening Post.*

" A work which constitutes in many ways the most instructive review that has ever been written of the evolution of human knowledge in its conflict with dogmatic belief. . . . As a contribution to the literature of liberal thought, the book is one the importance of which can not be easily overrated."—*Boston Beacon.*

"The most valuable contribution that has yet been made to the history of the conflicts between the theologians and the scientists."—*Buffalo Commercial.*

"Undoubtedly the most exhaustive treatise which has been written on this subject. . . . Able, scholarly, critical, impartial in tone and exhaustive in treatment."—*Boston Advertiser.*

---

New York : D. APPLETON & CO., 72 Fifth Avenue.

# D. APPLETON & CO.'S PUBLICATIONS.

*GERMANY AND THE GERMANS.* By WILLIAM HARBUTT DAWSON, author of "German Socialism and Ferdinand Lassalle," "Prince Bismarck and State Socialism," etc. 2 vols., 8vo. Cloth, $6.00.

"This excellent work—a literary monument of intelligent and conscientious labor—deals with every phase and aspect of state and political activity, public and private, in the Fatherland. . . . Teems with entertaining anecdotes and introspective *aperçus* of character."—*London Telegraph.*

"With Mr. Dawson's two volumes before him, the ordinary reader may well dispense with the perusal of previous authorities. . . . His work, on the whole, is comprehensive, conscientious, and eminently fair."—*London Chronicle.*

"Mr. Dawson has made a remarkably close and discriminating study of German life and institutions at the present day, and the results of his observations are set forth in a most interesting manner."—*Brooklyn Times.*

"There is scarcely any phase of German national life unnoticed in his comprehensive survey. . . . Mr. Dawson has endeavored to write from the view-point of a sincere yet candid well-wisher, of an unprejudiced observer, who, even when he is unable to approve, speaks his mind in soberness and kindness."—*New York Sun.*

"There is much in German character to admire; much in Germany's life and institutions from which Americans may learn. William Harbutt Dawson has succeeded in making this fact clearer, and his work will go far to help Americans and Germans to know each other better and to respect each other more. . . . It is a remarkable and a fascinating work."—*Chicago Evening Post.*

"One of the very best works on this subject which has been published up to date."—*New York Herald.*

*A HISTORY OF GERMANY, from the Earliest Times to the Present Day.* By BAYARD TAYLOR. With an Additional Chapter by MARIE HANSEN-TAYLOR. With Portrait and Maps. 12mo. Cloth, $1.50.

"There is, perhaps, no work of equal size in any language which gives a better view of the tortuous course of German history. Now that the story of a race is to be in good earnest a story of a nation as well, it begins, as every one, whether German or foreign, sees, to furnish unexpected and wonderful lessons. But these can only be understood in the light of the past. Taylor could end his work with the birth of the Empire, but the additional narrative merely foreshadows the events of the future. It may be that all the doings of the past ages on German soil are but the introduction of what is to come. That is certainly the thought which grows upon one as he peruses this volume."—*New York Tribune.*

"When one considers the confused, complicated, and sporadic elements of German history, it seems scarcely possible to present a clear, continuous narrative. Yet this is what Bayard Taylor did. He omitted no episode of importance, and yet managed to preserve a main line of connection from century to century throughout the narrative."—*Philadelphia Ledger.*

"A most excellent short history of Germany. . . . Mrs. Taylor has done well the work she reluctantly consented to undertake. Her story is not only clearly told, but told in a style that is quite consistent with that of the work which she completes. . . . As a matter of course the history excels in its literary style. Mr. Taylor could not have written an unentertaining book. This book arouses interest in its opening chapter and maintains it to the very end."—*New York Times.*

"Probably the best work of its kind adapted for school purposes that can be had in English."—*Boston Herald.*

New York: D. APPLETON & CO., 72 Fifth Avenue.

# D. APPLETON & CO.'S PUBLICATIONS.

### BOOKS BY PROF. G. FREDERICK WRIGHT.

*GREENLAND ICEFIELDS, AND LIFE IN THE NORTH ATLANTIC.* With a New Discussion of the Causes of the Ice Age. By G. FREDERICK WRIGHT, D. D., LL. D., F. G. S. A., author of "The Ice Age in North America," "Man and the Glacial Period," etc., and WARREN UPHAM, A. M., F. G. S. A., late of the Geological Surveys of New Hampshire, Minnesota, and the United States. With numerous Maps and Illustrations. 12mo. Cloth, $2.00.

The immediate impulse to the preparation of this volume arose in connection with a trip to Greenland by Professor Wright in the summer of 1894 on the steamer Miranda. The work aims to give within moderate limits a comprehensive view of the scenery, the glacial phenomena, the natural history, the people, and the explorations of Greenland. The photographs are all original, and the maps have been prepared to show the latest state of knowledge concerning the region. The volume treats of the ice of the Labrador current, the coast of Labrador, Spitzbergen ice in Davis Strait, the Greenland Eskimos, Europeans in Greenland, explorations of the inland ice, the plants and animals of Greenland, changes of level since the advent of the Glacial period; and includes a summary of the bearing of the facts upon glacial theories. The work is of both popular and scientific interest.

*THE ICE AGE IN NORTH AMERICA, and its Bearings upon the Antiquity of Man.* With an appendix on "The Probable Cause of Glaciation," by WARREN UPHAM, F. G. S. A., Assistant on the Geological Surveys of New Hampshire, Minnesota, and the United States. New and enlarged edition. With 150 Maps and Illustrations. 8vo, 625 pages, and Index. Cloth, $5.00.

"The author has seen with his own eyes the most important phenomena of the Ice age on this continent from Maine to Alaska. In the work itself, elementary description is combined with a broad, scientific, and philosophic method, without abandoning for a moment the purely scientific character. Professor Wright has contrived to give the whole a philosophical direction which lends interest and inspiration to it, and which in the chapters on Man and the Glacial Period rises to something like dramatic intensity."—*The Independent.*

*MAN AND THE GLACIAL PERIOD.* International Scientific Series. With numerous Illustrations. 12mo. Cloth, $1.75.

"The earlier chapters describing glacial action, and the traces of it in North America—especially the defining of its limits, such as the terminal moraine of the great movement itself—are of great interest and value. The maps and diagrams are of much assistance in enabling the reader to grasp the vast extent of the movement."—*London Spectator.*

---

New York: D. APPLETON & CO., 72 Fifth Avenue.

## D. APPLETON & CO.'S PUBLICATIONS.

*THE DAWN OF CIVILIZATION.* (EGYPT AND CHALDÆA.) By Prof. G. MASPERO. Edited by Rev. Prof. A. H. SAYCE. Translated by M. L. McCLURE. Revised and brought up to date by the Author. With Map and over 470 Illustrations. Quarto. Cloth, $7.50.

"The most sumptuous and elaborate work which has yet appeared on this theme. . . . The book should be in every well-equipped Oriental library, as the most complete work on the dawn of civilization. Its careful reading and studying will open a world of thought to any diligent student, and very largely broaden and enlarge his views of the grandeur, the stability, and the positive contributions of the civilization of that early day to the life and culture of our own times."—*Chicago Standard.*

"By all odds the best account of Egyptian and Assyrian theology, or, more properly speaking, theosophy, with which we are acquainted . . . The book will arouse many enthusiasms. Its solid learning will enchant the scholar— its brilliancy will charm the general reader and tempt him into a region which he may have hesitated to enter."—*The Outlook.*

"For a general comprehension of the dawn of civilization we know of no stronger work."—*New York Times.*

"You no sooner open it at random than you discover that every paragraph is alluring and instructive. You may not hope to read it through, even in a dozen sittings, but you can not give a glance at any one of its pages without having your attention specially challenged."—*New York Herald.*

"The most complete reconstruction of that ancient life which has yet appeared in print. Maspero's great book will remain the standard work for a long time to come."—*London Daily News.*

*LIFE IN ANCIENT EGYPT AND ASSYRIA.* By G. MASPERO, late Director of Archæology in Egypt, and Member of the Institute of France. Translated by ALICE MORTON. With 188 Illustrations. 12mo. Cloth, $1.50.

"A lucid sketch, at once popular and learned, of daily life in Egypt at the time of Rameses II, and of Assyria in that of Assurbanipal. . . . As an Orientalist, M. Maspero stands in the front rank, and his learning is so well digested and so admirably subdued to the service of popular exposition, that it nowhere overwhelms and always interests the reader."—*London Times.*

"Only a writer who had distinguished himself as a student of Egyptian and Assyrian antiquities could have produced this work, which has none of the features of a modern book of travels in the East, but is an attempt to deal with ancient life as if one had been a contemporary with the people whose civilization and social usages are very largely restored."—*Boston Herald.*

"A most interesting and instructive book. Excellent and most impressive ideas also, of the architecture of the two countries and of the other rude but powerful art of the Assyrians, are to be got from it."—*Brooklyn Eagle.*

"The ancient artists are copied with the utmost fidelity, and verify the narrative so attractively presented."—*Cincinnati Times-Star.*

---

New York: D. APPLETON & CO., 72 Fifth Avenue.

# D. APPLETON & CO.'S PUBLICATIONS.

*NEW EDITION OF PROF. HUXLEY'S ESSAYS.*

**COLLECTED ESSAYS.** By THOMAS H. HUXLEY. New complete edition, with revisions, the Essays being grouped according to general subject. In nine volumes, a new Introduction accompanying each volume. 12mo. Cloth, $1.25 per volume.

- VOL. I.—METHOD AND RESULTS.
- VOL. II.—DARWINIANA.
- VOL. III.—SCIENCE AND EDUCATION.
- VOL. IV.—SCIENCE AND HEBREW TRADITION.
- VOL. V.—SCIENCE AND CHRISTIAN TRADITION.
- VOL. VI.—HUME.
- VOL. VII.—MAN'S PLACE IN NATURE.
- VOL. VIII.—DISCOURSES, BIOLOGICAL AND GEOLOGICAL.
- VOL. IX.—EVOLUTION AND ETHICS, AND OTHER ESSAYS.

"Mr. Huxley has covered a vast variety of topics during the last quarter of a century. It gives one an agreeable surprise to look over the tables of contents and note the immense territory which he has explored. To read these books carefully and studiously is to become thoroughly acquainted with the most advanced thought on a large number of topics."—*New York Herald.*

"The series will be a welcome one. There are few writings on the more abstruse problems of science better adapted to reading by the general public, and in this form the books will be well in the reach of the investigator. . . . The revisions are the last expected to be made by the author, and his introductions are none of earlier date than a few months ago [1893], so they may be considered his final and most authoritative utterances."—*Chicago Times.*

"It was inevitable that his essays should be called for in a completed form, and they will be a source of delight and profit to all who read them. He has always commanded a hearing, and as a master of the literary style in writing scientific essays he is worthy of a place among the great English essayists of the day. This edition of his essays will be widely read, and gives his scientific work a permanent form."—*Boston Herald.*

"A man whose brilliancy is so constant as that of Prof. Huxley will always command readers; and the utterances which are here collected are not the least in weight and luminous beauty of those with which the author has long delighted the reading world."—*Philadelphia Press.*

"The connected arrangement of the essays which their reissue permits brings into fuller relief Mr. Huxley's masterly powers of exposition. Sweeping the subject-matter clear of all logomachies, he lets the light of common day fall upon it. He shows that the place of hypothesis in science, as the starting point of verification of the phenomena to be explained, is but an extension of the assumptions which underlie actions in every-day affairs; and that the method of scientific investigation is only the method which rules the ordinary business of life."—*London Chronicle.*

New York: D. APPLETON & CO., 72 Fifth Avenue.

## D. APPLETON & CO.'S PUBLICATIONS.

### MISCELLANEOUS WORKS OF HERBERT SPENCER.

*SOCIAL STATICS.* New and revised edition, including "The Man *versus* The State," a series of essays on political tendencies heretofore published separately. 12mo, 420 pages. Cloth, $2.00.

CONTENTS.—Happiness as an Immediate Aim.—Unguided Expediency.—The Moral-Sense Doctrine.—What is Morality?—The Evanescence [? Diminution] of Evil.—-Greatest Happiness must be sought indirectly.—Derivation of a First Principle.—Secondary Derivation of a First Principle.—First Principle.—Application of the First Principle.—The Right of Property.—Socialism.—The Right of Property in Ideas.—The Rights of Women.—The Rights of Children.—Political Rights.—The Constitution of the State.—The Duty of the State.—The Limit of State-Duty.—The Regulation of Commerce.—Religious Establishments.—Poor-Laws.—National Education.—Government Colonization.—Sanitary Supervision.—Currency, Postal Arrangements, etc.—General Considerations.—The New Toryism.—The Coming Slavery.—The Sins of Legislators.—The Great Political Superstition.

"Mr. Spencer has thoroughly studied the issues which are behind the social and political life of our own time, not exactly those issues which are discussed in Parliament or in Congress, but the principles of all modern government, which are slowly changing in response to the broader industrial and general development of human experience. One will obtain no suggestions out of this book for guiding a political party or carrying a point in economics, but he will find the principles of sociology, as they pertain to the whole of life, better stated in these pages than he can find them expressed anywhere else. It is in this sense that this work is important and fresh and vitalizing. It goes constantly to the foundation of things."—*Boston Herald.*

*EDUCATION : Intellectual, Moral, and Physical.* 12mo. Paper, 50 cents ; cloth, $1.25.

CONTENTS: What Knowledge is of most Worth?—Intellectual Education.—Moral Education.—Physical Education.

*THE STUDY OF SOCIOLOGY.* The fifth volume in the International Scientific Series. 12mo. Cloth, $1.50.

CONTENTS: Our Need of it.—Is there a Social Science?—Nature of the Social Science.—Difficulties of the Social Science.—Objective Difficulties.—Subjective Difficulties, Intellectual.—Subjective Difficulties, Emotional.—The Educational Bias.—The Bias of Patriotism.—The Class-Bias.—The Political Bias.—The Theological Bias.—Discipline.—Preparation in Biology.—Preparation in Psychology.—Conclusion.

*THE INADEQUACY OF "NATURAL SELECTION."* 12mo. Paper, 30 cents.

This essay, in which Prof. Weismann's theories are criticised, is reprinted from the *Contemporary Review*, and comprises a forcible presentation of Mr. Spencer's views upon the general subject indicated in the title.

New York: D. APPLETON & CO., 72 Fifth Avenue.

www.ingramcontent.com/pod-product-compliance
Lightning Source LLC
Chambersburg PA
CBHW020228240426
43672CB00006B/453